China's Information and Communications Technology Revolution

In recent years, China has experienced a revolution in information and communications technology (ICT), in 2003 surpassing the USA as the world's largest telephone market, and as of February 2008, the number of Chinese Internet users has become the largest in the world. At the same time, China has overtaken the USA as the world's biggest supplier of information technology goods. However, this transformation has occurred against the backdrop of a resolutely authoritarian political system and strict censorship by the Party-state. This book examines China's ICT revolution, exploring the social, cultural and political implications of China's transition to a more information-rich and communication-intensive society. The pace of the development of ICT in China has precipitated much speculation about political change and democratisation. This book explores the reality of ICT in China, showing clearly that whilst China remains a one-party state, with an ever-present and sophisticated regime of censorship, substantial social and political changes have taken place. It considers the ICT revolution in all its aspects, outlining the dominant trends, the impact on other countries of China as an ICT exporter, strategies of government censorship and use of ICT for propaganda, the implications of censorship for Chinese governance, the political implications of Internet culture and blogging, and the role of domestic and foreign NGOs. Overall, this book is a vital resource for anyone seeking to understand a rapidly transforming China, both today and in the years to come.

Xiaoling Zhang is a lecturer in the School of Contemporary Chinese Studies, the University of Nottingham, UK. She researches on the transformation of media, culture and society in China. **Yongnian Zheng** is Professor and Director of Research in the School of Contemporary Chinese Studies, University of Nottingham, UK. He is the author of 13 books, including *Technological Empowerment*, *De facto Federalism in China*, *Discovering Chinese Nationalism in China* and *Globalization and State Transformation in China*, and co-editor of, amongst other books, *The Chinese Communist Party in Reform*.

China policy series

Series Editor: Zheng Yongnian

China Policy Institute, University of Nottingham, UK

1 **China and the New International Order**
Edited by Wang Gungwu and Zheng Yongnian

2 **China's Opening Society**
The non-state sector and governance
Edited by Zheng Yongnian and Joseph Fewsmith

3 **Zhao Ziyang and China's Political Future**
Edited by Guoguang Wu and Helen Lansdowne

4 **Hainan – State, Society, and Business in a Chinese Province**
Kjeld Erik Brodsgaard

5 **Non-Governmental Organizations in China**
The rise of dependent autonomy
Yiyi Lu

6 **Power and Sustainability of the Chinese State**
Edited by Keun Lee, Joon-Han Kim and Wing Thye Woo

7 **China's Information and Communications Technology Revolution**
Social changes and state responses
Edited by Xiaoling Zhang and Yongnian Zheng

China's Information and Communications Technology Revolution

Social changes and state responses

Edited by Xiaoling Zhang and Yongnian Zheng

LONDON AND NEW YORK

First published 2009
by Routledge
4 Park Square, Milton Park, Abingdon, Oxon OX14 4RN
605 Third Avenue, New York, NY 10017

Routledge is an imprint of the Taylor & Francis Group, an informa business

Typeset in Times by Wearset Ltd, Boldon, Tyne and Wear

British Library Cataloguing in Publication Data
A catalogue record for this book is available from the British Library

Library of Congress Cataloging-in-Publication Data
China's information and communications technology revolution: social changes and state responses/edited by Xiaoling Zhang and Yongnian Zheng.
p. cm. – (China policy series; 7)
Includes bibliographical references and index.

1. Information technology–China. 2. Communication–Technological innovations–China. 3. Internet–China. 4. Social change–China.
5. Freedom of information–China. 6. Freedom of expression–China.
I. Zhang, Xiaoling. II. Zheng, Yongnian.

HC430.I55C455 2009
303.48'330951–dc22
2008039438

ISBN13: 978-0-415-46230-3 (hbk)
ISBN13: 978-0-203-88113-2 (ebk)

Contents

List of figures viii
List of tables ix
List of contributors x
Acknowledgements xi

Introduction 1
YONGNIAN ZHENG AND XIAOLING ZHANG

ICT development, state and society 2
Digital civil society and digital governance 6
Selective digital control and regime legitimacy 8
The development of ICT in China and its implications for the world 11
Whither China's digital control? 14

1 Historical imagination in the study of Chinese digital civil society 17
GUOBIN YANG

The logic of complex interdependence and the origins of digital civil society 18
Digital formations and Chinese digital civil society 19
Periodization and the study of the Chinese Internet 20
Two stages of digital civil society development 22
Persistent dynamics of digital civil society 24
New dynamics in the period of expansion 27
Conclusion 29

2 Dancing thumbs: mobile telephony in contemporary China 34
ZHENZHI GUO AND MEI WU

Introduction 34

Mobile telephony and "combined modernization" 35
From pre-industrial to mobile communication: the "great leap forward" in telephone development 38
Social and cultural implications of mobile phone use: three cases 41
Conclusion: the future use of the mobile phone 46

3 Regulating *e gao*: futile efforts of recentralization? 52
BINGCHUN MENG

From parody to culture jamming 53
Deconstructing authorship 55
Decentralized production and distribution 58
Carnival in the virtual space 60
Conclusion 62

4 In the name of good governance: e-government, Internet pornography and political censorship in China 68
GUOGUANG WU

Web governance in China: institutions and discourses 70
Big-government online with little service 73
How and why web pornography prevails 76
Political censorship, political reform and Internet hypocrisy 79
Sophistications of censorship, failures of governance: conclusions 81

5 Chinese intellectuals and the Internet in the formation of a new collective memory 86
JUNHUA ZHANG

Introduction 86
Collective memory and its functions 87
The development of Chinese blogs 89
China's memory policy 93
The older generation of intellectuals and the official memory policy 95
Findings from a content analysis of Chinese bloggers 96
Conclusion 100

6 From "foreign propaganda" to "international communication": China's promotion of soft power in the age of information and communication technologies 103
XIAOLING ZHANG

Introduction 103
From defensive to offensive – changing goals and strategies 103
The expansion of ICT capacity 106
CCTV-9 and China National Network 109
Discussions 113

7 Web engineering in the Chinese context: "let a hundred flowers bloom, a hundred schools of thought contend" 121
KIERON O'HARA

Introduction 121
The history and architecture of the Web 121
Properties of the WWW 127
China and the WWW 131
Conclusion: a dilemma 133

8 The political cost of information control in China: the nation-state and governance 136
YONGNIAN ZHENG

Information distribution and nation-state building 137
Information control and governance 144
Conclusion 152

Index 156

Figures

1.1	"Nail house" in Chongqing, 2007	23
1.2	Number of active blogs in China, 2002–2006	25
2.1	Fixed phone and mobile phone population comparison	40
5.1	Age structure of Internet users in China	90
5.2	Increasing number of bloggers (10,000 persons)	90
5.3	Active and inactive bloggers	91
5.4	Share of bloggers among the Internet users	91
5.5	Composition of professions among the bloggers	92
5.6	Age structure of China's bloggers (%)	92
5.7	Motives of Chinese bloggers while compiling the weblog (%)	93
5.8	Dos and Don'ts – red line	94
5.9	Age structure of the "storytellers"	96
5.10	Professions of the "storytellers"	97
5.11	Stance taken by the bloggers	98
5.12	Scientific degree of the stories	98
5.13	Time period of the stories	99
5.14	Blogs within or outside the "red line"	100
7.1	Getting information from A to B in a compromised network	123

Tables

1.1 Selected indicators of Internet growth in China, 2002 and 2007 25
1.2 Most frequently used network services in China (multiple options), June 1999–June 2004 26
1.3 Most frequently used network services in China (multiple options), June 2003–June 2007 26
4.1 Comparison of government online services in China and EU, 2006 74
5.1 Top ten countries with highest number of Internet users 89
5.2 Number of graduates having obtained bachelor degrees in China 91

Contributors

Bingchun Meng, Lecturer, the Department of Media and Communications at the London School of Economics and Political Science.

Guobin Yang, Associate Professor, the Department of Asian and Middle Eastern Cultures at Barnard College, Columbia University. He is also a faculty in the Weatherhead East Asian Institute and an affiliated faculty in the Department of Sociology of Columbia University.

Guoguang Wu, Associate Professor and Chair in China and Asia-Pacific Relations Centre for Asia-Pacific Initiatives, the University of Victoria, Canada.

Junhua Zhang, Research Associate, Otto-Suhr Institute of Political Science, Center for Chinese and East Asian Politics, as well as at the Institute of East Asian Studies of the Freie Universität Berlin, Germany.

Kieron O'Hara, Senior research fellow in Electronics and Computer Science, the University of Southampton, UK.

Mei Wu, Assistant Professor and Coordinator of English Communication, Department of Communication, Faculty of Social Sciences and Humanities, University of Macau, Macau Special Administrative Region, China.

Xiaoling Zhang, Lecturer, School of Contemporary Chinese Studies, the University of Nottingham, UK.

Yongnian Zheng, Professor and Director of Research, China Policy Institute, School of Contemporary Chinese Studies, the University of Nottingham, UK.

Zhenzhi Guo, Professor, School of Journalism and Communication, Tsinghua University, China.

Acknowledgements

Most of the chapters in this volume were selected from *the International Symposium on Information and Communication Technologies (ICT) and Transformation in China* in the University of Nottingham, Nottingham, UK, on 14–15 June, 2007. So our first thanks go to the Research Community of the University of Nottingham and the School of Contemporary Chinese Studies, University of Nottingham, which co-sponsored the symposium. We would also like to thank the Universities China Committee in London which helped bring two Chinese speakers to the symposium. Special thanks go to Richard Pascoe, Elizabeth Wright and Shujie Yao for their great support. We are also very grateful to Sow Keat Tok, Minjia Chen, Mei Yan and Davina Malcolm for making the symposium run smoothly. Finally we are grateful to Mr Peter Sowden and Mr Tom Bates at Routledge who have provided valuable guidance and support from the beginning to the end of the project.

Xiaoling Zhang
Yongnian Zheng

Introduction

Yongnian Zheng and Xiaoling Zhang

The rise of information and communication technologies (ICT) in China since the early 1990s has been exponential. From February 2008, according to BDA China,[1] the number of Chinese Internet users has become the largest in the world. Over half of these Internet users have broadband. China also has the largest group of mobile phone users, reaching 574.63 million in March 2008.[2] The number of Chinese using instant messaging systems has more than doubled in the past few years. By the end of 2007, Chinese blogs (online personal diaries) numbered more than 47 million.[3] The new information technology has also reached China's hinterland. Almost every county (and indeed many towns and villages) now has broadband. Internet cafés with high-speed connections are ubiquitous and cheap even in remote towns. Fixed-line Internet access is still uncommon in rural homes, but in many parts of the countryside it is possible to surf the Internet at landline modem speeds using a mobile handset.

The rapid development of ICT in China, which has been influencing political, economic, cultural change and social behaviour, has become an increasingly hot topic, not only in academic and policy circles, but also in business circles, both in China and in the West. Indeed never before has the rise of a new form of information technology stimulated such heated debates. Central to all the debates are the potential socio-political consequences that the new ICT could bring to China's authoritarian system. However, amidst all the debates concerning the relationship between ICT and political and social changes in China is another issue of great concern: what implications will the rapid development of ICT in China have on the rest of the world? Given the size of the Chinese population and the country's rapid economic growth, the use of the Internet and other forms of ICT will continue to increase. After all, despite the current large number of Internet users in China, Internet penetration rate (the number of people in the population using the Internet) is still very low, at 16 per cent, compared to the relatively mature markets such as the United States (penetration 69.7 per cent), the United Kingdom (62.3 per cent), South Korea (66.5 per cent) and Japan (67.1 per cent), meaning that China has significant room to grow.

Appraising different aspects of the development of ICT in China from multidisciplinary perspectives, the authors of this volume provide much to think about as they offer their views on the development of ICT in China in relation to political change and democracy, the link between communication and social behaviour in a multidimension transition country and the implications for the rest of the world.

ICT development, state and society

Obviously China recognizes the importance of the prosperity of the ICT industry: China must integrate into the global economy in order to strengthen itself for competition, and integration requires not only economic and administrative reform but also absorption of advanced technologies, including the potentially subversive Internet, which not only revolutionizes the way we communicate, but the nature of communication itself.

The Chinese government worries about the undesirable political consequences of the free flow of information facilitated by the new ICT. For decades, the government has ruthlessly suppressed any organized dissent inside China through information control and other coercive measures. However, from the very beginning, there have been high expectations of the ICT, especially the Internet, in China. Many have hoped that the Internet would facilitate political change and transform China, not only into an open society, but also into an open and democratic regime. But the reality lags far behind these expectations. The ICT so far has not been able to promote democratic development in China; instead, the new ICT seems to have become an effective instrument of control for the Chinese Communist Party (CCP). Some have thus begun to blame multinational firms that have facilitated ICT development in China, including Cisco, Google, Microsoft and Yahoo. Some analysts suggest that China's sophisticated Internet infrastructure would not be possible without technology and equipment imported from the US and other Western companies.

While pessimists view the new ICT in China as merely a tool for governmental control, optimists point out the almost unlimited potential of the new technology to generate liberating effects. They believe that Chinese ICT users can always use newly developed technology to make government control less effective. Take blogs as an example. Blogs make the censors' work much more difficult, if not impossible. China's fast-growing blog users know how they can get past censorship by avoiding using taboo keywords, including those programmed into the Chinese version of MSN Spaces. As China's Internet companies engage in fierce competition to draw blog traffic to their portals, few checks seem to be made on who is writing them. A blog can easily and quickly be set up on a Chinese portal, and no one will ask for verifiable personal information.

Compared to more traditional media such as newspapers, television and broadcasting, the new ICT are inherently 'societalizing' because they directly transfer from the state to individuals and groups in society the power to initiate, send and receive messages. Anyone with access to the telecommunications network can formulate a message and send it to anyone else on the network. The mobile phone, text and instant messaging, Windows messenger (Microsoft's instant-messaging system), and QQ (a messaging service provided by a Chinese company, Tencent) have all helped people to form networks on a scale and with a speed that is beyond the government's ability to control.

Furthermore, the freedom of information associated with the Internet is a reflection of contradictions between the market and politics. On one hand, due to various market factors, multinational firms and domestic firms alike have to cooperate with the Chinese government. On the other hand, exactly for market reasons, firms have to 'liberalize' the regulations and requirements set up by the government in order to be competitive in the market. For example, a few years ago, the Chinese government issued a regulation to limit phone-card sales. According to that regulation, sellers have to check buyers' ID cards. But the Chinese soon found that this regulation was extremely difficult to enforce. Limiting phone-card sales to just a few shops with the ability to process registration requirements would be a blow to mobile-phone companies and huge numbers of private vendors who thrive on such business. Competition between the market and politics becomes intensive. The government can make frequent attempts to limit the functioning of the market, but the market tends to prevail over politics eventually.

The government does control the new ICT, but it also uses the technology to mobilize social support for its own cause. The pessimists seem to have focused excessively on the technical ability of the government to control the new ICT. However, once the government uses the technology for social mobilization, opportunities are created for other social forces to further their own causes, which are not necessarily in line with the government. This can be exemplified by the rise of Internet nationalism. Since nationalism has become an increasingly important source for the political legitimacy of the communist state, nationalist diatribes have a better chance of getting past the censors than other forms of political comment. But nationalism has also provided a convenient cover for experimenting with new forms of activism on the part of social forces. The power of instant messaging, for instance, became evident in April 2005, when it was used to organize anti-Japanese protests in several Chinese cities, including Beijing, Shanghai, Guangzhou and Shenzhen. In the build-up to the protests, Sina organized an online campaign aimed at demonstrating public opposition to Japan's bid for permanent membership of the UN Security Council. Some 20 million people submitted their names. In competing with Sina, Sohu also gathered more than 15 million names. These Internet-based nationalistic campaigns certainly provided strong support for the government's Japan policy. Nevertheless, the government soon found that it had to contain such nationalistic mobilizations since, once social forces were mobilized, they began to exercise strong pressure on the government.[4]

There are also many other cases in which the new technology was used by the government to mobilize social support. The government now desires to expose various forms of malfeasance, such as corruption and mine disasters. Since the Hu Jintao-Wen Jiabao leadership came into power, the shift to a more 'people-centred' approach to governance has legitimized certain forms of exposure, which means that citizens can push those limits. The boundary between what is legitimate to expose and illegitimate is always shifting. So this opens up possibilities for Chinese activists to bring about political change. This is especially true when the government is divided. For instance, in the Sun Zhigang case, there were many internal discussions about changing the custody and repatriation regulations, but nothing changed until the Sun Zhigang case came out.[5] Then those in favour of changing these regulations were able to prevail upon those who had resisted. Shifting issues and policy agendas have allowed reform to emerge in the interstices of the system. The Internet and other information technologies are certainly able to strengthen these tendencies.

Due to its fast growing influence, even the party leadership now has to pay attention to the deluge of public comment. Eager to acquire some legitimacy, but anxious to avoid democracy, it is trying to appeal to populism via the new technology. Premier Wen Jiabao said during the National People's Congress in March 2006 that the government should listen extensively to views expressed on the Internet. With few other ways of assessing the public mood, the Internet is indeed a barometer, even though surveys suggest that users are hardly representative of the general population, being mainly young, highly educated and male.

Apparently, while optimists usually see the benefits that potential civil society can gain from ICT development, pessimists focus on how the government benefits during this process. Both pessimists and optimists can find empirical evidence to support their arguments. Their opposite views are indeed understandable due to the complicatedness of the ICT. In reality, the ICT in general and the Internet in particular can stimulate certain types of political change but not others. For example, the ICT is more likely to promote what political science literature calls 'political liberalization' than what is called 'political democratization'. Accordingly, certain types of ICT-facilitated challenges to the state are likely to facilitate political reform on the part of the government, but other types of challenge are likely to be repressed. At this stage, it is too early to say which actor, the state or society, will win the battle over the ICT. In the multiple ICT-mediated meeting grounds between the state and society, sometimes the state wins, and sometimes society wins. Such a situation is likely to continue in China for the foreseeable future.

We believe that the ICT is not only a tool which can be used by both the state and society in their interaction. More importantly, the ICT is a new and unexplored political realm where both the state and society try to expand their own political space. In doing so, the game between the two actors is not always a zero-sum one. ICT development could be a win-win game between the state and society and, when some conditions are present, it is mutually empowering between the two actors.[6]

A mutually empowering argument requires us to reconsider state–society relations. For many years, scholars treated the state and society as a dichotomy.[7] The state was regarded as a critical agent of socioeconomic transformation, and a condition of strong states and weak societies was believed to facilitate socioeconomic transformation, and that of strong societies and weak states pose a severe structural barrier for such a transformation.[8] In the state-centred literature, the strength of the state is often equated with its autonomy from society and with its ability to ignore other social actors or to impose its will on society.[9] The state-centred theory had an impact on policy-makers and scholars in developing countries like China. Apparently, it greatly influenced a Chinese version of statism.[10] Frequently, for political elites in the third world, it is a simple solution to centralize all powers in order to engage in socioeconomic changes, even though centralization might not be an effective solution.

In the recent decade, scholars have found that some dimension of state power has more to do with the state's ability to work through and with other social actors; that a state's apparent disconnectedness from social groups turns out to be associated in many cases with weakness rather than strength. The state itself is a part of a given society, and it needs society's cooperation to achieve its objectives. Increasingly, scholars have realized that when certain conditions are present, states and social forces can become mutually empowering, and interactions, not separation, between the state and social forces can have the effect of creating more power for both sides.[11]

Needless to say, state capacity is important in developing countries. States are facing the double tasks of socioeconomic transformation and political democratization simultaneously. On the one hand, rapid and sustained economic development requires a strong state capable of going beyond the shortsightedness of special interest groups with long-term developmental strategies. On the other hand, political development often requires and depends on the emergence of a robust sphere of civil associational life and the consolidation of social power in their state organizations. Political reforms often entail the weakening of the power of pre-existing states during a period when these states are promoting economic transformation and providing for effective governance.[12] Nevertheless, socioeconomic transformation and political reforms are not necessarily in conflict with one another in certain circumstances. For instance, it is found that transition to democracy does not necessarily reduce the role of the state and weaken its capacity; instead, a capable state is an important condition in sustaining substantial democracy.[13] Joint efforts on the part of civil society and the state might offer the most efficient way of carrying out political reforms. Strong and robust civil associations can go hand-in-hand with powerful and resilient states.

We believe that the ICT provides an area for mutual empowering between the state and society to take place. We also believe that the degree of mutual empowering is rather different in different areas of state–society relations since the impact of the ICT varies in different areas. Needless to say, the argument of mutual empowering does not mean in any sense that there is no conflicting interests over the ICT between the state and society. Technological empowerment is also a form of politics between the state and society. There are areas in which the state and society clash. However, even in the areas with conflicting interests, who will win the game between the state and society is not a straightforward question. There are cases in which social groups lose their battles in challenging the state but there are also cases in which social groups have successfully challenged the state.

Most of the chapters collected in this volume were selected from the international conference on China's ICT development which was held in Nottingham in June 2007. In these chapters, scholars attempt to demonstrate how the state and society interact over different ICT-mediated public spaces. They explore the role of different new technologies such as the Internet and mobile phones from different perspectives including social, cultural, political and international. Our aim is not only to spell out main social and political implications of ICT development in China, but also to explore new research agendas related to ICT development.

Digital civil society and digital governance

Without doubt, one key issue surrounding the ICT is whether Chinese civil society can be empowered in its relations to state power. While the Chinese state has played an important role in guiding and promoting the development of the ICT, the development of digital civil society – a social product of ICT development – has to be understood in the context of its relations to the state. The state facilitates the development of digital civil society on one hand, and constrains its challenges to state power on the other hand. In Chapter 1, Guobin Yang examines the complicated relations among Internet development, the state and digital civil society.

Yang divides the development of digital civil society into two stages in China. The first stage, from the mid-1990s when China began to develop the Internet to about 2002, was the stage of emergence. The second stage, from 2003 to the present, is a period of expansion. It is important to note, as Yang mentioned, that while this periodization is somehow arbitrary, it does help researchers to highlight both continuities and discontinuities of main characteristics associated with ICT development. Yang then looks into how 'the logic of complex interaction among multiple institutional actors' has provided driving forces behind the development of digital civil society. In each period, digital civil society has shown its unique characteristics which are consequences of changing strategies taken by all the major actors in responding to changing socioeconomic and political conditions. The state has continuously to refine its strategies of control on one hand, and to recognize the importance of the prosperity of the Internet industry on the other hand. Business people know the political limits even as they are pursuing benefits, and they have learned how to facilitate Internet development by working with the government. Meanwhile, digital civil society actors are also fully aware of political limits even as they often span the boundaries. Different forms of Internet activism such as online rights defence, with their emphasis on legal and rights-based resistance, are responses to refined political control. Yang thus explains how and why the dynamics of digital civil society have been characterized by multiple interaction, negotiation and evolution. By placing digital civil society into a set of institutional factors, Yang shows that not only does civic use of the Internet constantly undergo change, but the politics and business of the Internet also change. Interactions among different institutional factors lead to changes in digital space, and these changes often give rise to new social conditions, which in turn impinge on the dynamics of a fledgling digital civil society.

Such a dynamic perspective helps us foresee the future challenges and opportunities of digital civil society in China. The main challenges identified by Yang include digital divide, commercialization and digital control. More often than not, commercialization of the media is viewed as a corrupting influence given the fact that the Internet has been excessively used for entertainment and advertising. Digital divide exists between the rural and the urban population. More importantly, the state has learned how to exercise its control over the Internet more efficiently. For example, Internet control is shifting from punitive power to disciplinary power in a Foucaultian perspective. However, Yang believes that all these challenges should not lead us to be pessimistic since they are also opportunities. Internet control has been there ever since the beginning of the Internet, but it has not slowed down the evolution of the Internet and civil society. More interesting and important is, as Yang points out, that much of the dynamism, energy and creativity of the Chinese Internet culture has been generated in reaction to regulations and control. Moreover, the commercialization of the Internet is somehow inevitable since it is unreasonable to expect Chinese Internet users to use the technology only or even mainly for political purposes. As fun spaces, cyberspace attracts a critical mass of people and often leads to identity formation and cultural creativity which often help collective civic action when occasions arise. Similarly, digital divide also contains opportunities, since it implies that China has room for the further diffusion of the Internet. More importantly, according to Yang, the digital divide also reflects the conditions of a fractured society and thus social divide. Citizens and citizen groups will find themselves increasingly called upon to mobilize their available resources to fight poverty, social injustice, corruption and other social ills. The ICT is indeed becoming increasingly integrated into citizen struggles. Therefore, the future of Chinese digital civil society is open.

Another important issue related to the ICT is digital governance. While the ICT promotes free flow of information in every respect, it can also generate undesirable consequences. A simple question arises here: when information becomes excessive, how can the users of information cope with it? In Chapter 2, Zhenzhi Guo and Mei Wu explore the social and cultural implications of mobile telephony in China. In less than two decades, China has become the world's largest mobile phone population: one in every three Chinese has a handset, meaning that the country has leapt from a pre-industrial stage of minimum landline penetration to the top position in the information age. While mobile telephony is mainly instrumental for economic development, it has been rapidly integrated into society and become a part of people's everyday lives and thus affects a wide range of reconfigurations of social relations, cultural representation and symbolic re-creation. Guo and Wu attempt to interpret such social and cultural consequences through three case studies, including the *Super Girls* (a television show), the 'Bus Uncle' (video-clip) and the *Cell Phone* (film) since all these cases reflect the reality related to the use of mobile phones in China.

According to Guo and Wu, while the mobile phone has become the most convenient device for information and connection, its users also face the worst consequence of the new media technologies – information and contact explosion. It is not so clear whether all the information can help people to truly connect with each other, to understand the world better, and to engage in meaningful social practices. The endless information and ubiquitous communication have already overwhelmed many users.

Furthermore, the excessively mediated relations lack personal intimacy. Mass produced and distributed messages do not necessarily benefit social interactions. In many cases, they are just another source for mobile phone companies to make money, like in the case of the *Super Girls* event, during which the intimate rapport hundreds of thousands of fans built through SMS and the Internet with their *Super Girl* idol is merely symbolic, imaginary and, of course, virtual. Another example is mobile greetings. In early stages of mobile telephony, when people received holiday greetings through their mobile phones, they often felt delighted. However, today, getting more and more mobile greetings has become a great burden for many people. Therefore, in recent years, people began to advocate boycotting mobile phone greetings, especially during holidays.

There are also other social consequences of the new technology, such as spam (mainly advertising) disturbance, text message fraud, examination cheating, secret filming, pornographic photos, virus spreading and ringtone disturbance in public locations. In China, more and more mobile phone-made public events have little to do with the public good; rather, they tend to be a short-lived social farce.

While Yang emphasizes how Internet control affects the development of digital civil society in China, Guo and Wu show how the lack of regulations over the use of mobile phone can affect people's daily lives. While hundreds of millions of mobile phone users benefit from this technology, they also have to bear unwanted consequences. When the cost becomes excessive, the government has to regulate the use of mobile phones. Here, one can find what role the Chinese government should play and can play in the future development of the ICT: less political control, more digital regulation.

Selective digital control and regime legitimacy

The potential of the ICT is still far beyond one's imagination in China. The Internet and other related technologies have not only empowered social forces as in the case of the formation and development of digital civil society, but also generated various forms of cultural products such as *e gao*, reality shows and blogging. Such products are usually produced through a bottom-up process, implying the participation by different social actors. Understandably, these products are associated with different social and political meanings in the Chinese political context. In other words, social actors create these products in their relations to state power. When social forces attempt to use these products to influence the state, state power in turn comes to regulate these products.

In Chapter 3, Bingchun Meng discusses *e gao* as one form of Internet products and the regulation of *e gao*. *E gao* (literally, 'reckless doings') first appeared in China in 2006, and soon became a widespread cultural phenomenon. Meng attempts to analyse the cultural and political implications of *e gao* as a decentralized form of communication, which challenges the established mechanisms of media production and distribution as well as the officially sanctioned norms of media content in China. She first traces how this pop culture phenomenon came into formation in China and its genealogical relationships with other artistic and cultural genres, and then discusses the subversive potentials of *e gao* by focusing on three major aspects: the issue of authorship, the production and distribution mechanism, and the rhetorical strategies of *e gao* texts.

One major factor that the Internet can empower social forces is because of the decentralized nature of this technology. However, many scholars are suspicious of the decentralizing and democratizing effects of the Internet, since the key issue, as Meng points out, is how these potentials can be realized and how the dialectic of control vs. change will play out on the digital front. More often than not, a concentrated media ownership structure, be it controlled either by government or a few private media conglomerates, can become an antithetical force against the decentralizing potential of new media. The struggles between the establishment and social forces have also taken place over *e gao*.

According to Meng, the rise of the *e gao* phenomenon suggests the existence of the multiple dimensions of the control mechanism. Control does not always come in the form of censorship. As in the *e gao* case, copyright law could be as effective in curbing the availability of certain content. Moreover, *e gao* also shows that political communication could also take place in non-conventional formats with non-conventional styles.

Due to its decentralization nature, *e gao* practices are dispersed and those who engage in this activity do not have a common agenda or coherent strategy, let alone any explicit political goals. However, Meng reminds us that not having political agenda does not mean *e gao* is void of political significance. She tells us that a closer examination of the relationship between media and power structure reveals that online spoofs do at least magnify some major tensions with regard to the digital communication environment in China. Regulatory attempts have been made to deal with many issues related to *e gao*, such as who can be recognized as an author and enjoy corresponding legal protection, how media content should be produced and distributed, and what kind of content is allowed and in which style it should be presented. Such efforts can be exemplified by China's recent new online video and audio regulation.[14]

However, Meng cautions us that while it is still too early to draw any conclusions on the effect of the new regulation on online audio-video services, one should not be too hasty in celebrating the political function of *e gao* either. In a similar vein to Yang, Meng stresses that the negotiation between decentralized forms of communication and the state's constant effort of recentralizing will continue in the digital environment and the openness of the network is always contingent upon social, political and legal conditions.

In examining the relations between the ICT and politics, it is vital to note that the ICT has been an integral part of the government, meaning that the ICT has become part and parcel of the government, just as for social forces. To a great degree, the free flow of information has also become a prerequisite for the functioning of the government. In this sense, a total control of information flow will undermine the government itself, and thus prevents it from exercising power over social forces. The fact that the government can exercise its control over society does not mean good governance based on free flow of information. To cope with this dilemma, the Chinese government has adopted a strategy that can be called selective control, meaning that the government controls the information which is regarded as vital to regime stability but lets social forces access other information freely.

In Chapter 4, on Internet censorship, Guoguang Wu examines how the Chinese government has tackled this dilemma. Apparently, as many have observed, while the Internet has made governmental censorship of mass communication more difficult than before, it has also made such censorship more sophisticated. Wu argues that this sophistication of governmental control of the Internet has complicated the political ramifications in the context of globalization for both Chinese domestic politics and foreign relations.

Wu found that one trait of such sophistication lies in the Chinese government's intentional mix-up of Internet governance and political censorship. According to Wu, the Chinese government has developed what he calls the Chinese 'trinity' of Internet management, namely, a combination of Internet industrial development, legitimate regulations of digital communications, and political censorship of the web. Such a trinity has become an efficient strategy for the Chinese government to deal with the multifaceted challenge brought by the Internet.

Wu first investigates how the Chinese government has developed institutional control of the Internet and the discourse to legitimize such control in the name of Internet governance. He then develops two parameters for measuring the successes or failures of good governance of the Internet: a positive parameter, by which one can look at how the Internet, particularly through e-government, provides public services to citizens; and a negative one, by which one can examine how the governmental regulations of the Internet help reduce pornography, an annoying problem but a cause that powerfully legitimizes state control and censorship of the websites. Furthermore, he contrasts the Chinese government's effort at and impact on the online political discussions against the measurements of the above two tasks. From this three-dimensional investigation of how the Chinese state works to govern the Internet, Wu finds that the Chinese government has performed much better in political censorship, while its performance in e-government services and Internet pornography containment is relatively poor.

Indeed, one can reasonably argue that such imbalance – effective political censorship and poor governance – is deliberate on the part of the Chinese government. For the government, effective political censorship is a must to ensure political stability; meanwhile poor e-government services and Internet pornography containment is not a surprise either since society gains more leeway in the unregulated cyberspace. However, as Wu correctly points out, such imbalance in practice often victimizes good governance while benefiting the single party's monopoly of political power.

In a similar vein, Junhua Zhang examines China's memory policy over blogs in Chapter 5. The development of blogs has been rapid in China ever since this Internet-generated technology came into being. As with the Internet, the use of blogs is also characterized by decentralization. In principle, this technology enables bloggers to express themselves freely. However, the Chinese government has also exercised control over blogs, just as it does over other Internet-generated space.

The Internet as a form of informal media is surely providing people with a great variety of participatory activities in creating collective memories, be they public or private. However, Zhang tells us that in China, the dominance of officially mediated collective memory is so strong that people are forgetting things exactly as the authorities have wished. Moreover, the unwritten regulations on the part of the government such as the arbitrary restriction of narrative topics have effectively kept bloggers away from the so-called critical issues. With the enforcement of the selective memory policy, the young generations of the Chinese do not know what they should remember regarding the contemporary history, and they thus tend to be indifferent to China's authoritarian system.

To a certain extent, Zhang argues, blogs have contributed to shaping a collective memory designed by the leading political elites, and bloggers become victims of the official memory policy. As a consequence, the existing collective memory is largely politically harmless to the existing power. Needless to say, the one-sided narratives of history could be the basis of legitimacy of the government. Surely, such narratives have motivated young Chinese's nationalistic sentiments towards their perceived enemies, be it Western societies or other ethnic groups, as demonstrated in waves of nationalistic movements in recent years.

Zhang argues that a new 'patched' collective memory is not compatible with an open society where people enjoy more autonomy in deciding what they like to know and how to judge the false and correct information by themselves. However, it is important to note that the Chinese government, while enforcing the biased memory policy, could also become a victim of its own policy. For instance, when young people become increasingly nationalistic, China's nationalistic movements tend to be beyond the control of the government. Nowadays, authorities have found it increasingly difficult to bring popular nationalistic movements under control. Whenever a nationalistic movement arises, social stability becomes a major concern.

The development of ICT in China and its implications for the world

The ICT, as means of communication and information flow, has enabled China not only to get information outside China, but also to 'export' information about

China to the outside world. However, the importance of the ICT for China is far beyond communication. The Chinese government has efficiently taken advantage of the ICT to project the country onto the international stage. In Chapter 6, Xiaoling Zhang explores how the Chinese government has employed the ICT to promote the country's soft power in an increasingly globalized world.

As Zhang observed, China's rise in economic power has been accompanied by a shift from being on the defensive to the offensive in its 'foreign propaganda'. With its rapid socioeconomic transformation, China is now focusing on projecting its image as a country dedicated to international cooperation and the safeguard of peace. This shift has been greatly facilitated by the technical condition created by the rapid growth and development of the ICT in China. In other words, the new ICT – from the individualized computer to the more mass-oriented radio and television – has offered China unparalleled opportunities to reconsider conventional ways for the construction of its international image.

Zhang examines in detail how the growth of ICTs has empowered China to 'have a bigger voice' in the global competition for influencing, if not controlling, the political environment. She looks at China's infrastructure, changing policies and strategies on one hand, and the content on the key satellite channels and websites for foreign propaganda on the other. The Chinese political system has helped its 'foreign propaganda' and the pursuit for soft power in world affairs. She notes that in a liberal society, many soft-power resources are separate from the government. NGOs such as firms, universities, foundations and churches often develop soft power of their own that may reinforce or be at odds with official foreign policy goals. In contrast, in China, the government can always draw symbolic resources from the cultural and ethnic nationalism to strengthen and legitimize its statist claim of representing the Chinese, and can orchestrate 'all-dimensional, multi-channelled, wide-ranging and deep-levelled' patterns of 'foreign propaganda'.

However, Zhang cautions us that what has helped in the expansion of soft-power resources may also turn against it. ICTs are often a resource that helps produce soft power, but no mistake should be made in confusing soft power with resources. The expansion of soft power is not only about having the 'hardware', the best facilities, but also about 'software', i.e. cultural and political values, something that China is not unaware of. To pursue soft power on the world stage, what China has to offer to the world are not just quality manufacturing goods but also distinctive and attractive cultural values and products. In convincing the outside world of its peaceful intentions China faces tremendous challenges. The nature of media in China continues to go against the nature of real-time global communication by satellite television and the Internet which requires accuracy, objectivity and above all timeliness. As part of China's state-run news media they are to conform to the government's guidelines. China's international reach of media remains primarily a government undertaking, driven by the government's political imperatives. Moreover, the lines between domestic propaganda and international communication are not always sharply drawn. The Chinese government makes a difference between Chinese domestic propaganda and international communication: more relaxed to outsiders and stricter with insiders for the sake of domestic political and social stability. In reality, however, propaganda for domestic purposes has been simply carried over into international communication. The old-fashioned Chinese propaganda will hardly be acceptable in the international community. In short, civil liberty has been the foundation of all soft powers in the West, including the media itself. Without the development of civil liberty first, China will find it ineffective to project itself on the world stage in a favourable light.

In Chapter 7, on web engineering, Kieron O'Hara examines the political philosophy behind the design of the World Wide Web (WWW), and expresses his concerns over China's information control in the long run. According to O'Hara, the revolutionary aspect of the WWW is that it is a decentralized information structure. This democratic decentralization is a key factor in the added value that the Web provides, because it facilitates the serendipitous re-use of information in new and unanticipated contexts. Embedded in the design of the WWW is political liberalism. The WWW has grown because of its support of the free and democratic flow of information. Indeed, it is the free flow where value is added to information. However, the Chinese government is much more interested in the value than the freedom. This is a serious issue for those steering the development of the WWW, especially when China becomes more involved in global affairs, including global Internet governance. As the number of its users outgrows other countries, it is an important question how it will choose to increase its impact on global Internet governance.

According to O'Hara, the globe-wise hands-off strategy developed during the 1990s to support the use of the WWW in science, research and commerce, which restricted the regulation of the Web, has allowed China (and other illiberal regimes) to flout liberal principles in this way. Also due to liberal principles, there are no affirmative globally-recognized principles governing the flow of information online. The basic principle of free flow of information packets and a very simple set of rules and standards underpinning these complex structures could be undermined by attempts to restrict information flow. As use of the Web has spread, many illiberal regimes such as China feel threatened. China's political censorship of the Internet is pervasive and its policy-makers show no sign of willingness to change this. Increasingly, China is itself becoming a manufacturer of Internet backbone equipment and related information technology, and it has a vested interest in doing more of its own research and development and in promoting its own information technology standards globally. How China will approach the issue of global standards for the future design and development of the Internet is likely to be an important issue for Western nations, and especially the European Union, as China's economic power and political influence grows.

China now regularly uses Internet filtering technologies, looking for specific keywords or IP addresses, while regulating bloggers and Internet cafés and suborning big Western Internet firms such as Yahoo! and Google to censor sensitive content, and all the while employing web-policemen to trawl the Web for content of which it disapproves. O'Hara points out, what is worrying about the Chinese model in the context of the WWW is that it is particularly pernicious. The Chinese approach is centralized, and more importantly, opaque, making the operation of the Web unclear. The frequency and scale of the censorship is invisible to users, and therefore the extent of it may not be fully known to the Chinese public.

China tends to play an increasingly important role in global Internet governance. How to deal with an authoritarian China? China will clearly remain in charge of its own laws, and is entitled as a sovereign nation to regulate behaviour within its borders. This cannot be wished away. According to O'Hara, an engagement policy will be inevitable. A 'principled' approach to China on the part of the West could result in a vast reduction of digital contact. Needless to say, this does ignore the possibility of using the WWW to ease China into a more liberal stance, as well as – given the size of the Chinese online presence – risking the integrity and connectivity of the WWW itself. A hard-line approach to China could split the WWW into two more or less separate networks; currently it is not clear how damaging this might be. Apparently, one has to wait and see how the West will engage China over cyberspace and how such engagement will transform China.

Whither China's digital control?

An ultimate question to be asked is whither China's digital control? Its engagement with the West continues to be important, as it was in the past. However, it will be unrealistic to expect that China can be transformed by external forces. Therefore, it is more important to look into the internal dynamics for changes over cyberspace. In Chapter 8, Yongnian Zheng attempts to search for the internal dynamics for changes over digital control on the part of the Chinese government.

Zheng explores the political cost of information control in China. Yes, the Chinese government has exercised tight information control in order to maintain its dominance over social forces. However, information control involves high political costs of different types. More often than not, it leads to poor performance in governance. Zheng argues that it is seemingly 'rational' for the Chinese government to maximize the benefit from Internet development while minimizing its cost. Nevertheless, in reality, it is difficult to define what the benefits are and what the costs are. To look at the political cost of information control will lead one to rethink the sustainability of information control. At a certain point, the cost of information control might become larger than the benefit. If this is the case, the government, as a rational actor, will have to allow freer flow of information, and liberalize information control.

Zheng identifies different forms of cost associated with information control. He focuses on the political cost of information control from two perspectives: first, how information control prevents China from developing rational forms of nationalism and thus modernizing the nation-state; and second, how information control prevents China from developing good governance, as exemplified by the SARS epidemic in 2003. According to Zheng, information control has led to a distorted Chinese nation-state. In terms of national integration, information control has perhaps prevented any independence movements among ethnic groups, but in the long run it can also prevent the development of any shared values and thus state identity among different ethnic groups. At the international level, information control has distorted Chinese nationalism, and thus affects China's relations with other countries.

Furthermore, information control has had a seriously negative impact on governance in China. Information control seemingly enables the state to control society and leads to a situation of a 'strong state and weak society'. However, in reality, both the state and society can be weakened because of information control by the state. Good governance results from the effective interaction between the state and society under a condition of free flow of information.

Zheng believes that the distorted nation-state and bad governance imply that information control is not sustainable in the long run. Many factors have come into being to facilitate a greater degree of information liberalization in China. China has rapidly developed a market economy. The functioning of the market economy depends on the free flow of information. All individuals within this market make decisions according to the information they collect. China has now been integrated into the world economy. Information control will not only affect the Chinese economy, but also the whole world economy. Furthermore, Chinese society is becoming increasingly open, meaning that the functioning of society is also dependent on the free flow of information. This is also true in terms of political participation. Without the free flow of information, there will be no meaningful political participation. All these developments require information liberalization. Zheng seems to be optimistic about cyberspace liberalization in China. But his optimism has a sound rationale: when the cost of information control is becoming increasingly high, control becomes unsustainable.

Notes

1 From the website of Xinhua News Agency, at http://news.xinhuanet.com/internet/2008–03/14/content_7786806.htm (accessed 18 May 2008).

2 From the website of the Ministry of Information Industry of the People's Republic of China, at www.mii.gov.cn/art/2008/04/25/art_27_37173.html (accessed 16 May 2008).

3 From the website of China Internet Network Information Centre (CNNIC), at www.cnnic.net.cn/html/Dir/2007/12/27/4954.htm (accessed 18 May 2008).

4 For some latest works on Internet nationalism in China, see, Xu Wu, *Chinese Cyber Nationalism: Evolution, Characteristics, and Implications* (Lanham, Boulder: Lexington Books, 2007); and Simon Shen, *Redefining Nationalism in Modern China: Sino-American Relations and the Emergence of Chinese Public Opinion in the 21st Century* (New York: Palgrave, 2007).

5 In 2003, Sun Zhigang died in police custody in Guangzhou after being detained illegally with a temporary resident permit under custody and repatriation (C&R) regulations. The spreading of the news on the Internet led to a public outcry against the practice. Senior Chinese legal scholars wrote to the legislature, questioning the constitutionality of this regulation. One particular problem with the regulations was that they were adopted as regulations by the State Council and not as a law by the full National People's Congress (NPC), and as a result it was argued that the law was

unconstitutional on the grounds that it violated Article 8 of the Legislation Law of the People's Republic of China. In June 2003, Premier Wen Jiabao announced that C&R regulations were abolished and would be replaced by Measures for Assisting Vagrants and Beggars with No Means of Support in Cities.

6 This brief discussion also appears in Yongnian Zheng, *Technological Empowerment: The Internet, State, and Society in China* (Stanford: Stanford University Press, 2008), Chapter 1.

7 For example, Peter B. Evans, Dietrich Rueschemeyer and Theda Skocpol, eds, *Bringing the State Back In* (New York: Cambridge University Press, 1985).

8 For example, Joel S. Migdal, *Strong Societies and Weak States: State-Society Relations and State Capabilities in the Third World* (Princeton: Princeton University Press, 1988); and Atul Kohli, ed., *The State and Development in the Third World* (Princeton: Princeton University Press, 1986).

9 For a useful review, see Xu Wang, 'Mutual Empowerment of State and Society: Its Nature, Conditions, Mechanisms, and Limits', *Comparative Politics*, vol. 31, no. 2 (1999), pp. 231–49.

10 For example, Shaoguang Wang and Hu Angang, *The Chinese Economy in Crisis: State Capacity and Tax Reform* (Armonk: M. E. Sharpe, 2001). The original Chinese version was published in 1993 when the Chinese government began to recentralize its fiscal power, see Wang Shaoguang and Hu Angang, *Zhongguo guojia nengli baogao* (A Report on State Capacity in China) (Shenyang: Liaoning renmin chubanshe, 1993). For a discussion of statism in China, see, Yongnian Zheng, *Discovering Chinese Nationalism in China: Modernization, Identity and International Relations* (Cambridge: Cambridge University Press, 1999), pp. 38–44.

11 For example, Joel S. Migdal, Atul Kohli and Vivienne Shue, eds, *State Power and Social Forces: Domination and Transformation in the Third World* (New York: Cambridge University Press, 1994); Peter Evans, *Embedded Autonomy: States and Industrial Transformation* (Princeton: Princeton University Press, 1995); Joel S. Migdal, *State in Society: Studying How States and Societies Transform and Constitute One Another* (New York: Cambridge University Press, 2001).

12 Wang, 'Mutual Empowerment of State and Society', p. 232.

13 Adam Przeworski, Pranab Bardhan, Luiz Carlos, Bresser Pereira, Laszlo Bruszt, Jang Jip Choi, Ellen Turkish Comisso and Zhiyuan Cui, *Sustainable Democracy* (New York: Cambridge University Press, 1995).

14 Yongnian Zheng, 'Online Audio and Video Regulations: Analysis', *E-Commerce Law and Policy*, The E-Commerce Newsletter for Lawyers, March 2008, pp. 7–9.

1 Historical imagination in the study of Chinese digital civil society[1]

Guobin Yang

For years, media scholars have lamented the lack of historical methods and sensibilities in communication studies, especially in political communication. They have called for more attention to the culture and institutions of communication.[2] Current studies of the Chinese Internet suffer from a similar deficit of historical imagination. This is partly because the Internet has only a short history in China. It is partly also because the Internet scene changes so fast that it may appear as a moving target. With the rush to catch the target, there is little time left to look back. But the Internet is no more a moving target than other social processes. Historical imagination is just as important for understanding it.

Historical imagination is not just about providing the historical background for what is happening at present. Nor is it about discovering historical precedents of a new phenomenon and thereby implying that nothing under the sun is new. Historical sociology views social formations as the outcomes of the interactions between social action and social structure. It is about how people make history under conditions not of their own making. Such analysis is about changes and processes. In them, the past is neither just data nor background, but the very conditions that constitute the present.[3]

One way of infusing historical imagination into studies of the Chinese Internet is to stop viewing its history as a continuous flow of time still unfolding before our eyes. Such a view ironically gives the wrong impression of an eternity and minimizes the sense of change. Although the history of the Internet in China is short, it is possible to analyze it by breaking it down into smaller sections using the strategy of periodization, thus making it possible to highlight both continuities and discontinuities and to identify their underlying conditions. It can reveal change.

My analysis will focus on digital civil society, a new social formation that has emerged from the interactions between the Internet and civil society. I will make a distinction between two periods of digital civil society development in China. The period of emergence dates from the mid-1990s to 2002. Beginning in 2003, Chinese digital civil society entered a stage of expansion. The two periods evince the same logic of complex interactions among multiple actors, especially the interactions among the state, market and civil society actors. This explains both the emergence of digital civil society in the first period and its expansion in the second. Yet the dynamics of interactions assume some new features in the second period with all the major actors modifying their strategies, partly in response to the first stage of development. This complicates the interaction dynamics in the second stage.

The logic of complex interdependence and the origins of digital civil society

Lester M. Salamon and Helmut K. Anheier proposed an influential "social origins" theory of civil society to explain national variations in non-profit sector development. Their theory is instructive for understanding the development of a Chinese digital civil society. Salamon and Anheier argue that while most other theories are single-factor explanations, the "social origins theory" takes into account the complex constellation of conditions that shape the non-profit sector. They trace their theoretical roots to Barrington Moore's theory of the origins of fascism and democracy and Esping-Anderson's theory of the origins of the modern welfare state. As they put it,

> complex social phenomena – for example, the emergence of the "welfare state" or "democracy" – cannot be easily understood as the product of the unilinear extension of a single factor, such as industrialization, diversity, or education. Rather, much more complex interrelationships among social classes and social institutions are involved.[4]

One weakness in current studies of the socio-political impact of the Internet is a focus on single factors – typically the Internet technology or the state. This leads to the ironical result of either exaggerating the influence of technology at the expense of politics or the other way round. The tensions, contradictions and synergies that arise out of the interactions among multiple arenas of technology, politics, culture, society and economy are often neglected. The formation of Chinese digital civil society is a historical process involving the interactions between civil society and the Internet under conditions of complex interdependence. These conditions provide the structure of opportunities and constraints for social action, but do not determine it. Rather, structure and action are mutually constitutive. This means that the historical formation of a Chinese digital civil society has no teleology. Its path is not predetermined but is open to struggle and negotiation.

Political, economic, technological and social conditions act on the development of digital civil society, but also react to it. Interaction is the dominant dynamics. The concept of complex interdependence helps to capture these interactions. Complex interdependence refers to the mutual influences among multiple actors. Developed for the study of international relations, the theory of complex interdependence originally refers to mutual influences resulting from "international transactions – flows of money, goods, people and messages across international boundaries."[5] The emphasis is on the interactions and interdependence among multiple actors and the ascending role of civil society actors.

The information revolution has changed one feature of complex interdependence by vastly increasing the number of channels of contact between societies.[6] Because of the plenitude of free information, credibility becomes an essential basis of influence. Thus the influence of states will depend increasingly on their ability to remain credible. This ability can now be more easily challenged by non-state actors, however, because the information revolution gives citizens the means to transmit critical information across vast distances more easily.

The concept of complex interdependence can be extended to the study of national politics. In China, economic reform has moved Chinese society increasingly closer to conditions of complex interdependence. Whereas the state dominated Chinese economy and society in earlier times, the reform has brought about structural differentiation. A "halting" pluralism appeared that provided the structural conditions for the co-evolution of the Internet and civil society.[7] Although the state remains dominant, it is increasingly subject to pressure from non-state actors such as business interests and citizens. Complex interdependence means that in the age of information, total control of information is impossible. The potential to expose false information and reveal hidden information always exists, while citizens and citizen groups will use multiple information channels to challenge state actors. As some scholars have argued, the media revolution has put constraints on the Chinese government even in foreign policy,[8] a field that traditionally is insensitive to external pressure. It is in this context that the Internet and civil society have energized each other in their co-evolution, leading to the rise of a new social formation – a digital civil society.

Digital formations and Chinese digital civil society

Digital formations are social forms that emerge around and through the use of information technologies. In formulating this concept, Robert Latham and Saskia Sassen discuss such cases of digital formations as electronic markets, Internet-based large-scale conversations, and knowledge spaces arising out of NGO networks.[9] A focus on digital formations has the advantage of avoiding technological determinism. A common form of technological determinism makes statements like "television has altered our world."[10] The Internet version of such statements would run like: "the Internet has altered our world." Negative statements like "the Internet does not change anything" or "the Internet does not lead to democractization" are guided by similar assumptions of technological determinism. Indeed, they represent a more deceptive form of technological determinism because they make it appear as if they were opposed to it. An analytical focus on digital formations does not ask questions about the impact of the Internet per se. Instead, attention is directed at dynamics and outcomes of the interactions between technology and society. Such an analysis proceeds on the condition that the interactions have taken place for long enough to produce recognizable social formations.

The interactions between the Internet and Chinese civil society have been sustained for well over a decade. What are the main components of a Chinese digital civil society formation? When scholars talk about Chinese civil society, they focus, with varying degrees of emphasis, on civic organizations, popular resistance, or public channels and spaces for communication.[11] An important recent study of Asian civil societies follows a similar conceptualization, where civil society is broadly defined to include all the above components:

> as a distinct public sphere of organization, communication and reflective discourse, and governance among individuals and groups that take collective action deploying civil means to influence the state and its policies but not capture state power, and whose activities are not motivated by profit.[12]

Following this conceptualization, I will consider civic associations, civic spaces of communication and civic action as the core elements of civil society. With respect to civic associations, Chinese digital civil society encompasses the large numbers of online communities, web-based social networks and loose organizations, as well as the active online presence of offline civic associations. In terms of civic spaces of communication, it consists of numerous BBS forums, blogs and online magazines. Finally, I will consider Internet-based activism and contentious activities as the third element of a Chinese digital civil society.

Periodization and the study of the Chinese Internet

Periodization literally means identifying different periods of a historical process. It is based on the assumption that social processes have both continuities and discontinuities. By identifying periods, analysts can identify common and distinct features. As Bob Jessop puts it,

> The main aim of any periodization is to interpret an otherwise undifferentiated "flow" of historical time by classifying events and/or processes in terms of their internal affinities and external differences in order to identify successive periods of relative invariance and the transitions between them.[13]

The criteria of periodization vary with the object of analysis. In some cases, historical periods are ready-made and the analyst simply follows existing schemes. Historians of the Cultural Revolution in China, for example, follow the officially established periodization of the Cultural Revolution as the decade from 1966 to 1976. Periodization is often contested because it can have important political implications. Thus for some analysts of the Cultural Revolution, it did not last until 1976 but ended in 1969. My point is that there are no "objective" criteria for cutting up history. And yet periodization is a useful way of framing history. In this sense, periodization serves the same function as a picture frame. It is best seen as a heuristic analytic tool.

Several attempts have been made to periodize the history of the Internet in China. The "official" attempt was made in a public exhibit about the development of the Internet. This exhibit was organized by the Chinese Internet Network Information Center on the occasion of the Third China Internet Conference in September 2004. The exhibit divided the history into five periods. The first period, from 1987 to 1994, was the exploratory stage.[14] The second period, from 1994 to 1996, was called the stage of "readiness" (*xushi daifa*). Between 1996 and 1998, the third period, the Internet began to take off. The fourth period was from 1999 to 2002, when the Internet gathered momentum. Finally, the Internet entered a fifth period in 2003. This is the period of prosperity.[15]

Ernest Wilson's comparative study of the information revolution in developing countries contains a periodization of the commercial development of the Internet in China. He identifies four phases of market structuring. The first, precommercial phase was from 1987 to about 1993. The second, from 1993 to 1995, was a transitional period to the commercial. The third phase, from 1996 to 1997, was commercialization. The fourth, from 1998 to 2000, was the competitive period. Although Wilson's study ends around 2000 and therefore does not have a fifth phase, he does suggest that following the competitive period will be a phase of consolidation and expansion of the Chinese Internet market.[16]

What about the history of the political regulation and control of the Internet in China? No periodization has been proposed, but three periods are recognizable. In the first period, from 1994 to 1999, the Chinese state built a basic legal and administrative framework for regulating computer networks and information security. In 1994, for example, the State Council issued "Safety and Protection Regulations for Computer Information Systems." In 1997, the Ministry of Public Security issued "Computer Information Network and Internet Security, Protection and Management Regulations," which outlines the duties and responsibilities of China's Internet service providers. In the second stage, from 2000 to 2003, the state introduced a set of policies to control contents through the regulation and registration of ISPs, ICPs and ordinary users. For example, regulations specifically targeting BBS were announced in November 2000, stipulating that bulletin board services should follow a licensing procedure.[17] The third phase, from 2004 to the present, marks the expansion of Internet regulation and control from government to governance and governmentality.[18] Examples are official initiatives to promote self-discipline and professional code of conduct targeting both IT businesses and consumers.

These periodizations of the history, business and politics of the Chinese Internet reveal an important historical pattern, which is a historical paradox. Ernest Wilson puts it in the following terms:

> As the markets in Beijing, Shanghai, Guangzhou, and other cities grew more competitive and structurally sophisticated and the Internet's versatility became more obvious to ordinary consumers, the information revolution became increasingly problematic for government and party officials. As Internet diffusion exploded, the Beijing government imposed some of the harshest restrictions in the world.... Rapid technological growth was simultaneously combined with hard policy restrictions.[19]

As I will argue below, the same paradox of development and control pertains to the development of Chinese digital civil society. Indeed, the development of digital civil society parallels remarkably the three stages of Internet regulation and control, indicating a strangely symbiotic relationship between these two processes.

Two stages of digital civil society development

The contours of a Chinese digital civil society appeared in the period from the mid-1990s to 2002. During this period, the number of Internet users in China increased from about 670,000 in 1997 to 59 million in 2002. New types of civil society organizations, such as environmental NGOs, multiplied. New forms of citizen activism, known as rights defense (*weiquan*), became common. More and more international NGOs set up offices in China. Communication and interactions between Chinese civil society groups and international communities proliferated. Chinese society as a whole became increasingly contentious.[20] All these contributed to the marriage of civil society with new information and communication technologies, leading to the rise of a digital civil society. This fledgling digital civil society was evident in three areas.[21] First was the proliferation of BBS (bulletin board system) forums and online publics engaged in discussions and debates about social issues. One study published in 2003 finds that online discussions in chatrooms were helping to set public agendas.[22] Yongming Zhou's study of the influential intellectual website the "Realm of Ideas" similarly provides evidence of public discussions fostered by website publications.[23] Second, civic associations began to go online[24] while web-based civic organizations and online communities multiplied.[25] Third was the emergence of online activism, namely, the use of the Internet for contentious activities. Cyber-nationalism is among the earliest instances of Chinese online activism.[26] In addition, many other forms of online activism appeared then, including the extensive use of the Internet for expressing dissent and political opposition by transnational actors on the global stage.[27]

In 2003, the fledgling digital civil society entered a stage of expansion. Since then, not only have BBS forums and online publics grown, but online public opinion has attained greater influence. Internet incidents (*wangluo shijian*), a form of Internet-centered political contention, has become a major source of online public opinion. In ordinary times, the vast majority of Chinese netizens are engaged in routinized online communication. Such communication may become radicalized as netizens respond fervently to offline events and crises involving cases of social injustice, corruption, disadvantaged social groups and nationalism. Such cases of online activism were already happening in the late 1990s and early 2000s, but they have increased in frequency and impact since 2003. In 2003 alone, several major cases happened, including the Sun Zhigang case, the BMW case and the Liu Yong case.[28]

Since 2003, online activism has not only grown in frequency, but has also diversified in form. The above-mentioned cases are relatively spontaneous forms of contention in reaction to social crises. Their impact depends on intensified, but episodic, mass participation. Two interesting new forms have appeared in recent years. One is blog-based citizen journalism, where individual citizens use their personal blogs to cover critical social issues. The most prominent case of such citizen journalism was Zola Zhou's coverage of the "nail household" incident in Chongqing in 2007. In perhaps the first scholarly study of *dingzihu* in Chinese villages, Lianjiang Li and Kevin O'Brien consider them as "recalcitrants" who "react vigorously to state extraction and cadre demands," "direct their attacks against dishonest, incompetent, and partial cadres," and "often respond to mistreatment (or perceived mistreatment) with threats to disrupt cadre assignments."[29] "Nail-like" persons are rightful resisters. They challenge authorities on the basis of laws and official policies. The "nail household" incident in the city of Chongqing concerned specifically a couple who refused to relocate because they were unhappy with the compensation package. With all the neighborhood driven away and the construction project already under way, their house stuck out from the ground like a stubborn nail, refusing to budge (see Figure 1.1). When blogger Zola Zhou, a 26-year-old man from Hunan province, learned about this, he traveled a long way from his hometown to Chongqing. There, he blogged live about the house, its owners and local citizens' views about the incident. His lengthy and detailed blog entries directed a great deal of attention, including international media attention, to the incident, and was instrumental in helping the owners win a more favorable compensation package.

The other new form of online activism is a more routinized and organized form of online contention known as online rights defense (*wangluo weiquan*). The use of the Internet for rights defense already appeared in the late 1990s.[30] Yet the scale and impact of online rights defense have significantly expanded in recent years.[31] On December 10, 2007, I conducted a keyword search of the Chinese characters for *weiquan wang*, or rights defense websites, using China's popular engine baidu.com. The search generated 2,820,000 results. Another key word search of *wangluo weiquan* (Internet rights defense) generated 261,000

Figure 1.1 "Nail house" in Chongqing, 2007.

results. There are now so many websites, BBS forums and blogs devoted fully or partially to rights defense that online rights defense has become a notable new phenomenon.

The past few years have also seen the expansion of online communities. Tianya.com and the online communities in major portal sites are obvious examples. Web-based social networks and voluntary associations that organize offline civic activities have proliferated. A case study of citizen-organized ceremonies in memory of Confucius shows that the Internet is central to trans-local voluntary organizing.[32] Other examples include the influential online organization 1kg.org launched in 2004. The organization combines tourism with charity and calls on its members, mostly young tourists, to carry "one more kilo" when they travel to poor regions of the country. This one kilo could be books, stationery and such things that might be donated to the poor children in those regions. Together, the growing number of online communities and web-based organizations and networks constitute part of an associational revolution unfolding in China in recent years.[33]

What has made it possible for Chinese digital civil society to continue to expand since 2003? There are important reasons for asking this question. For in appearance, Chinese digital civil society should not have easily expanded. After the high tide of online activism in 2003, state control of the Internet became tightened and more refined. In September 2004, Yitahutu (YTHT), a bulletin board forum hosted by Beijing University and one of the most influential of its kind in China, was closed down by an administrative order jointly issued by several government agencies. Toward the end of the year, procedures for the annual inspection of registered non-governmental organizations were tightened.[34] "Public intellectuals" came under assault in official media.[35] In 2005, the influential intellectual website Yannan was closed. And following the closure of Yitahutu in the previous year, many university-based BBS forums were overhauled or closed to users from outside the university communities. This included the closure of SMTH, the earliest and most influential university BBS in China. At the same time, new state initiatives were launched in 2004 aimed both at containing the Internet and channeling users to officially endorsed sources of online information. All these developments indicate shrinking political opportunities for digital civil society. And yet, as I showed above, digital civil society has continued to expand. Why?

Persistent dynamics of digital civil society

The continuing evolution of digital civil society suggests that the conditions that originally created it still pertain today. First, institutionalized channels for public participation (e.g. the petition system) are still weak or ineffective. Thus citizens need alternative channels of communication. The Internet meets this need better than official channels. Second, the social issues that initially fed Internet discussions have not been solved, but have become exacerbated. The issues are broad-ranging, but of utmost concern to ordinary citizens are social injustice, corruption, social inequality and the abuse of power. They reflect social discontents about the negative effects of China's economic development. The third factor is the parallel growth of the Internet and civil society. All three conditions are present in the two periods under study. Yet the third condition, especially the Internet, significantly expanded in the second stage such that its power has grown relative to the first period.

The Internet has sustained the momentum of growth since 2003. As Table 1.1 shows, at the end of 2002, there were 59.1 million Internet users in China. By June 2007, this number had exceeded 162 million. The number of computer hosts grew from 20.8 in December 2002 to 67.1 million in June 2007 while the number of websites increased from 371,600 to 1,310,000.

Besides, there have appeared some new developments since 2003. The most important for our purposes is the rapid expansion of SMS, broadband and blogs. In June 2007, over 75 percent of Chinese Internet users were using broadband access and over 34 percent were using wireless or mobile phone access. In 2002, there were about 230,000 active blogs in China. As Figure 1.2 shows, this number increased to over 7.6 million in 2006.[36]

Table 1.1 Selected indicators of Internet growth in China, 2002 and 2007

	December 2002	*June 2007*
Number of Internet users	59.1 million	162 million
Number of computer hosts	20.8 million	67.1 million
Number of websites	371,600	1.3 million

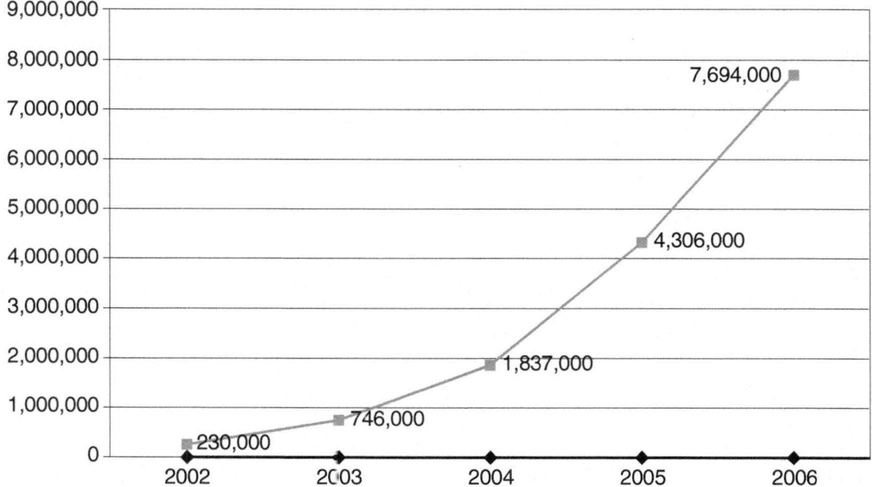

Figure 1.2 Number of active blogs in China, 2002–2006 (source: www.cnnic.net.co).

In the first period, e-civil society in China was ahead of e-government and e-commerce. This trend still holds in the second period. People still use the Internet far more for social purposes than for commercial purposes or for interacting with the government. E-government practices have improved,[37] but remain limited in scale and influence.[38] E-commerce has grown but is seriously underdeveloped. Table 1.2 shows that for the period 1999–2002, more people used BBS and newsgroups than online shopping and online payment. Table 1.3 shows that from 2003 to the present, the trend remains much the same. Both the uses of BBS and online shopping have grown in parallel fashion, but online shopping still lags behind the use of BBS and online communities.

Table 1.2 Most frequently used network services in China (multiple options), June 1999–June 2004 (in percent)

	Email	*Newsgroups*	*BBS*	*Online shopping*	*Online payment*
June 1999	90.9	21.4	28.0	3.2	N/A
December 1999	71.7	17.0	16.3	7.8	1.8
June 2000	87.7	25.4	21.2	14.1	3.7
December 2000	87.7	19.3	16.7	12.5	2.7
June 2001	74.9	10.7	9.0	8.0	1.8
December 2001	92.2	13.4	9.8	7.8	2.1
June 2002	92.9	20.4	18.9	10.3	N/A
December 2002	92.6	21.3	18.9	11.5	N/A
June 2003	91.8	20.7	22.6	11.7	N/A
December 2003	88.4	N/A	18.8	7.3	N/A
June 2004	84.3	N/A	21.3	7.3	N/A

Source: CNNIC survey reports. See www.cnnic.net.cn.

Table 1.3 Most frequently used network services in China (multiple options), June 2003–June 2007 (in percent)

	Email community	*BBS*	*Blog*	*Online shopping*
June 2003	91.8	22.6	N/A	11.7
December 2003	88.4	18.8	N/A	7.3
June 2004	84.3	21.3	N/A	7.3
December 2004	85.6	20.8	N/A	6.7
June 2005	91.3	40.6	10.5	19.6
December 2005	64.7	41.6	14.2	24.5
June 2006	64.2	43.2	23.7	26.0
December 2006	56.1	36.9	25.3	23.6
June 2007	55.4	69.8 (online chat etc.)	19.1	25.5

Source: CNNIC survey reports. See www.cnnic.net.cn.

In the past five years, civil society has experienced some ups and downs due to changing political conditions, but many indicators suggest that expansion is the general trend. For one thing, traditional types of civic and grassroots associations have been undergoing a renaissance. Second, the number of civic associations continues to grow. Officially registered civic organizations numbered at 360,000 at the end of 2006, although estimates put the actual numbers at about three million.[39] Take environmental NGOs for example. In April 2001, there were about 184 student environmental organizations in China. In 2002, there were fewer than 100 non-student ENGOs. By 2005, the number of grassroots ENGOs had doubled to more than 200 while student environmental associations exceeded 1,000.[40] Spaces for environmental civic action have increased.[41] These developments prompted Chinese scholars to claim, in a *Blue Book of Civil Society Development in China* compiled in 2007, that "China has crossed the doorsteps of a civil society."[42]

Despite setbacks such as the removal of the editor of the well-known "Freezing Point" magazine under the *Beijing Youth Daily*, the space for public communication and discussion has expanded. Again take environmental issues as an example. Public discussions about environmental issues have become more extensive and contentious, as evidenced in the debates surrounding dam-building on the Nu River and the "Respect Nature" debate in 2005. Debates about all sorts of other critical social issues not only fill cyberspace, but have become important sources of information for mainstream mass media. Other examples include the public debates surrounding the so-called "black kiln" case, a case which indicated both the intensity and scale of public debates and the growing trend of the convergence of the Internet and the mass media in generating public opinion.[43]

Third, a citizens' rights defense movement has been gaining momentum. All forms of citizen action, radical or moderate, have been happening, involving migrants, peasants, workers and homeowners. The struggles for citizen rights already started in the 1980s, but they have taken on new forms in the recent decade. This prompted the Chinese scholar Fan Yafeng to suggest that after 2003, citizenship struggles "went social."[44] They became a general social phenomenon instead of being limited to small intellectual and activist circles. The expansion of online rights defense I discussed above is closely related to the broader trend of rights defense in China today.

New dynamics in the period of expansion

Besides these pre-existing conditions, several new conditions become salient in the second period and complicate the dynamics of digital civil society development. First, developments in the IT industry present new economic conditions. The success of China's major dotcom companies cannot be separated from the entrepreneurs' understanding of people's social and communication needs. When the Internet began to be commercialized in China in the mid-1990s, the most astute IT entrepreneurs saw the importance of social networking. The most successful network services, from bulletin board systems to online chatting and online communities, are based on business strategies aimed at meeting these communicative needs. In recent years, the salience of citizen-consumers in the consciousness and business strategies of dotcom companies has never been more evident. More than ever before, dotcom CEOs have realized the centrality of user-generated content (UGC) to website traffic. This partly explains the recent buzz about Web 2.0.[45]

The second new condition is the changing forms of political control. The second stage of digital civil society development began with a regime change. In September 2002, Hu Jintao replaced Jiang Zemin as the general secretary of the Chinese Communist Party. Soon, in March 2003, Hu also took over as the head of the state. The fourth generation of Chinese leadership thus took power. This has profound implications for all areas of Chinese life, including digital civil society. The new wave of Internet control mentioned earlier took place under the new regime. This indicates continuity with the previous regime under Jiang Zemin when institutions and mechanisms of Internet control first began to be built. Another continuity is that while exercising control, the Chinese government continues to support the IT industry. State authorities have become increasingly aware of the centrality of web content to the industry and are not prepared to dissolve the prosperity of the Internet by controlling all content. On June 3 and 4, 2007, the Chinese government convened a national conference on Internet culture construction and management. According to the cover story in the July 2007 issue of the magazine *New Media*, a main theme of the conference was to promote a Chinese-style Internet culture that combines prosperity and control. This theme conveyed the message about the importance of both a thriving and a controlled Internet, despite the seemingly impossible mission of trying to maintain both prosperity and control.

Internet control also has an important new feature in the second stage. As I mentioned earlier, from 2004 to the present, Internet regulation and control have expanded. The broad pattern of expansion is from government to governance and governmentality. This expansion is reflected in new government initiatives to refine strategies of governance. Specifically, there is more emphasis on the use of legal mechanisms as a means of regulation and control and on promoting the online influence of official mass media. In addition, there are new initiatives to promote corporate social responsibility among IT businesses and ethical conduct among Internet users. For example, in 2004, China Internet Society, an NGO under state sponsorship (GONGO), launched a website for ordinary users to voluntarily report on cases involving Internet violations.

The third new condition is risk society. More than any other time, the year 2003 marked China's entry into the age of risk society. Disasters, emergencies, environmental risks, industrial accidents and all sorts of crisis situations have happened before, but they are not as frequent and as fateful as in recent years. The SARS crisis in 2003 drove home the message of the risk society.[46] The Songhua River pollution in 2005 served as an additional reminder. These accidents have strengthened the awareness, both among government leaders and ordinary citizens, that risks are becoming a part of life and that managing risks require more effective, more accountable and more transparent institutions. In such a risk society, information disclosure and citizen participation become essential for rapid state response. At the same time, the expansion of new information technologies makes it more difficult for the state to control the spread of local sources of information.

Conclusion

To summarize, what does the combination of old and new conditions mean for the expansion of digital civil society? It creates a situation of complex interactions in which digital civil society faces both opportunities and constraints. The state has refined its strategies of control but recognizes the importance of the prosperity of the Internet industry. Business interests know the political limits even as they are pursuing benefits. The same applies to digital civil society. In their use of the Internet, civil society actors are fully aware of political limits even as they often span the boundaries.[47] Thus the new forms of Internet activism such as online rights defense, with their emphasis on legal and rights-based resistance, are responses to refined political control. The dynamics of digital civil society are characterized by multiple interaction, negotiation and evolution.

One goal of this chapter is to explore the possibilities of using the strategy of periodization to introduce a historical sensibility into the study of the Chinese Internet. I divided the history of a Chinese digital civil society into two periods. The period of emergence covered the years from the mid-1990s to 2002, whereas the period of expansion covers the years from 2003 to the present (the end of 2007 as of this writing). In some sense, this is a heuristic distinction. Other authors may divide the history in different ways. My main purpose, however, is to demonstrate that periodization is a useful method of infusing history into current scholarship on the Chinese Internet. By viewing the development of a Chinese digital civil society in two different periods, I have shown that both the shape of this digital civil society and the conditions that help to mold it contain differences as well as continuities in the two periods.

This finding adds nuance to the understanding of a host of issues related to a Chinese digital civil society. It shows that not only does civic use of the Internet constantly undergo changes, but the politics and business of the Internet also change. New social conditions keep appearing that impinge on the dynamics of a fledgling digital civil society. Identifying the persistent and new conditions is essential for understanding the changing dynamics of Chinese digital civil society. Periodization helps to highlight these conditions.

Finally, my analysis of the multidimensional conditions underlying the two periods has implications for understanding the future challenges and opportunities of Chinese digital civil society. The challenges are threefold – digital divide, commercialization and digital control. Commercialization of the media, both in China and elsewhere, has often been viewed as a corrupting influence. The commercialization of the Internet, for example, may lead to the excessive use of the Internet for entertainment and advertising. Digital divide refers mainly to the digital gap between the rural and the urban population. The rural Internet survey report issued by CNNIC in August 2007 shows that only 5.1 percent of the 737 million rural population is online while 21.6 percent of the urban population is online. Finally, the evolving regime of political control, with its constant refining of strategies and tactics of control, suggests that a shift is taking place from punitive power to disciplinary power, which a Foucaultian perspective might view as biopower. The essence of biopower is to harness human subjects in the service of the state's agendas. It is a *productive* power because it enables the production of particular kinds of knowledge, subjects and needs. Examples of this biopower regime include efforts to shift to "soft control" (*roushi guanli*) and to make use of the Internet in the inculcation of dominant values. A future challenge here is the extent to which the biopower regime will mold digital civil society in its own image.

The challenges therefore are formidable. But, paradoxically, they are also opportunities because of their internal tension and contradictions. Political control of the Internet has not slowed down the evolution of the Internet and civil society in the past. It will not in the future. In fact, much of the dynamism, energy and creativity of the Chinese Internet culture is generated in reaction to regulations and control. This suggests that control can backfire. Oppression always meets with resistance. The symbiosis between the Internet and civil society in a broader institutional environment of complex interdependence contains a dynamism that resists control. Similarly, the commercialization of the Internet may have its positive side. It is unreasonable to expect Chinese Internet users to use the Internet only or even mainly for political purposes. Cyberspace should provide fun spaces and fun spaces can be spaces of identity formation and cultural creativity. As such, they attract critical masses of people, who may turn (and have often turned) to civic action when occasions arise.

Even the existing digital divide contains opportunities, for it means there is an extraordinary room for the further diffusion of the Internet.[48] With hundreds of millions of rural population still unwired, one need not be very imaginative to see the enormous possibilities ahead. The vast digital divide also means another kind of opportunity for the continuing evolution of the digital civil society. The digital divide reflects the conditions of a fractured society. It reflects the social divide. In the face of this social divide, citizens and citizen groups will find themselves increasingly called upon to mobilize their available resources to fight poverty, social injustice, corruption and other social ills. They will increasingly find themselves fighting to articulate and defend their interests and rights. Thus new information and communication technologies will become increasingly integrated into citizen struggles. The future of Chinese digital civil society is open.

Notes

1 Earlier versions were presented at the International Conference on Information Technology and Social Responsibility at the Chinese University of Hong Kong, December 17–18, 2007 and the International Conference on Social Stratification, ICT and Media in China at the Annenberg School for Communication of the University of Pennsylvania, January 25, 2008. For their support and comments, the author thanks

Joseph Chan, Paul DiMaggio, Monroe Price, Jack Qiu, Stefaan Verhulst, Jing Wang, Xiaoling Zhang and Yongnian Zheng. Part of the research was made possible by a grant from the Weatherhead East Asian Institute of Columbia University.

2 David Michael Ryfe, "History and Political Communication: An Introduction," *Political Communication* 18 (2000), pp. 407–20.

3 For a classic statement on the principles and methods of historical sociology, see Philip Abrams, *Historical Sociology* (Ithaca: Cornell University Press, 1982).

4 Lester M. Salamon and Helmut K. Anheier, "Social Origins of Civil Society: Explaining the Nonprofit Sector Cross-Nationally," *Voluntas: International Journal of Voluntary and Nonprofit Organizations*, Vol. 9, No. 3 (September, 1998), p. 226.

5 Robert O. Keohane and Joseph S. Nye, Jr., *Power and Interdependence*, 2nd edn (Glenview: Little Brown, 1989), pp. 8–9.

6 Robert O. Keohane and Joseph S. Nye, Jr., "Power and Interdependence in the Information Age," *Foreign Affairs*, Vol. 77, No. 5 (1998), pp. 81–94.

7 Harry Harding, "Will China Democratize? The Halting Advance of Pluralism," *Journal of Democracy*, Vol. 9, No. 1 (1998), pp. 11–17.

8 Susan Shirk, "Changing Media, Changing Foreign Policy in China," *Japanese Journal of Political Science*, Vol. 8, No. 1 (2007), pp. 43–70.

9 Robert Latham and Saskia Sassen, "Introduction: Digital Formations: Constructing an Object of Study," in Robert Latham and Saskia Sassen, eds., *Digital Formations: IT and New Architectures in the Global Realm* (Princeton: Princeton University Press, 2005), p. 9.

10 Raymond Williams, *Television: Technology and Cultural Form* (London: Routledge, 1974), p. 5.

11 Guobin Yang, "Civil Society in China: A Dynamic Field of Study," *China Review International*, Vol. 9, No. 1 (Spring 2002), pp. 1–16.

12 Muthiah Alagappa, "Introduction," in Muthiah Alagappa, ed., *Civil Society and Political Change in Asia* (Stanford: Stanford University Press, 2004), pp. 1–21.

13 Bob Jessop, "Recent Societal and Urban Change: Principles of Periodization and their Application on the Current Period," in Tom Nielsen, Niels Albertsen and Peter Hemmersam, eds., *Urban Mutations: Periodization, Scale, Mobility* (Aarhus: Arkitektskolens Forlag, 2004).

14 In 1987, the first email was sent from China to an address in Germany. See CNNIC timeline.

15 www.cnnic.cn/html/Dir/2004/12/16/2642.htm (accessed April 17, 2007).

16 Ernest J. Wilson III, *The Information Revolution and Developing Countries* (Cambridge: MIT Press, 2004), pp. 241–2.

17 For a complete list of Internet regulations in China, see CNNIC's official webiste, www.cnnic.net.cn.

18 If government refers to the formal institutions, rules and practices of the state, then governance refers to the formal and informal institutions, rules and practices of both the state and non-state actors while governmentality denotes "the cultural and social context out of which modes of governance arise and by which they are sustained." Sandra Braman, "The Emergent Global Information Policy Regime," in Sandra Braman, ed., *The Emergent Global Information Policy Regime* (Houndmills: Palgrave Macmillan, 2004), p. 13.

19 Ernest J. Wilson III, *The Information Revolution and Developing Countries*, p. 238.

20 Elizabeth J. Perry and Mark Selden, eds., *Chinese Society: Change, Conflict and Resistance*, 2nd edn (London: Routledge, 2003).

21 I discussed these three areas of development in detail in Guobin Yang, "The Internet and Civil Society in China: A Preliminary Assessment," *Journal of Contemporary China*, Vol. 12, No. 36 (2003), pp. 453–75, and Guobin Yang, "The Co-evolution of the Internet and Civil Society in China," *Asian Survey*, Vol. 43, No. 3 (2003), pp. 405–22.

22 Li Xiguang, Xuan Qin and Randolph Kluver, "Who Is Setting the Chinese Agenda? The Impact of Online Chatrooms on Party Press in China," in K.C. Ho, Randolph Kluver and Kenneth C.C. Yang, eds., *Asia.com. Asia Encounters the Internet* (London and New York: RoutledgeCurzon, 2003), pp. 143–58.
23 Yongming Zhou, *Historicizing Online Politics: Telegraphy, The Internet, and Political Participation in China* (Stanford: Stanford University Press, 2006), Chapter 7.
24 Guobin Yang, "How Do Chinese Civic Associations Respond to the Internet: Findings from a Survey," *The China Quarterly*, No. 189 (2007), p. 131.
25 Despite the large size and growing influence of online communities in Chinese cyberspace, there are few scholarly studies of them. For a few exceptions, see Michel Hockx, "Links with the Past: Mainland China's Online Literary Communities and their Antecedents," *Journal of Contemporary China*, 13 (2004), pp. 105–27; Liu Huaqin, *Tianya Shequ: Hulianwang shang jiyu wenben de shehui hudong yanjiu* (Tianya Communities: A Study of Text-based Social Interaction on the Internet) (Beijing: Minzhu chubanshe, 2005); and Guobin Yang, "The Co-evolution of the Internet and Civil Society in China," *Asian Survey*, Vol. 43, No. 3 (2003), pp. 405–22.
26 Xu Wu, *Chinese Cyber Nationalism: Evolution, Characteristics, and Implications* (Lanham: Lexington Books, 2007).
27 Michael S. Chase and James C. Mulvenon, *You've Got Dissent! Chinese Dissident Use of the Internet and Beijing's Counter-Strategies* (Santa Monica: RAND, 2002). Guobin Yang, "The Internet and Civil Society in China: A Peliminary Assessment," *Journal of Contemporary China*, Vol. 12, No. 36 (2003), pp. 453–75. Yuezhi Zhao, "Falun Gong, Identity, and the Struggle over Meaning Inside and Outside China," in Nick Couldry and James Curran, eds., *Contesting Media Power: Alternative Media in a Networked World* (Lanham: Rowman & Littlefield, 2003), pp. 209–23.
28 Sun Zhigang died of beating while in police custody. Public protests led to the cancellation of China's regulations about the urban vagrants which were first introduced in the 1950s. In the BMW case, a BMW driver allegedly deliberately ran over and killed a peasant woman after the peasant woman and her husband accidentally scratched the BMW automobile with their tractor. A light sentence given by the court to the BMW driver angered Chinese netizens and triggered protests. Liu Yong was a crime lord with murder charges. He got a death sentence from an intermediate court trial. A provincial higher court changed the ruling to death sentence with a two-year reprieve, which provoked widespread public opposition on the Internet. In response, China's Supreme Court upheld the original ruling of death penalty with no reprieve. For detailed discussions of these cases, see Yongnian Zheng, *Technological Empowerment: The Internet, State, and Society in China* (Stanford: Stanford University Press, 2007).
29 Lianjiang Li and Kevin O'Brien, "Villagers and Popular Resistance in Contemporary China," *Modern China*, Vol. 22, No. 1 (1996), p. 35.
30 Beverley Hooper's study of consumer activism mentions consumers using the Internet to defend their interests back in 1998. See Beverley Hooper, "Consumer Voices: Asserting Rights in Maoist China," *China Information*, Vol. 14, No. 2 (2000), p. 106. Deborah Davis has observed the use of Internet by homeowners to defend their interests. See Deborah Davis, "Urban Chinese Homeowners as Citizen-Consumers," in S. Garon and P. Maclachlan, eds., *The Ambivalent Consumer* (Ithaca: Cornell University Press, 2006), pp. 281–99.
31 For case studies, see Jonathan Benny, "Rights Defence and the Virtual China," *Asian Studies Review*, Vol. 31 (December 2007), pp. 435–46.
32 Han Heng, "Hulian wang yu jiti xingdong de dacheng – yi Qufu minjian jikong weili" (The Internet and the Achievement of Collective Action – a Case Study of Non-official Commemorations of Confucius). Unpublished manuscript.
33 Shaoguang Wang and Jianyu He, "Associational Revolution in China: Mapping the Landscapes," *Korea Observer: A Quarterly Journal*, Vol. 35, No. 3 (Autumn 2004), pp. 485–533.

34 Interview with Chinese environmentalist, December 17, 2004.
35 For example, *Guangming Daily*, China's leading official newspaper targeting an educated audience, published such an article on December 14, 2004. The attacks on "public intellectuals" (*gonggong zhishi fenzi*) were a response to a cultural trend in recent years to call upon Chinese intellectuals to engage in public activities aimed at tackling contemporary social and political problems. This cultural trend is reminiscent of the culture fever in the late 1980s that influenced the rise of the 1989 student movement.
36 CNNIC defines an active blog as one that is updated at least once a month on average.
37 Kathleen Hartford, "Dear Mayor: Online Communications with Local Governments in Hangzhou and Nanjing," *China Information*, Vol. 19, No. 2 (2005), pp. 217–60. Ian Holliday and Ray Yep, "E-government in China," *Public Administration and Development*, Vol. 25, No. 3 (2005), pp. 239–49.
38 A recent survey finds that familiarity with e-government websites is very low among Chinese Internet users. See the CASS Internet Report 2007, "Surveying Internet Usage and Impact in Seven Chinese Cities," directed by Guo Liang, October 2007.
39 Gao Bingzhong and Yuan Ruijun, "Introduction: Stepping into Civil Society," in Beijing University Civil Society Research Center, *Zhongguo gongmin shehui fazhan lanpi shu* (Blue Book of Civil Society Development in China) (Beijing: Beijing University Press, forthcoming).
40 All-China Environmental Protection Federation, "Blue Book on the Conditions of Environmental NGOs in China" (Beijing, 2006). Unpublished report.
41 Peter Ho and Richard Louis Edmonds, "Perspectives of Time and Change: Rethinking Embedded Environmental Activism in China," *China Information*, Vol. 21, No. 2 (2007), pp. 331–44.
42 Gao Bingzhong and Yuan Ruijun, "Introduction: Stepping into Civil Society."
43 Shi and Yang provide an excellent case study of this incident. See Shi Zengzhi and Yang Boxu, "Civicness as Reflected in Recent 'Internet Incidents' and Its Significance," in Beijing University Civil Society Research Center, ed., *Zhongguo gongmin shehui fazhan lanpi shu* (Blue Book of Civil Society Development in China) (Beijing: Beijing University Press, forthcoming).
44 Cited in David Kelly, "Citizen Movements and China's Public Intellectuals in the Hu-Wen Era," *Pacific Affairs*, Vol. 79, No. 2 (2006), pp. 183–204.
45 An interesting related development for future study is the growing role of dotcom companies in public agenda-setting through the control of front-page postings. Nowadays, web editors have the power to determine the influence of a posting by giving it prominence on the first page.
46 On the use of SMS during the SARS crisis, see Haiqing Yu, "Talking, Linking, Clicking: The Politics of AIDS and SARS in Urban China," *positions*, Vol. 15, No. 1 (2007), pp. 35–63.
47 Kevin O'Brien and Lianjiang Li, *Rightful Resistance in Rural China* (Cambridge: Cambridge University Press, 2006).
48 Recent work on working-class ICT use by Jack Qiu suggests new ways of understanding the digital divide in China. Whereas nationally the digital divide remains a grave reality, the working-class population by no means remain passive observers waiting for the arrival of an information revolution. On the contrary, through active use of cell phones and SMS (rather than broadband internet), working-class people are actively bringing about their own form of information revolution. See Jack Linchuan Qiu, "Information Society: Theory, Reality, Model, Reflections," paper presented at Beijing Forum, Beijing University, November 2007.

2 Dancing thumbs

Mobile telephony in contemporary China

Zhenzhi Guo and Mei Wu

Introduction

Although not a pioneer in information communication technologies (ICT) innovations, China now has the world's largest mobile phone population of 547 million, plus 365 million landline households[1] and 162 million netizens.[2] One in every three Chinese has a handset, and this number is larger than the whole population of the United States. It is important to note that China leaped from a pre-industrial stage of minimum landline penetration to this top position in the information age in less than two decades. This is different from the Western course of ICT development where mobile communication started a century later after telephony. China's diffusion of mobile telephony, the Internet, digital video and wireless networks occurred when the country was impoverished with basic landline telephones. This expansion also resonates with the country's unprecedented economic growth, rapid industrialization, sprawling urbanization, gigantic migration, mass consumerism and information overload. What China has experienced is so unparalleled in the world history that the social bearings of this mobile-telephony-centered "media-volution" remain virtually unfathomed.

This chapter examines the social and cultural implications of the development of mobile telephony in China from the perspective of "combined modernization." It argues that mobile telephony, although an information and communication technology of the post-industrial age, attains a completely new set of social significance in China. It is above all instrumental for economic development as it advances in a society which, lacking essential industrial facilities such as a universal telephone service, highway system and public transit network, is under great pressure of industrial imperatives. However, as it is rapidly integrated into society and people's everyday life, it imparts a wide range of reconfigurations of social relations, cultural representation and symbolic re-creation which are characterized as post-modern or "second modernity."

The chapter starts with a theoretical construct of the combined process of modernization. It is followed by a historical overview of telephone development with the mobile phone as the second phase in a sequence of telecommunication evolution. The third section explores in detail three mobile-related cases – the *Super Girls* television show, one of the most successful TV shows which employs SMS as its promotional scheme, the "Bus Uncle" video, a mobile phone-made and Internet-distributed video, and the movie *Cell Phone*, the first box-office film on the mobile phone.

Mobile telephony and "combined modernization"

According to a report in *The Economist*,[3] the mobile phone has twice the impact on society in the developing world as compared to developed countries. Every ten phones per 100 people in a developing society generate an economic growth of 0.6 percentage points as measured in the Gross Domestic Product. Not only so, the mobile phone, with all its advantages in use and attractiveness as an individual consumer product, has also a greater impact on the developing world than the Internet as an essential means of human communication in modern society.

This mobile-led development is strikingly different from the developed world in that it comes almost hand-in-hand with the landline development. In many areas, it comes even prior to the installation of fixed line infrastructure. In Western society, the universal telephone service was achieved in the 1970s. In the US for example, the household telephone penetration was 25 percent as early as in 1909. It reached 40 percent in 1942, 62 percent in 1950, 78 percent in 1960 and 90 percent in 1970 and remained at 93 percent between the 1980s and 1990s.[4] In contrast, there were only 300,000 telephone users[5] in China when the People's Republic was founded in 1949. By 1978, when the country was about to embark on the economic reform, the number of its telephone users reached 1.93 million,[6] a penetration rate of only 0.4 percent.[7] However, by June 2004, China registered the world's largest population of landline and mobile phone users with 295 million fixed line users and 305 million mobile phone users.[8] The fixed line penetration rate per 100 persons increased from seven in 1998 to 21.2 in 2003.[9] Yet although the Chinese level is comparable only to that of the US in the 1940s–1950s, China has a mobile phone population larger than the whole population of the US.

Although there are increasing academic studies on the social implications of the use of mobile phones,[10] theoretical approaches on mobile communication lack a macro-framework to conceptualize the social meanings of mobile communication in developing countries in general, and China in particular. They are limited to an implied presupposition that the mobile phone is a phenomenon of information society, a sort of post-industrial, post-modern experience as none of them takes into consideration the synchronous nature of the mobile communication expansion which goes side-by-side with the landline development in these countries. In addition, the existing paradigms also lack a frame of reference to comprehensively analyze the unprecedented influence of mobile phones in Chinese society where the scale of mobile population, the penetration of its use, the multitude of its service, and the degree of its embeddedness in communication and socialization are unparalleled in the world's human history.

Some Chinese scholars[11] have attempted to theorize the Chinese development with reference to Ulrich Beck's notion of "second modernity."[12] Beck *et al.*, in an effort to reformulate the theory of reflective modernization, argue that Western society has undergone two phases of modernity: the "first modernity" characterized by a series of institutions including the nation-state, the industrial corporation, the nuclear family and the authority of science,[13] and the "second modernity" involving a radical process of modernization in which the logic and order of the first modernity, such as clarity, linearity, the institutional system and the idea of controllability are challenged and incapable of providing solutions to global risks under increased globalization and individualization.[14] In Western society, according to Beck, there is a sequential link between the two phases of modernization. However, this pattern of two-phased modernization, according to Deng Zhenglai, does not happen in non-Western societies, particularly in China. What is being witnessed is a process of modernization which combines the characteristics of both the "first modernity" and the "second modernity."[15]

In this combined process of modernization, new communication technologies such as mobile communication, the Internet, television and personal computers, which are closely linked with the "second modernity" in developed countries, play a distinguishing role. They are introduced, adopted and diffused at a phenomenal speed in the countries which missed out on the first phase of modernization that was normally symbolized by the invention of the steam engine, electricity, telegraphy and telephony and sequentially the rise and establishment of the industrial world. As a result, new social phenomena and significance are emerging which vary from the Western experience. In other words, the roles and effects these new media technologies play in the developing countries are different from those in the developed world.[16]

Drawing reference from these notions, we redefine the "second modernity" in China not simply as a sequence to the "first modernity," but a process of social development which combines the characteristics of social and cultural phenomena witnessed in both industrial society and post-industrial information society.[17] It is a course of industrialization that was long overdue, but arrived in conjunction with the advent of the information revolution. Different from the sequential procession of the "industrial society" and "information society," this is a "combined movement" of modernization. We argue that in developed countries, mobile communication, the Internet and other media gizmos are closely associated with the "second modernity" while fixed line telephony is connected with the "first modernity" as one of the key innovations of communication technology. For these countries which have long established a sophisticated communication system of landlines and public telephones, mobile communication and the Internet are usually "adding flowers to the brocade" (*jinshang tianhua*). They play mainly a complementary role in social development. In contrast, mobile phones are introduced and diffused almost simultaneously or even in advance of land phones in developing countries. Their impact on a society which had basically no telephone system is not only spectacular, but also greatly different from the experiences of developed countries. This synchronized development of landline and mobile telephone has contributed to the emergence of a new socio-techno phenomenon characterized by the "combined modernization" of both the "first modernity" and the "second modernity," which generates a range of social and cultural implications epitomizing a sophisticated mélange of attributes of industrialization, modernity, post-modernity and information society.

Hence, within the paradigm of social construction of ICT, scholarly works that examine mobile phone systems in the West focus on post-modern characteristics of the artifact. They accentuate it as a series of arenas for negotiating issues essential for the post-modern social phenomena such as the sustenance of social life and re-creation of cultural representations like self identity, micro-social community, power, resistance and mobilization. The mobile phone, while becoming an increasingly ubiquitous part of everyday life, plays sophisticated roles in social interaction, alters the way people manage time and space and reinforces an individual identity.[18]

On the other hand, there is a vacuum of clear conceptualization of the social role of mobile communication in the developing world where the mobile phone has developed simultaneously with, or even ahead of, landline telephones and the social-techno phenomenon embodies both industrial and post-industrial elements. Approaches are often limited to political instrumentalism. For instance, the mobile handset is seen as an enabler for negotiating political mobilization and resistance[19] as in the cases of political activism in the Philippines[20] and Nigeria.[21] It also facilitates affordable contacts, information exchange and social networking for the underprivileged population, like villagers in India,[22] rural women in Bangladesh,[23] migrant workers in southern China,[24] guest laborers in Singapore,[25] small businessmen in Rwanda,[26] and grassroots religious groups in the Philippines[27] and Nigeria.[28] Another set of studies explores the mobile phone as a symbol of tension between tradition and modernity, rural values and urban norms, local affinity and foreign infringement, communal rapport and diasporic dispersion, familial kinship and virtual networks, individualism and globalization.[29] Such arguments, to some extent, point to the mixed characteristics of modernization and post-modernization in the use of mobile communication in the developing world.

Within China, the mainstream rhetoric in academia and mass media on mobile phones is dominated by technological utopianism. It is widely touted as a symbol of progress, betterment of human life and advancement of society. The rapid expansion of mobile phones in China is hailed as a great success of the economic reform and an indicator of China's economic rise. However, a different view does exist, albeit held by a few only, which is skeptical of the utopian claims of the mobile phone and attempts to evaluate its impact from the social shaping perspective. One constructive study comes from Yang Boxu in 2007. He draws a connection between the development of the mobile phone and that of the fixed line phone and elucidates how each phase is associated with specific social attributes. He argues that the fixed line phone emerges with the societal change from community to social networks, a process of industrialization, while the mobile phone comes with change over time – globalization, from social networks to Barry Wellman's "networked individualism."[30]

The following section, set within the perspective of the "combined modernization," presents a historical overview of the telephone development with the mobile phone as the second phase in a sequential development. However, as stated above, the mobile telephony plays a dual set of roles. It is on one hand an instrument for industrialization, and yet on the other hand, it stands as a complexity of symbols, individualized interpretations and production and reproduction of cultural representations in an information society. The rest of the chapter explores three sets of socio-cultural meanings of mobile telephony in China by examining three mobile-related examples – the *Super Girls* TV show which demonstrates the mobile phone as an instrument of commercial entertainment, the "Bus Uncle" video which epitomizes how the ubiquity of the mobile phone effects the creation of a pseudo public interest, a phenomenon of information-ridden, post-modern society, and the movie *Cell Phone*, which illustrates the mixed feeling that contemporary Chinese harbor about the dilemma of modernization and post-modernization, clearly symbolized by the use of the handset.

From pre-industrial to mobile communication: the "great leap forward" in telephone development

The development of telephony (both fixed and mobile phones) in China, which has witnessed an extraordinarily long period of adoption and penetration, covers over 100 years. It went through five major periods:

1 the introduction period (1882–1912);
2 the slow adoption period (1912–1949);
3 the stagnant period (1949–1979);
4 the new development (1980–1990s); and
5 the leapfrog period (2000–present).

Its evolution in fact exemplifies the country's modern history, which is ridden with crises and challenges.

Telephony was introduced to China in the late nineteenth century by a Danish telecommunication company (Great Northern Telegraph Co.). The company set up, without permission of the imperial court, the first telephone switchboard in a Shanghai foreign concession in 1882 with about 20 users.[31] However, for the next six decades, telephone services remained limited to the metropolis, dominated by foreign technology and controlled by the nationalist government, owing mostly to technological deficiency and social, political and economic turmoil in the country.[32] Landline networks and telephone services, although slowly spreading with the industrial development and urban expansion in the country in the first half of the twentieth century, covered only 311,681 users in Chinese cities in 1949 when the communists took over power.[33]

The new People's Republic first turned to the USSR for telecommunication technology to upgrade its poor telecommunication infrastructure. However, the pace of development was interrupted when the two countries split in 1960. In a planned economy, the communist government considered telecommunication technology and its service primarily as state military facilities. Thus, the telecommunication infrastructure was restricted to bureaucratic use. The telephone service was mostly limited to those officials who had important positions and ranked high in the administrative hierarchy. During the pre-reform era from the early 1950s to the end of the 1970s, the telephony industry stagnated. There were only about two million telephone users, a penetration rate of only 0.43 percent[34] in China until the early 1980s.

In the 1980s and 1990s, with the reform policy and foreign-loan funded purchases of telecommunication technology and facilities from developed countries, such as Germany, France, Japan and the US, the Chinese telephone capacity quickly expanded, enhancing the number of landline users from 1.9 million in 1978 to 108.7 million in 1999.[35]

The mobile phone, a latecomer on the scene, developed even faster. First appearing in China in 1988 with only 3,200 users[36] (called *Dageda* in Chinese, meaning big, big brother), it enjoyed a skyrocketing increase during the 1990s and in the first few years of the new millennium, it jumped from 18,300 in 1990 to 43.3 million in 1999[37] and 206 million in 2002.[38] In 2002 digital technology became dominant in the mobile phone industry, replacing analog technology in the international market. The Chinese mobile phone industry, accordingly, rode on this digital wave, as the Ministry of Information Industry (MII) issued a state regulation banning the manufacture and sales of analog mobile phones on July 1, 2001 and analog network on January 1, 2002.

In a sense 2003 was a watershed. By the end of 2003, the number of Chinese mobile phone users had, for the first time, surpassed that of landline sets. While there were only 144.8 million mobile phone users in 2001 (179 million landline users),[39] the number nearly doubled to 268.7 million in 2003. Meanwhile there were 263 million landline users.[40] This indicates the beginning of the mobile phone era in China (see Figure 2.1).

While the landline was still far from widespread (a penetration of only 28.1 percent) by April 2007, the mobile reached 35.3 percent of the population.[41] The fixed line telephone, seen as the most common household facility in Western homes, has a different status in China. Its penetration rate is much lower than that of television and is losing the competition with the mobile. People even worried whether landline telephones would be totally replaced by mobile phones.[42] According to the latest statistics, the number of landline users declined by 2.34 million in 2007, the first decrease in 40 years. Meanwhile mobile users registered a record increase of 86.23 million, reaching a total population of 547.3 million.[43]

The mobile phone, at the time, developed nearly hand-in-hand with the Internet in China. On February 1, 2003, when the American space shuttle Columbia crashed during landing, mobile phone subscribers were among the first to receive the news through SMS. The message was sent by www.sina.com, one of the two biggest Chinese portals, at 22:32, 16 minutes after the accident happened.[44] In fact,

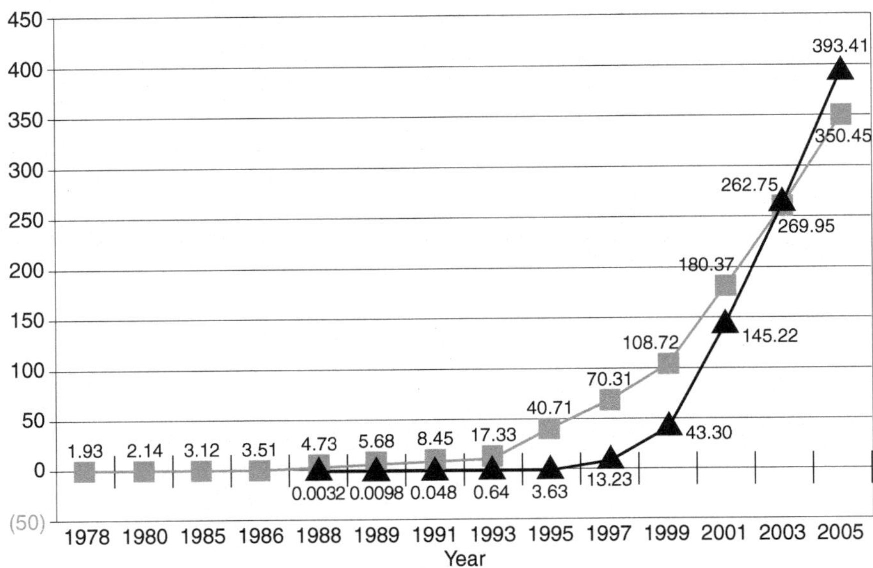

Figure 2.1 Fixed phone and mobile phone population comparison (source: From yearbooks of the National Bureau of Statistics of China).

when the global Internet bubble burst in the late 1990s, it was mobile phone users who helped to save the tottering Internet companies in China as they started to incorporate into their service some new mobile phone functions, including message exchange (text at first, then audio and video), and ringtone downloading. Mobile phone accounts were also used to pay Internet bills. For a few years, the service of mobile phone ringtone downloading contributed to one of the largest revenues for many Internet websites.

The mobile phone has brought the "great leap forward" for both itself and the Internet. This is happening in a unique Chinese circumstance. In the 1990s China was on a new "long march" toward a market economy, transforming from a pre-industrial society into a brand new information society. The first-generation mobile phones – the brick-like "Big, Big Brother," which was once a prestigious status symbol, was soon replaced by a variety of cheaper, lighter and more fashionable handsets. The mobile phone has become part of everybody's life, be they migrant workers, who use it as a symbol of success, or university students who are the biggest fans of new mobile phone usage, or even primary school students – whose parents want to keep an eye on their whereabouts. Thumbs that used to be clumsy have now become dexterous, "dancing" in text messaging (SMS). Indeed the mobile phone popularity has also given rise to such terms as the "thumb group," "thumb economy," "thumb culture," "thumb revolution."[45]

Social and cultural implications of mobile phone use: three cases

Mobile telephony plays many social roles in the current transitional Chinese society. As stated previously, it first functions as the most convenient and economical means of communication in business activities in the country's drive from an economic reform to a market economy. In addition, it also generates a profitable "thumb economy." The most prominent example is SMS service. Compared to rather expensive mobile phone calls (40 or 60 *fen* a minute, plus a roaming service fee if not used locally), fees for text messaging in China – ten *fen* a message anywhere in the country – is fairly low. So it becomes the first choice among mobile phone users, especially youngsters and university students who have less money and more text messaging skills. SMS thus becomes the most important source for telecom companies' revenues.[46] In 2006, 429.67 billion messages were sent nationwide, an increase of 41.0 percent from the previous year.[47] The messages sent in March 2007 alone reached 182.6 billion, 38.1 percent more than that of December 2006.[48] During traditional holiday seasons such as the Chinese Spring Festival and Mid-autumn Festival, greetings messages bring in a huge income to China's telecommunication oligarchs like China Mobile and China Unicom. During the Spring Festival in 2007, for example, 15.2 billion greetings messages were sent in seven days, generating at least 1.52 billion RMB for the telecom companies.[49]

Besides the instrumental functions for the economic development (especially the telecom companies), the mobile phone is also reshaping the social interaction and cultural expression of Chinese society, affecting both the social norms, personal behaviors and cultural representation of the Chinese people. With increasingly reduced costs, people talk more and more casually over the mobile phone: seasons' greetings, call-in participations, sentimental long chats, all creating a post-modern phenomenon of an excessive, trivial and meaningless information overload. Symbols are constantly created and overturned; identities are shifted and reconstructed; and elite narratives are ridiculed and recreated into parodies. Silly humor is prevalent. SMS for instance has contributed to the creation of a new web/mobile language. "I love you" in Mandarin is now replaced by "521" (*wo ai ni*) in SMS, and "531" means "I miss you" (*wo xiang ni*). "478" is a curse meaning "drop dead" or "damn you" (*si qu ba*) in some contexts and an affectionate gesture amongst friends.[50] The mischievous creations, both in the form of humorous messages (*duanzi*) and in podcasting video spoofs (*e gao*), are different from the traditional way of expression, and have a tendency of spreading over mobile phones as quickly as epidemics.

In the following part, we will focus on three exemplary cases to illustrate how the mobile phone is connected to a complicated phenomenon of the combined modernity in current China, which incorporates characteristics of industrial society, such as market development and commercialization, with those of information society including an excess of information, a trivialization of the public agenda and a critical reflection of communication technology as a symbol of progress. First, mobile phone use develops with the market economy when commercialization goes hand-in-hand with mass entertainment. Market-orientated and profit-driven *Super Girls*, a star-making reality show, is typical of this mobile phone-stimulated consumerism. Second, mobile phone use is becoming omnipresent; it is common and casual, at ease and at will, either in public places or at home, whether in speaking, messaging or taking pictures. To study this ubiquitous and informal use of the mobile phone, the "Bus Uncle," an amateur podcasting video clip, is a good case in point. Third, mobile phone use is often connected with changing social values and moralities. The tension between the highly sophisticated technology and the moral degeneration is dramatically demonstrated in the movie *Cell Phone* (director Feng Xiaogang, 2004).

The reality show of the **Super Girls***: whose carnival?*

In 2005, Hunan Satellite Television (HSTV), a provincial satellite station in central China, was racing ahead in the Chinese TV market with its *Super Girls* reality show, the most successful commercial program, or entertainment media event. From the very beginning, appeal to audience was a principal concern. The program is not different from its American model – *American Idol*. Chinese producers also adopted the American ways of selecting players through unlimited nationwide participation in the initial stage, sharp comments by showy committee members, clumsy performances of amateur singers. The Chinese who used to be considered shy by nature, however, developed their own commercial strategies to make the games more competitive: taking increasingly breath-taking competition steps, different kinds of voting (committee experts, reviewers made by previously failed players, audience, TV viewers), and eliminating procedures of one-to-one competition. There were also sentimental moments showing the great sorrow of losers and immense joy of winners, as well as the girls' friendship with each other, especially between winners and losers.

Apart from the advertisement that was the main source of TV show revenue, *Super Girls* invented many commercial approaches, of which the most profitable was mass voting by fans via mobile phone messages, which accounted for one-third of the income.[51] Mobile phone voting has since become the most cited and most studied subject of commercial practices[52] employed by this media event.

It is the mass participation in SMS voting that brought in big money. The way of mobile phone voting was: first fans registered as "members" of HSTV – with only one *yuan*. Then each member had the right to send 15 voting messages for free. In the meantime, however, they automatically became receivers of the event messages with additional fees.[53]

The *Super Girls* 2005 was a big commercial success. According to news reports,[54] there were 150,000 participants for mass selection in several cities in 2005 alone and millions of voters. All in all, HSTV made RMB30 million from the SMS service in this event, while it received RMB60 million from advertising, the SMS income accounted for one-third of the total revenue.[55] It is worth noting that the mobile phone voting cost was very minimal for individual fans. But billions of text messages could make a huge profit for the organizers.

SMS is surely the most profitable scheme used in the *Super Girls*. But it is also the most successful use of the mobile phone by Chinese to break through their usual reservation and shyness in expressing their affection or opinions face-to-face.

At the rate of ten *fen* per message, the *Super Girls* voters didn't hesitate to vote and to promote their idols. Fan clubs, in turn, kept sending information about their stars through SMS and the Internet. A huge amount of money was generated from fan networks; and the thumb economy, accordingly, became a new buzzword.

There is also another new word – "mobile democracy."[56] Some critics claim that fans were in power when voting through their handsets. Some even predicted, on the basis of free participation, that mass voting in the form of *Super Girls* would encourage political democracy in China.[57] But it is hard to link commercially organized entertainment involvement like the *Super Girls* with active political participation. Some people are even worried that activities like this might distract young people from serious public participation.[58]

It is evident that the liberalistic claims about the *Super Girls* are exaggerated. All the media fanfare was carried out with promotional purposes. On one hand, it is clear that the huge SMS income actually came from a relatively small group of fans, who had borrowed or bought mobile phone SIM cards to promote their idols, as there was a limit for voting from each mobile phone number while buying mobile phone cards was unlimited and anonymous.

On the other hand, this kind of individual participation was dwarfed by mobile-phone-organized professional promotional practices. During the second season of the *Super Girls* in 2006 the fan activities became institutionalized. Fans were organized and mobilized by "professional fans" whose task was to promote different girls by way of off-stage activities of all kinds. SMS played a key role in mobilizing and coordinating these activities.

Some people suggested that as the *Super Girls* generated billions of revenue, it contributed to the national economy.[59] The *Super Girls* did encourage spending. The real question, however, is: who pays whom for what?

HSTV and its telecommunication collaborators were real winners in the game. What did the fans get? In this commercial game they lost money, time, energy and enthusiasm while getting basically nothing except mobile-phone-and-TV-enabled entertainment. This is not a people's festival, but a carnival of money and big corporations.

A story of the "Bus Uncle:" what for ubiquitous eyes?

In mid-2006, a six-minute video clip was spread on the web and attracted millions of hits. It was known as the "Bus Uncle," an amateur video shot by a mobile phone of a common scene in China – a quarrel on a bus. But this time it was caught by a mobile phone: a 50-something man in a Hong Kong bus was talking loudly over his mobile phone. A youngster sitting behind patted him on his shoulder, asking him to keep his voice down. Feeling insulted, the older man exploded in anger. Turning back to the young man he burst into angry curses and dirty words. The enraged monologue lasted for nearly six minutes; and was recorded by a passenger with a mobile phone camera. Then the video was put on YouTube, and became wildly popular overnight. The two most impressive soundbites – "Not solved! Not solved! Not solved!" (in Cantonese) and "You have pressure, and I have pressure, why do you find faults with me?" – became so popular that they immediately became hit phrases for a couple of months.

The Bus Uncle, middle-aged and unemployed, became famous for "a fit of curse" overnight. It was rumored that he was offered a new job soon after the incident and charged high fees for requested interviews. A seeming "underdog" became a short-time celebrity – all thanks to the mobile phone.

The quality of the video does not meet professional standards – the picture is blurry and unstable. The sound is not quite clear, either. The words were uttered in Cantonese, a dialect that most Chinese can't understand. But as a media-enabled "public event," it was received without barriers – people voluntarily transcribed the quarrel into a text, translated it into *putonghua* (the standard Chinese language), and even added subtitles to the video. There are also many variation parodies made from the original video clip.

The original video-maker, however, was never well known. The event he covered was so common in everyday life that it would never be considered newsworthy enough to be made into a "public media event." How could a common scene like a bus quarrel and an ordinary character like the Bus Uncle become a "hot event" if it had not been for the mobile phone? The new media technology such as the handset camera, YouTube and the Internet has made a common occurrence a news event. And this could only happen in an age of multimedia mobile phones as they become so ubiquitous in our daily life and so easily operational as a possible tool to record common events, disseminate them, and thus make news. But what is behind the mobile-phone-generated news?

This clip of the Bus Uncle is definitely not meaningless. It shows the new technology's ability to create eye-catching public topics from what was conventionally regarded "trivial affairs." The mobile phone now has become a ubiquitous artifact in our environment. When this device is in everyone's hands, there is a possibility that anyone can document and publicize something for the attention and amusement of a larger audience. Hence, topics for public consumption may become contingent, casual and harder to predict. The outcome might be that we are surrounded and overwhelmed with an information overload which becomes even more fragmented, trivialized and meaningless. While such eye-catching pieces may be short-lived, the random and spontaneous nature in recoding, and the ease in publicizing such daily occurrences are challenging the traditional model of constructing public interest and discussion agenda, and creating mobile-phone-age media events, public topics and even public celebrities. With television, we amuse ourselves, with the mobile phone the amusement becomes even more trivialized, short-lived, yet possibly ubiquitous – it could be done anywhere and at any time.

The dramatic metaphor of the movie **Cell Phone***: what "progress"?*

In December 2004, Feng Xiaogang, a well-known Chinese film director, presented his New Year comedy movie – *Cell Phone*. The timely movie was wildly popular, as the mobile handset, a new fancy communication tool, was just getting popular in China.

When Shouyi Yan, the leading character in the movie, first "used" the telephone he was accompanying a young woman, a fellow villager, to call her newly-wed husband using a public phone. The call was not really a private and affectionate phone conversation: the message was delivered first to an old man who was in charge of a public phone on the other end, and then was broadcast several times via a high-pitched loudspeaker. The message was thus heard by everyone on the spot – apart from the husband. This was a typical scene in a community-bound society where nobody would mind that personal messages were made public. In a new time when people pay more respect to privacy Yan became a well-known host of a famous TV talk show *You Yi Shuo Yi* ("Say it as it is") which is supposed to be a truth-revealing programme. Behind the scene he is actually a disloyal husband and a "two timer." The mobile phone calls, short messages and finally a mobile-phone-shot video betrayed him time and again. In the end both his wife, with their newborn son, and the woman he loves leave him for good. The third woman, with whom he has an affair, finally replaces him as the hostess of the popular show, making him redundant.

In the movie, the cell phone is a collection of multiple metaphors – progress, freedom, seduction, betrayal and misfortune, which represent an inextricable confusion of social values and moral integrity in China's rapid transformation. In Yan's view, all the bad luck seems to result from the mobile phone: the flirting calls and SMS from the secret lover were found by his wife, the secretly shot photo revealing He's disloyalty was seen by his girlfriend. Ironically when some really urgent call/message is coming – his grandma, the most beloved person in his life, was dying and yearning to see him for the last time – Yan missed the call. Being surrounded by many destructive messages while missing the most important one, this seems to be the message delivered by the movie.

The movie dramatically challenges the dominant notion of "progress" and vividly reflects the tension between technology and changing social morals of Chinese society today. Yan's story is not so rare in the transforming China where people have more personal choices and fewer social restrictions. People are increasingly "open" (in a Chinese context, it often means sexually active without much restriction) to all attractions, seeking happiness for their own benefit. This transition is often labeled as "progress" by some critics.

There is another embodiment of "progress" – the technological progress from the no-phone village to the mobile-phone-ubiquitous cosmopolis. From a mainstream perspective, this technological advancement is an enabler of the social "progress" of more individual freedom and openness. Ironically enough, however, the movie depicts another scenario. While people have more "secrets" from all kinds of choices, high technologies become increasingly sophisticated in peeping into the lives of others, including the most private secrets. Contrary to the common notion, what is being experienced by the contemporary Chinese who have more freedom to seek self-indulgence is that the progress of technology has also made ICT tools more and more smart at spying/revealing the private lives of these happiness seekers. The cell phone becomes a "time bomb" in a palm. The "progress" is double-edged. At the end of the movie, Yan throws his cell phone into a fire in his home village. This amplifies the complicated feelings contemporary Chinese have about the cell phone – a complex of fascination, boredom, distress, reprimand and rejection.

Conclusion: the future use of the mobile phone

As the mobile phone has become a platform that combines all the media (newspaper, radio, television and the Internet), and as more functions of mobile phones have been developed and promoted by manufacturers, most people would choose the mobile phone when they were asked to keep only one communication tool from a list of media devices, according to a survey by P. Levinson.[60] The mobile phone has become the most convenient device for information and connection. It is the media center, playing a pivotal role in both personal and mass information and communication.

However, we may face the worst consequence of the new media technologies – information and contact overloading. Does all the information really help people to truly contact each other, to understand the world better, and to engage in meaningful social practices? In fact, the endless information and ubiquitous communication may overwhelm us. Then, just like Yan in the movie *Cell Phone*, people might miss the most important information while immersed in a sea of useless or even harmful messages.

The excessive mediated relations lack personal intimacy as well. When people initially received holiday greetings through their mobile phones – mostly from close friends and relatives – they were delighted and responded actively. Not for long though. Getting more and more mobile greetings nearly every holiday – most of them distributed without specific receivers – becomes a great burden for many people to respond to. During the Spring Festival of 2007, some people even advocated boycotting mobile phone greetings![61] Mass produced, mass distributed messages do not necessarily benefit social interactions. In many cases, they are just another source for mobile phone companies to make money, like in the case of the *Super Girls* event, the intimate rapport hundreds of thousands of fans built through SMS and the Internet with their *Super Girl* idol is merely symbolic, imaginary and, of course, virtual.

There are social consequences of the new technology, too. A number of negative phenomena of mobile phone use include spam (mainly advertising) disturbance, text message fraud, examination cheating, secret filming, pornographic photos, virus spreading and messaging, ringtone disturbance in public locations, etc.[62] From the "Bus Uncle" case we come to know that some mobile-phone-made public events may have little to do with the public good; rather, they tend to be a short-lived social farce.

Mobile telephony has swept China within a very short period of time. This is also the time when the nation is being transformed, for better or worse, in every aspect and at a phenomenal speed. In this wave of combined modernization with both "first modernity" and "second modernity" communication technologies, China and other developing countries are undergoing a joint course of industrialization, urbanization, information ubiquity and global tribalism. The mobile phone is at the core of society's communication system with hundreds of millions of people holding a mobile handset and communicating anywhere and at any time. The social significance of this artifact and how it affects Chinese society remains to be fathomed. This chapter has outlined only a few strands of analysis in this field. Further studies are needed for our understanding of the new communication technologies and social transformation in China.

Notes

1 China Information Industry website: *2007 quanguo tongxinye fazhan tongji gongbao* (2007 National Telecommunication Development Statistic Report). Online, available at: www.mii.gov.cn/art/2008/02/19/art_169_36206.html.

2 China Internet Network Information Center: *Zhongguo hulianwangluo fazhan zhuangkuang tongji baogao* (China Internet Network Development Status Statistic Report, 2008–01). Online, available at: www.cnnic.org.cn/uploadfiles/pdf/2008/1/17/104156.pdf.

3 *The Economist*: "The Real Digital Divide" (March 10, 2005). Online, available at: www.economist.com/opinion/displaystory.cfm?story_id=3742817 (accessed December 30, 2007).

4 Claude S. Fischer, *American Calling: A Social History of the Telephone to 1940* (Berkeley: University of California Press, 1992).

5 The number also includes those with switchboards which could have multi-individual users.

6 Yearbooks of the National Bureau of Statistics of China. Online, available at: www.stats.gov.cn/tjsj/ndsj/.

7 National Bureau of Statistics of China: *youdian tongxin shuiping* (Development of Postal and Telecommunications Services). Online, available at: www.stats.gov.cn/ndsj/information/zh1/n471a. Telephone penetration rates in China are often calculated by per 100 persons, not by households. And the statistics in the 1950s–1970s are often different due to a lack of standardized method of calculation.

8 China Information Industry website: *2004 1–6 tongxin hangye yunxing zhuangkuang* (2004 January–June Telecommunication Industry Operation Status). "The increase continued in the new century to 144.8 million in 2000, 179 million in 2001, 214 million in 2002, and 263 million in 2003" (2003).

9 China Information Industry website: *1998 tongxinye fazhan tongji gongbao* (1998 Telecommunication Industry Development Statistic Report). Online, available at: www.mii.gov.cn/art/2005/12/15/art_169_1481_2.html. *2003 1–12 tongxin hangye jingji yunxing zhuangkuang* (2003 January–December Telecommunication Industry Economic Operation Status). Online, available at: www.mii.gov.cn/art/2005/12/15/art_169_1288.html.

10 For example, James E. Katz and Mark A. Aakhus (eds.), *Perpetual Contact: Mobile Communication, Private Talk, Public Performance* (Port Chester: Cambridge University Press, 2002); Manuel Castells, Mireia Fernandez-Ardevol, Qiu Linchuan and Araba Sey, *The Mobile Communication Society* (Annenberg Research Network on International Communication. A Research Report Prepared for the International Workshop on Wireless Communication Policies and Prospects: A Global Perspective. Los Angeles, 2004); Richard C. Ling, *The Mobile Connection: The Cell Phone's Impact on Society* (San Francisco: Morgan Kaufmann, 2004); Mizuko Ito, Daisuke Okabe and Misa Matsuda, eds., *Personal, Portable, Pedestrian: Mobile Phones in Japanese Life* (Cambridge: MIT Press, 2005); Ran Wei and Lo Ven-Hwei, "Staying Connected while on the Move: Cell Phone use and Social Connectedness," *New Media & Society*, Vol. 8(1) (2006), pp. 53–72; Wenbo Kuang, *Shouji meiti gailun* (On Generalities of Mobile Phone Media) (Beijing: Renmin University Press, 2006); and Yuezhi Zhao, "After Mobile Phones, What Re-embedding the Social in China's 'Digital Revolution'," *International Journal of Communication*, Vol. 1, (2007), pp. 92–120.

11 Deng Zhenglai "Zhongguo falii zhexue dangxia jiben shiming de qiantixing fenxi – zuowei lishi tiaojian de 'shijie jiegou'" (Preliminary Analysis of Basic Missions of China's Legal Philosophy), *Faxue yanjiu* (Law Studies), Vol. 5 (2006), online, available at: www.tecn.cn/data/detail.php?id=11557; Chen Weixing, "Hulianwang chuanbo de quanli boyi" (Power Contestation in Communication), *2007 Zhongguo wangluo chuanboxue nianhuiji "xinxin luntan* (2007 China Computer-Mediated Communication Association Annual Conference and Xin Xin Forum) (Wuhan: Central China University of Science and Technology, 2007).

12 Ulrich Beck and Christoph Lau, "Second Modernity as a Research Agenda: Theoretical and Empirical Explorations in the 'Meta-change' of Modern Society," *The British Journal of Sociology*, Vol. 56, No. 4 (2005), pp. 525–57.

13 Ibid.

14 Ibid.

15 Deng Zhenglai, "Zhongguo falii zhexue dangxia jiben shiming de qiantixing fenxi."

16 Chen Weixing, "Hulianwang chuanbo de quanli boyi."

17 There are various terms used to characterize social transformation undergoing since the 1980s in the West, such as post-industrial society (Daniel Bell), post-modern society (Fredric Jameson, Jean-François Lyotard) or various concepts of information society. Beck's "second modernity" adds another version to the conceptualization of societal reconfiguration although it rejects the idea of post-modernity. In this chapter, we use the term "post-industrial," "post-modern" and "information society" interchangeably to indicate a form of society which we believe is intrinsically different from the enlightenment-based and mechanically oriented industrial society.

18 B. Brown, N. Green and R. Harper, eds., *Wireless World; Social and Interactional Aspects of the Mobile Age* (London: Springer, 2002); Castells *et al.*, *The Mobile Communication Society*; Diana Gant and S. Kiesler, "Blurring the Boundaries: Cell Phones, Mobility and the Line between Work and Personal Life," in *Wireless World: Social and Interactional Aspects of the Mobile Age*, edited by Barry Brown, Nicola Green and Richard Harper (London: Springer-Verlag, 2001); Hans Geser, "Towards a Sociological Theory of the Mobile Phone," (2004), online, available at: http://socio.ch/mobile/t_geser1.htm (accessed August 11, 2007); Rich Ling and Leslie Haddon, "Mobile Telephony, Mobility and the Coordination of Everyday Life," paper presented at the Conference "Machines that Become Us" (New Brunswick, New Jersey: Rutgers University, 2001); P. Glotz, S. Bertschi and C. Locke, eds., *Thumb Culture. The Meaning of Mobile Phones in Society* (Bielefeld: Transcript, 2005).

19 Howard Rheingold, *Smart Mobs* (Cambridge: Perseus Books, 2002).

20 L.S. Uy-Tioco, "The Cell Phone and Edsa 2: The Role of a Communication Technology in Ousting a President," paper presented at the Fourth Critical Themes in Media Studies Conference (New York: New School University, 2003).

21 Okoth Fredrick Mudhai, "Exploring the Potential for More Strategic Civil Society Use of Mobile Phones" (2003), online, available at: http://programs.ssrc.org/itic/publications/knowledge_report/memos/okoth.pdf (accessed August 11, 2007).

22 Harmeet Sawhney, "Mobiles, Local Connectivity, and Negotiation of Asian Modernities," paper presented at the International Conference on Mobile Communication and Asian Modernities (Hong Kong: City University of Hong Kong, 2005).

23 Salahuddin Aminuzzaman, "Mobile Phone and its Impact on Empowerment of Women in Rural Bangladesh," paper presented at the International Conference on Mobile Communication and Asian Modernities (Hong Kong: City University of Hong Kong, 2005).

24 Linchuan Qiu, *The Mobile Communication Society* (Annenberg Research Network on International Communication. A Research Report Prepared for the International Workshop on Wireless Communication Policies and Prospects: A Global Perspective. Los Angeles, 2004); and Patrick Law and Y. Peng, "The Use of Cellphones amongst Migrant Workers in Southern China," paper presented at the 2004 International Conference on Mobile Communication: Mobile Communication and Social Change (Seoul, 2004).

25 Eric C. Thompson, "Reaching Home by Hand-phone: Foreign Worker Communities and Mobile Communication in Singapore," paper presented at the International Conference on Mobile Communication and Asian Modernities (Hong Kong: City University of Hong Kong, 2005).

26 Jonathan Donner, "Microentrepreneurs and Mobiles: An Exploration of the Uses of Mobile Phones by Small Business Owners in Rwanda," *Information Technologies for International Development*, Vol. 2, No. 1 (2005), pp. 1–21.

27 B. Ellwood-Clayton, "Virtual Strangers: Young Love and Texting in the Filipino Archipelago of Cyberspace," in *Mobile Democracy: Essays on Society, Self, and Politics*, edited by K. Nyiri (Vienna: Passagen Verlag, 2003), pp. 225–39.

28 J.F. Agbu, "From 'Koro' to GSM 'Killer Calls' Scare in Nigeria: A Psychological View," *CORESERIA Bulletin*, 3–4 (2004), pp. 16–19.

29 C. Snowden, "Blinded by Text: Re-evaluating the Oral Imperative in Communication," paper presented at the Communications Research Forum 2000 (Canberra, 2000); G. Strom, "The Telephone comes to a Filipino Village," in *Perpetual Contact: Mobile Communication, Private Talk, Public Performance*, edited by J.E. Katz and M. Aakhus (Cambridge: Cambridge University Press, 2002), pp. 274–83; Patrick Law and Y. Peng, "The Use of Cellphones amongst Migrant Workers in Southern China," paper presented at the 2004 International Conference on Mobile Communication: Mobile Communication and Social Change (Seoul, 2004); Yang Boxu, "Social Networks and Individualism: The Role of the Mobile Phone in Today's Social Transformation in Urban China," paper presented at the 2007 China Computer-Mediated Communication Association Annual Conference and Xin Xin Forum (Wuhan, 2007); Zhao, "After Mobile Phones"; A. Alhassan, *Development Communication Policy and Economic Fundamentalism in Ghana* (Tampere, Finland: University of Tampere Press, 2004); R. Pertierra, "Mobile Phones, Identity and Discursive Intimacy," *Human Technology*, Vol. 1, No. 1 (2005), pp. 23–44; and Xia Yang, *Dizhi Duanxin Bainian Yundong Lieju duanxin Qi Da Zuizhuang* (Call on Boycotting Movement, Listing 7 Charges of SMS New Year Greetings), online, available at: http://news.sohu.com/20070218/n248296024.shtml (accessed February 18, 2007).

30 Yang Boxu, "Social Networks and Individualism: The Role of the Mobile Phone in Today's Social Transformation in Urban China," paper presented at the 2007 China Computer-Mediated Communication Association Annual Conference and Xin Xin Forum (Wuhan, 2007).

31 *Youdianshi bianjishi: Zhongguo jindai youdianshi (*Editorial Office of Post and Telecommunication History: China's Modern History of Post and Telecommunication) (Beijing: People's Post and Telecommunication Press, 1984).
32 Ibid.
33 Ibid.
34 National Bureau of Statistics of China, *youdian tongxin shuiping* (Development of Postal and Telecommunications Services). Online, available at: www.stats.gov.cn/ndsj/information/zh1/n471a.
35 National Bureau of Statistics of China, *2002 quanguo tongji nianjian* (2002 Yearbook of National Statistics); *youdian yewuliang* (The Amount of Postal and Telecommunication Business), pp. 15–41. Online, available at: www.stats.gov.cn/yearbook2001/indexC.htm.
36 National Bureau of Statistics of China, *2000 quanguo tongji nianjian* (2000 Yearbook of National Statistics); *youdian yewuliang* (The Amount of Postal and Telecommunication Business), pp. 15–41. Online, available at: www.stats.gov.cn/ndsj/zgnj/2000/O41c.htm.
37 Ibid.
38 National Bureau of Statistics of China, *2005 quanguo tongji nianjian* (2005 Yearbook of National Statistics); *youdian yewuliang* (The Amount of Postal and Telecommunication Business), pp. 15–41. Online, available at: www.stats.gov.cn/tjsj/ndsj/2005/indexce.htm; and *2002 Zhongguo dianxin tongji niandu baogao* (2002 China Telecommunication Statistics Annual Report). The increase continued in the new century to 144.8 million in 2000, 179 million in 2001, 214 million in 2002, and 263 million in 2003.
39 *Zhonghua Renmin Gongheguo 2003 Nian Guomin Jingji he Shehui Fazhan Tongji Gongbao* (PRC Statistical Communiqué of National Economy and Social Development, 2003).
40 Ibid.
41 *Tongxin Hangye Tongji Yuebao 2007–04* (April 2007, Monthly Statistics of Communications Industry), MII website, May 23, 2007.
42 Xie Weiqun, "Guhua Hui Xiaoshi ma?" (Could Landline Phone Disappear?), *People's Daily*, May 31, 2007, p. 6.
43 *2007 quanguo tongxinye fazhan tongji gongbao* (2007 National Telecommunication Development Statistic Report), MII website, February 19, 2008.
44 Liu Hongqing, *Fengsheng Shuiqi, Diwu Meiti* (The Fifth Media is Getting Up), online, available at: http://qnjz.dzwww.com/zt/200609/t20060919_1766948.htm (accessed September 19, 2006).
45 See, Kong Wei Chao, online, available at: http://berkeleyabc.org/2004/thumbeconomy.htm; www.wordspy.com/words/thumbculture.asp; www.mobileactive.org/mobile-democracy.
46 "06 Nian Zhongguo Duanxin Liang Zeng 41%, Yindong Liantong Shouru Chao 400 Yi" (Short Messages in 06 China Increase 41%, Incomes of China Mobile and China Unicom reached 40 Billion), February 25, 2007, online, available at: http://news.xinhuanet.com/zgjx/2007–02/25/content_5770105.htm.
47 *2006 Nian QuanguoTongxin Ye Fazhan Tongji Gongbao* (Statistical Communiqué of National Telecommunications Development, 2006), MII website, February 9, 2007.
48 *Tongxin Hangye Tongji Yuebao* (April 2007) (Monthly Statistical Communiqué of Communications Industry), MII website, May 23, 2007.
49 Feng Xiaofang, "Chunjie 7 Tian Jiaqi Quanguo Shouji Duanxin Fasong Liang Chaoguo 150 Yi Tiao" (The Amount of Mobile Phone Short Message Exceeds 15 Billion during the Seven Days of Chinese New Year Holiday) Xinhuanet, February 27, 2007.
50 Sadie Plant, *On the Mobile, the Effects of Mobile Telephones on Social and Individual Life*, Motorola report, 2001, pp. 8–9. Online, available at: www.motorola.com/mot/doc/0/234_MotDoc.pdf.

51 Zhai Yu and Shen Jianbei, "Chaoji Niisheng Quzhong, You Duoshao Jiazhi Keyi Chonglai?" (*Super Girls* is over, how much more incomes can be resumed?), August 29, 2005, online, available at: www.yipu.com.cn.

52 Xu Linling, "Chaoji Niisheng Ruhe Zhuanqian – Duanxin shi Zhuyao de Lirun Laiyuan" (How did *Super Girls* make Money – Text Message was the Main Source), August 25, 2005, online, available at: www.yipu.com.cn.

53 Zhai Yu and Shen Jianbei, www.yipu.com.cn, August 29, 2005.

54 Ye Weimin and Duan Xianju, "Chaoji niisheng yi kuaile de fangshi chongji zhongguo yule dianshi" (*Super Girl* Impacts China's TV Entertainment with Happiness), XinhuaNet, August 27, 2005, online, available at: www.hunantv.com; *Seven Day Fortune*, "chaoji nvsheng fuzhili shi shengchanli" (The Reproduction Power of *Super Girl* is Productivity), August 29, 2005, online, available at: www.yipu.com.cn.

55 Zhai Yu and Shen Jianbei, www.yipu.com.cn, August 29, 2005.

56 B. Ellwood-Clayton, "Virtual Strangers: Young Love and Texting in the Filipino Archipelago of Cyberspace," in *Mobile Democracy: Essays on Society, Self, and Politics*, edited by K. Nyiri (Vienna: Passagen Verlag, 2003), pp. 225–39.

57 "Chaoji niisheng de minzhu yishilun" (Democratic Ideology of *Super Girl*), online, available at: www.em-cn.com/Article/200703/144782.htm; Retuxiaoxiang, "Chaoji niisheng – zhongguo minzhu gaige de shijinshi" (*Super Girl* – the Touchstone of China's Democratic Reform) Development forum www.XINHUANET.com, August 8, 2005.

58 Gao Tao, "Chaoji niisheng yu minzhu de faxue sikao" (*Super Girl* and the Thought on Democratic Law), March 11, 2007, online, available at: www.lawsalon.net/index.php/viewnews-241.html; Wang Xiaoyu, "Yule de cuileidan, minzhu de cuimianji – guanyu 'chaoji niisheng' de pinglun de pinglun" (Tear Bomb of Entertainment, Somnifacient of Democracy – Comment on the *Super Girl's* Comments), online, available at: www.xschina.org/show.php?id=4688.

59 Dong Wei, "Shekeyuan Wenhua Lanpishu Jiedu Chaonii Chanyelian, Chaonii Gongxian Shehui Jingji Zhishao Shushi Yi" (CCSC Blue Book on Culture Explains *Super Girls'* Industry Chain, *Super Girls* has Contributed Social Economy at Least Several Billions), January 12, 2006, online, available at: www.youth.cn.

60 Paul Levinson, *Cellphone: The Story of the World's Most Mobile Medium and How It Has Transformed Everything* (New York: Palgrave Macmillan, 2004).

61 Wang Rutang and Wang Haiying, "Bainian Duanxin Zaoyu 7 Zong Zui, 140 Yi Tiao Chuang Xingao" (On Seven Charges Though, 14 Billion Pieces of New Year Greetings Message Reach a New High), *Xinhua Daily News*, February 26, 2007, online, available at: http://news.xinhuanet.com/focus/2007–02/26/content_5772804_1.htm; Yang Xia "Dizhi Duanxin Bainian Yundong Lieju duanxin Qi Da Zuizhuang" (Call on Boycotting Movement, Listing 7 Charges of SMS New Year Greetings), February 18, 2007, online, available at: http://news.sohu.com/20070218/n248296024.shtml.

62 Ding Shi and Zhen Caiji, "Jiji Yingdui Shouji Meiti de Tiaozhan" (Respond Actively to the Challenge from Mobile Phone Media), *Qiushi Magazine*, June 2006, online, available at: www.qsjournal.com.cn/qs/20060316/GB/qs%5E427%5E0%5E21.htm; Kuang Wenbo, *Shouji meiti gailun* (On Generalities of Mobile Phone Media) (Beijing: Renmin University Press, 2006); Huang Hong, "Shilun Shouji Meiti de Fumian Yingxiang ji Kongzhi" (On Mobile Phone's Negative Effects and How to Control Them), *Journalists*, May 2004, online, available at: http://xwjz.eastday.com/eastday/xwjz/node19085/node19087/userobject1ai221520.html; Feng Yuyuan, "Diwu Meiti de Fazh Xainzhuang ji Quxiang Tanxi" (The Present Development and Trend Exploration), November 21, 2005, online, available at: www.ddcbxj.com/Article/ShowArticle.asp?ArticleID=906; Huang Yupeng, "Shouji Chuanbo de Xiaoji Yingxiang ji Duice" (On the Negative Effects of Mobile Communication and Responsive Strategies), *Journalism Lover*, November 2006.

3 Regulating *e gao*

Futile efforts of recentralization?

Bingchun Meng

In 2006, *e gao* (literally translated as "reckless doings") emerged within the Chinese cyberspace as a cultural phenomenon, which generally includes all types of audiovisual spoofs, oft-times by taking advantage of the transformative capability of digital technology as well as the distribution power of the Internet. A good indication of the pervasiveness of this new phenomenon is the hundreds and thousands of results you would get once typing in *e gao* in any Chinese-language search engine. Indeed, according to a survey jointly conducted by *China Youth Daily* and Tencent.com,[1] only 1.8 percent of the 6,290 participants were unaware of this new vocabulary by September 2006. What is parallel to the growing popularity of spoof culture is the escalating efforts made by both the state and some private parties to regulate such content based on various concerns, ranging from alleged moral degradation to copyright infringement. By the end of 2007, both the State Administration of Radio, Film and Television (SARFT) and the Ministry of Culture had issued regulations aiming to curb the spread of online video spoofs. The release of new regulations not only drew wide press coverage on mainstream newspapers, but also provoked extensive debates on the Internet with regard to the legitimacy and feasibility of such rules.

So what exactly is *e gao* and what should we make of this culture phenomenon? What are the major tensions that drive the state's regulatory efforts? And more generally, what are the implications this particular case has on the prospect of the Internet as a platform for generating and disseminating alternative creative content? This chapter intends to analyze the cultural and political implications of *e gao* as a decentralized form of communication, which challenges the established mechanisms of media production and distribution as well as the officially sanctioned norms of media content in China.

I will start by tracing how this pop culture phenomenon has come into formation in China and its genealogical relationships with other artistic and cultural genres. I then discuss the subversive potential of *e gao* by focusing on three major aspects: the issue of authorship, the production and distribution mechanism, and the rhetorical strategies of *e gao* texts. First, since *e gao* derives meaning from "remixing" existing creative works, it oft-times creates difficulty for identifying individual authorship and claiming the subsequent legal protection. The rich intertextuality of online spoofs problematizes the notion of individual authorship, which lays the foundation for copyright protection. By the same token, established authors are likely to invoke copyright infringement allegations once they find the parodies offensive and take interest in preventing the circulation of those parodies. In this sense, *e gao* questions the legitimacy of copyright law as a means to centralize cultural resources and to maintain the control over information flow.[2] Second, the grassroots production of online spoofs disturbs the hierarchical status quo of Chinese media. Although the commercialization and marketization since the late 1970s have contributed to the multiplicity of media outlets in China, the government still exerts tight control over media via both political (e.g. censorship) and economic means (e.g. ownership). *E gao* epitomizes the power of new media in lowering the entry barrier to and redistributing the resources for production and distribution. The strong governmental reaction toward *e gao* indicates the challenge this phenomenon poses to a centralized media system. Third, taking an iconoclastic attitude toward the grand narratives of anything "mainstream" or "official," *e gao* is also an alternative means of engaging with social political issues in a heavily censored discursive environment. For individuals who cannot always voice their opinions through an institutionalized channel, the Internet provides a less constrained environment for them to speak up. The parodic style adopted by most *e gao* works is in sharp contrast with the authoritative tone of official discourses and it articulates criticism and grievances in a rather non-conventional style. In the last section of this chapter, I go back to the issue of regulation and address the more general question of the Internet's potential of challenging the "actual concentration of media power"[3] and how that potential is always conditioned by the social, political and legal contexts.

From parody to culture jamming

An understanding of the *e gao* culture should start from the elaboration of its very name. This word is so new it is not even listed in Chinese dictionaries. However, it can be traced to the Japanese word "Kuso," which refers to an Internet subculture that deconstructs serious literature or artistic materials to entertain people. Depending on the context, "Kuso" has many meanings and "damned," "funny," "nonsense," "idiocy," "farces" and "mischievous tricks" are just some of them. In Taiwan's Internet subculture and video gamers' communities, "Kuso" has evolved into a new attitude toward life that suggests "making fun of everything and playing practical jokes."[4] Since being adopted by mainland China, it has become a popular form of entertainment and got the name *e'gao*. The character "e" in Chinese means "evil," or "bad" and "gao" means "to make changes" or "to deal with." Combined, the phrase refers to a new multimedia expression that makes fun of established works through parody, and the style of the new works could range from being satirical, camp to outrageous or grotesque. At first, *e gao* works were mostly Photoshop-transformed pictures, such as the famous *Little Fatty* (Xiao pang) series that inserts the face of a chubby teenage boy into many movie posters or news photos. Later on, ever since *The Bloody Case that Started from a Steamed Bun* became a big hit on the Internet in 2005, video spoof became the major format of *e gao* online. By the end of the year 2006, both of the two leading Chinese portal sites, sina.com and netease.com, came up with their own top-ten list of online video spoofs that utilized visual materials ranging from the black and white Soviet war film *Lenin in 1918* to the Hollywood blockbuster *Matrix* and the spoofs touched upon topics from media corruption in China to the war in Iraq.

In terms of artistic tradition, *e gao* is not essentially new. In literature, parody as a genre can be dated back to ancient Greece, where a *parodia* was a narrative poem imitating the style and prosody of epics "but treat[ing] light, satirical or mock-heroic subjects."[5] Hutcheon points out that to take some elements out of their original context and reuse them could generate more complex new meanings than just ridicule and that this practice is also common in twentieth-century literature, with *Ulysses* being the prominent example, in which James Joyce incorporates elements from Homer's *Odyssey*.[6] Parody adopts someone else's discourse but "introduces into that discourse a semantic intention that is directly opposed to the original one," the second voice clashing with the first and creating "an arena of battle between two voices."[7]

In visual art, Dadaism, Surrealism and Situationism all used innovative techniques trying to attribute new meanings to existing objects or artistic expressions. A famous example is Marcel Duchamp's Dadaist painting entitled *LHOOQ*, which added a goatee and a moustache to Da Vinci's *Mona Lisa*. Just like Dadaism and Surrealism before it, Situationism wants to supersede the categorization of art and culture as separate activities and to transform them into part of everyday life. In fact, Situationists Guy Debord and Gil Wolman called for a "serious parody" that provokes transgression and subversion

> It is therefore necessary to conceive of a parodic-serious stage where the accumulation of detoured elements, far from aiming to arouse indignation or laughter by alluding to some original work, will express our indifference toward a meaningless and forgotten original, and concern itself with rendering a certain sublimity.[8]

This idea of achieving certain "sublimity" by playfully rearranging elements became the major inspiration for contemporary practice of *cultural jamming*. According to Jordan, culture jamming is "an attempt to reverse and transgress the meaning of cultural codes whose primary aim is to persuade us to buy something or be someone."[9] Cultural jammers aim to question the political assumptions behind a highly commercialized culture through reconfiguring corporate logos, billboards, trademarks, product images, fashion statements, etc.[10] One famous examples of culture jamming is activist magazine *Adbusters*' Blackspot sneaker campaign, which intends to "uncool" sportswear giant Nike by offering an ethically produced "unswooshed" alternative to the Nike shoes. The shoes bear a large white spot where one would expect a Nike logo. *Adbusters* also encouraged its readers to help spread the "Blackspot virus" by graffiti-ing black spots on

Niketown windows and displays across the US and Canada. Another example was that after the *Exxon Valdez* disaster, the San Francisco-based Billboard Liberation Front appropriated a radio promotion poster so that instead of "Hits Happen. New X-100" it read "Shit Happens-New Exoon."[11]

Taking a historical perspective, *e gao* clearly demonstrates resemblance with its predecessors at both aesthetic and political dimensions. Nevertheless, to interpret this phenomenon merely as the digital extension of literary parody or the Chinese counterpart of culture jamming would not be adequate. Unlike culture jammers who often constitute civil activism groups,[12] *e gao* practicers hardly have any coherent agenda. While culture jamming targets commercial messages of big corporate and the consumerism ideology in general, *e gao* is a much dispersed practice of pranking that does not always have a "common enemy" – nothing is scared, and anything could be made fun of. In the following sections, I will re-embed *e gao* in the contemporary Chinese context and explicate the tensions this phenomenon bears with the regulatory environment of new media.

Deconstructing authorship

In December 2005, the veteran director Chen Kaige released his latest blockbuster *The Promise* (*Wu Ji*) after running a high-profile promotional campaign in all types of media outlets. Chen is among the so-called "Fifth Generation" Chinese directors who drew instant international attention with their early works. In 1993, Chen's film *Farewell My Concubine* won the Golden Palm award at the Cannes Film Festival, but his works in the last decade or so have not been very successful. *The Promise* topped all the previous domestic blockbusters with a budget of RMB300 million ($37.5 million), and the media coverage before the premiere all claimed this movie as the great coming back of one of the best Chinese directors. However, *The Promise* turned out to be a great disappointment instead. In addition to the negative reviews from both critics and audiences, what upset Chen Kaige most was a 20-minute video spoof that became a huge hit on the Chinese Internet soon after the movie's release.

Titled *The Bloody Case that Started from a Steamed Bun*, the video was made by a 31-year-old sound engineer and freelancer named Hu Ge. Hu told one of *The Times* reporters that he was so disappointed after seeing *The Promise* that he decided to have a little fun with the convoluted epic of a girl transformed into a princess.[13] Hu adopted the format of Central China Television Station's (CCTV's) famous program "China Legal Reports" to organize edited sequences of *The Promise*. He kept the names of the original characters, but dubbed them with different speeches to develop his own story. *The Steamed Bun* attracted millions of viewers on the Internet, almost certainly outnumbering those who paid to see *The Promise* in theatres. Countless blogs provided links to or direct downloading of the short film. Although Hu Ge allegedly told one reporter that the intention of making such a spoof was simply to entertain himself and some friends, he did become some sort of cyber hero in China overnight. In fact, Hu Ge's name has become permanently associated with the popularization of online spoofs ever since.

The director Chen Kaige on the other hand was infuriated. Chen accused Hu of having no sense of morality for destroying the integrity of his work.[14] It soon became widely reported that Chen filed a lawsuit against Hu Ge based upon copyright violation. Chinese netizens' support for Hu Ge was very strong. According to an online poll conducted by Netease, which is one of the biggest Internet portals in China, only 843 votes (4 percent) sided with Chen Kaige while 14,760 (85 percent) supported Hu Ge. Many online posts suggest that for one thing Chen's RMB300 million movie provided audiences with much less enjoyment than Hu's 20-minute spoof and for another, *The Steamed Bun* may actually hype up *The Promise*, as otherwise the original movie would have faded away soon after it went into public screening.[15] Although the case was eventually dropped, it provoked unprecedented debate on the relationship between parody and fair use under the Chinese copyright legislation. Opinions from legal experts are divided. Some insist that Hu Ge's work has tarnished the integrity of *The Promise* and the amount of clips it takes from the original movie has exceeded the limit of fair use. Others argue that parody is a completely legitimate way of making comments on literary and artistic works, hence should be protected under freedom of expression.[16] Two provisions in China's Copyright Law are particularly relevant here. Article 22 of the Copyright Law identifies 12 conditions under which a work may be used without permission from, and without payment of remuneration to, the copyright owner. The first two conditions specified are:

1 to use for the user's own private study, research and self-entertainment; and
2 to appropriate quotations from a published work for the purpose of making comments or demonstrating a point.[17]

This is what is often referred to as the fair use clause of China's Copyright Law. On the other hand, Article 10 of the Copyright Law codifies that the term "copyright" includes both property rights and personal rights, which include "the right of integrity, that is, the right to protect one's work against distortion and mutilation."[18] So the debate on *The Steamed Bun* video boils down to how the two provisions should be applied to this case: can the 20-minute spoof be deemed fair use or is it an infringement of the director's personal rights? Indeed, the tension between copyright protected authorship and creative activities is intensified in *e gao* practice, which relies on digitally enabled decontextualization and recontextualization of elements from existing works.

The romantic notion of authorship[19] – that an individual is solely responsible for the creation of a unique piece of literary or artistic work – is one of the cornerstones of copyright law. A copyrightable work is recognized as the fruit of an individual author's creative labor, thus shall be reproduced, distributed and reused only at the author's discretion. This basic assumption underlining the current legal system on intellectual products, however, turns out to be a problematic one, as has been pointed out by many literary critics. Roland Barthes states that "the text is a tissue of citations, resulting from the thousand sources of culture … the writer can only imitate a gesture forever anterior, never original."[20] Michel Foucault also deconstructed the idea that the author is the originator of something original by declaring the "death of the author" while emphasizing that "author" is the product or function of writing. Foucault contends that the author function is not formed spontaneously. Rather, it results from various cultural constructions, in which we choose certain attributes of an individual as "authorial" attributes, and dismiss others.[21] Even before the post-structuralist thinkers, Northrop Frye remarked that the conventionality of literature is "elaborately disguised by a law of copyright pretending that every work of art is an invention distinctive enough to be patented,"[22] while the literary tradition demonstrated that "poetry can only be made out of other poems novels out of other novels."[23] In her now classic "Genius and Copyright," Woodmansee traced the economic and legal conditions that lead to the emergence of "authorship" as we know it today. She pointed out that the modern notion of individual authorship was not "invented" until the eighteenth century, when a new group of writers began to seek a living from selling their writings to the new and rapidly expanding reading public.[24]

Once we acknowledge authorship as a constructed discourse contingent upon certain economic, cultural and legal conditions, we can better understand the challenges that *e gao* poses to copyright regulation at both practical and discursive levels. *E gao* is by definition an appropriation of some original works and it derives its meanings from intertextuality rather than textuality, from the dialogs among different voices rather than the monologue of the author. By revising and remixing bits and pieces from various texts, *e gao* practitioners break down the boundaries between individual works, thus further exposing the problematic of claiming individual authorship. With the aid of digital technologies, even less cost and effort are required to subvert and transgress any "original works of authorship fixed in any tangible medium of expression."[25] From Photoshop-edited pictures to re-dubbed movie sequences, *e gao* has made it more difficult to specify where one text ends and another one begins and what is "text" and what is "context."

Needless to say, it is in the interest of those established authors to maintain the boundaries that define individual authorship, so that they can continue to enjoy the benefits of monopolizing the creative resource.[26] Copyright law is the instrument for them to do so. Whenever the established author feels that an *e gao* piece could be detrimental to his or her interests for whatever reasons, they would invoke the power of copyright law in order to stop the creation and distribution of new texts, just as Chen Kaige was trying to do. In July 2006, China enacted a new Internet Copyright Regulation that specifically addresses online copyright infringement, including P2P file sharing. Later that year, the municipal government of Chongqing enacted a new information network regulation that for the first time included a provision aiming to curb *e gao* online. According to the new rule, posting online videos to satirize others or social phenomena could potentially be considered an act of defamation thus facing punishment.[27] According to a new regulation released by the Ministry of Culture in December 2006, all music that has been modified from its original form, including those for non-profit purposes, must first be submitted to the Ministry before being uploaded online.[28] In January 2008, Beijing Municipal Copyright Administration, the capital's regulatory body for copyright-related issues, announced that the top priority in the coming year is to strengthen Olympics-related intellectual property protection and to take strong action against any practice of *e gao* Olympic-related expressions, including symbols, slogans, mascots, songs, videos, etc.[29] These new regulations are just a few examples to indicate that as the stakes get higher for copyright protection, more attempts will be made to tame the disturbance of *e gao* by reclaiming individual authorship. In a digital communication environment that enables easier parody of others' works, the question that remains open is how effectively the regulations can be enforced. This leads to the discussion in the next section, as one major reason that contributes to the enforcement of regulations is the dispersed nature of *e gao* practice.

Decentralized production and distribution

Western commentators tend to adopt the liberal-democratic model when assessing the transformation of Chinese media industries since the 1980s. From numerous press coverage to proliferating academic writings on media in China, the framing question seems rather consistent: will marketization combined with new technology eventually democratize China? This kind of thinking has several pitfalls. First, it assumes that market and state are inherently in conflict, yet neglects the fact that marketization in China is a top-down process initiated by the state and it actually contributes to the legitimacy of the Party-state.[30] Second, it usually suggests a rather monolithic view toward the state and overlooks the tensions among different state agencies. In addition, control mechanism itself is also evolving from governance to governmentality, which takes effect at various non-state dimensions including the self-regulation of private sectors and self-censorship at the individual level.[31] Third, the liberal-democratic framework is based upon a more or less romantic notion of market being an autonomous and inclusive sphere. Such a notion overlooks the exclusion as a result of media ownership concentration and the bias created by any advertising-driven commercial media system.[32]

Although commercialization and marketization have led to the dramatic growth of media outlets and increased diversity of media content, resources for producing and distributing audiovisual content are still very much concentrated. Starting from the late 1990s, the Party initiated a series of new policies to consolidate the media sector by nurturing a handful of media conglomerates.[33] The rationale for such consolidation is twofold – achieving economic advantage and political control. In anticipation to China's accession to the WTO and the further opening up of the domestic media market as the result of global integration, the Chinese state aspired to forge its own multimedia giants so as to compete with transnational companies like News Corp or Viacom. Consequently, domestic media conglomerates such as Hunan Radio and Television Group and Shanghai Media Group came into formation, and they became the de facto monopolizer of broadcasting resources at provincial level. The consolidation also bears political concerns. After two decades' commercialization, the proliferation of media outlets had made it more difficult for the Party-state to exert control, therefore state-mandated conglomeration is a means of recentralization. For example, the number of television stations reduced from 1997's 4,000 to a total of 1,557 by the end of 2002, among which the 1,200 county stations lost rights to make programs or operate channels and only serve as transmission stations.[34]

Against this background, *e gao* works are ordinary people's attempts to "talk back" by appropriating products of those who dominate media industries. Since the success of the *Steamed Bun* video in December 2005, all the major domestic blockbusters were spoofed in one way or another by creative Chinese netizens, including *The Banquet*, *Curse of Golden Flowers*, *A World without Thieves*. Creators of online video spoofs are neither sanctioned by the political power of the state nor following the bottom line of the market. The videos are produced without any initial profit-seeking incentives and are available through free downloading. If we borrow George Gerbner's metaphor that media are electronic storytellers for the society,[35] then these are grassroots storytellers who do not necessarily represent state ideology or corporate interest. On the homepage of his personal blog, Hu Ge posted the following statement:

> I am an amateur in video production, which is simply a hobby of mine. These videos are just for expressing some of my personal comments on various issues and for entertaining my family and friends. From now on all my videos will be of this style. If you don't like them, then just don't watch them. But please do continue to support me if you like them. My videos, first of all, are not at the expense of any state resource; secondly I do not make a profit by selling any tickets, and I never impose them on any unwilling audience.[36]

This is very much reminiscent of another quote from media activist Matthew Arnison, who is a Sydney-based open source software developer as well as an advocate for open publishing and independent media:

> Old media technology creates a natural hierarchy between the storytellers and the audience. The storyteller has access to some piece of technology, such as a TV transmitter or a printing press. The audience don't ... somewhere along the way, this has been justified by assuming that most people aren't that creative that having only a handful of people to tell stories in a city of millions is a natural way of doing things. But is it?[37]

Digital technology shifted the relationship between storytellers and the audience, who now find it much easier to put their own stories into a proper format with presentable quality. More importantly, the Internet enables wide distribution of multimedia content across geographical boundaries.

The regulatory anxiety grew with the increasing popularity of online video spoofs. Starting from the second half of 2006, discussions on the forthcoming licensing scheme for online videos suddenly increased in the press. Some titles quoted here are: "China is Making New Iron Laws to Regulate Online Videos,"[38]

"The SARFT is Once Again Striking Down Heavily on Illegal Internet Videos,"[39] "*E gao* on the Web is against the Idea of Harmonious Society."[40] The SARFT in China occupies the dual role of being both the regulator and operator of broadcasting and film industries. Broadly speaking, the SARFT is responsible for controlling access to satellite and cable TV networks, approving the content of radio, television as well as films, and overseeing the operation of national TV networks. The Internet infrastructure on the other hand is regulated by the Ministry of Information Industries (MII). In the era of network convergence, just like a cable network could provide telecom service, the Internet also became a new platform for distributing audiovisual content. As a result, the turf war between the SARFT and the MII has been going on since the late 1990s in respect of who has the control over information transmitted on converged networks.[41] The SARFT's strong reaction against *e gao* from the very beginning was considered by many as an effort to reclaim its regulatory power over content on the Internet.

In December 2007, the SARFT and the MII co-published the new Regulation for Online Audio and Video Services, which cover the production, editing and aggregation of audio and video content and provision to the public through both the Internet and mobile networks. Under the new rule, all online audio and video service providers are required to apply for an "Online Audio-Visual Broadcasting License," key qualifications including: the majority being state-owned, having no record of violations in the three years up to application, and possessing a comprehensive program censoring system, legal program resources, legal funding sources and "standardized technology."[42] The new regulation prompted negative response in both online forums and mainstream media. The editorial of *Southern Metropolis Daily*, which is one of the most influential liberal newspapers in China, argued that the SARFT/MII regulations are a "shocking intrusion" no matter what the government's goal is, whether it is to promote cultural development and innovation or to ensure fair market competition. It is now too early to predict whether the new regulation could be effectively enforced given the dispersed nature of the Internet. By the end of 2006 there were more than 150 websites that provide online video sharing,[43] very few of them can be properly licensed based on the new rule. But it is unlikely that the state regulators would actually shut down the majority of those websites. Although the SARFT and the MII appeared uncharacteristically cooperative this time, the difference between their respective policy-orientation still exists. While the former has a higher political and economic stake in content regulation, the latter cares more about running an efficient network infrastructure. Hence the enforcement remains an open question.

Carnival in the virtual space

In *Rabelais and His World*, Mikhail Bakhtin pinpointed two important aspects of the Middle Ages folk culture: carnivalesque and grotesque realism.[44] According to Bakhtin, carnival is "a special type of communication impossible in everyday life," with "special forms of marketplace speech and gesture, frank and free, permitting no distance between those who came in contact with each other and liberating from norms of etiquette and decency imposed at other times."[45] Carnivalesque culture is characterized by grotesque realism, which includes parody and any other form of discourse that "brings down to earth" anything ineffable or authoritarian. Grotesque images of food and body in the Middle Ages carnivals were meant to generate laughter that "degrades and materializes." This laughter is not just the individual's reaction to some "comic event," it is "the laughter of all the people."[46] When carnival was taking place, nobody lived outside it. Hence carnival culture is neither a purely artistic form nor a spectacle that only belongs to the sphere of art. Instead, "It belongs to the borderline between art and life. In reality, it is life itself, but shaped according to a certain pattern of play."[47]

This notion of carnivalsque culture sheds light on our understanding of *e gao* in China. In a centralized and highly controlled media environment, Chinese people use spoofs and pranks, which sometimes are combined with vulgar elements, to "bring down to earth" anything related with the officialdom. Nothing is sacred and nothing can escape from being the object of laughter. As Hannah Arendt has stated, "The greatest enemy of authority is contempt, and the surest way to undermine it is laughter."[48] Running through the most popular spoof videos enlisted on either sina.com or netease.com, one can identify some general traits in both content and style. Most videos are innovative collages of clips from various movies or TV shows, with a few exceptions actually containing real-time performance of amateur actors/actresses. The aesthetic style is a mixture of satirical, parodic, camp and grotesque. Several common themes are quite prominent across different videos, such as the deconstruction of orthodox revolutionary stories and heroes (the so-called "red classics"), parody of the typical stone-faced style of the state broadcaster as well as the highly commercialized practice of contemporary Chinese media, and satirical comments on pertinent social and political issues.

In *The Bloody Case over a Steamed Bun*, Hu Ge edited and distorted sequences from the most expensive film ever made in China, and the outcome is a poignant yet also hilarious criticism on the implausibility of the original blockbuster. In addition, Hu pokes fun at the state broadcaster CCTV by using a poker-faced presenter and stuffy communist terminology when reporting on the investigation into the humble bun murder. As the story in the *Steamed Bun* video unfolds, Hu also managed to insert implicit comments on various social issues such as migrant workers not getting paid from their employers, product placement practice in commercial media, corruption of public security officers. Another popular video called *The Sparkling Red Star* is the parody of a household revolutionary movie with the same title. The creator gives him/herself a pseudo name "Hu Dao Ge," which interestingly enough is a parody of Hu Ge. Adding a new subtitle of *Pan Dongzi going for the singing contest*, this ten-minute spoof used clips from the original movie to tell a totally different story. This time the poor boy that joined the Red Army in struggles against the evil landlord was turned into a pop-star wannabe who is eager to become famous overnight by taking part in the singing contest hosted by CCTV. The evil landlord in the original movie became a bribe-taking judge working for CCTV and the boy's father is now a real-estate tycoon who is willing to buy the son's path to success. *The Sparkling Red Star* not only subverted the orthodox revolutionary narrative of oppressed farmers fighting against reactionary landlords, but also made a satire of the corrupted practice of state media. A more recent creation by Hu Ge that involves real-time performance made fun of "the war against terrorism." The 40-minute short movie tells the story of how Chief Director of World Police Qiao Bushi (referring to George Bush) tried every possible means to detect Da Shaqi (abridged Chinese expression for weapons of mass destruction) hidden by an evil terrorist Sha Damu (referring to Saddam). A wide range of issues all became targets of laughter, including the UN Security Council, prisoner abuse at Guantanamo, lip sync practice of pop stars during live performance, communist slogans, just to name a few.

The political and cultural elitists' condemnation of *e gao* is best represented by a lengthy report on a symposium held by a major Party organ *Guang Ming Daily* in August 2006.[49] The purpose of the symposium, according to the deputy chief-editor of the newspaper, was to "prevent *e gao* from spreading on the Internet." Participants of the symposium include university professors, editors from major newspapers, directors from state-owned studios and Party officials. Taking a unanimously negative attitude toward *e gao*, they offered criticism from various perspectives, which can be summarized in the following ways. First, *e gao* deconstructed noble ideals and heroic images, both of which are crucial to sustaining the "socialist spiritual civilization." It is neither humorous nor creative, but simply vulgar expressions with very bad taste. Second, *e gao* undermined the value of honesty and sincerity, and turned everything into a joke. By poking fun at everything with an often malicious intent, *e gao* blurred the boundary between the good and the evil and, third, *e gao* practice shows no respect toward authors of parodied works and is an infringement of their copyright. Ironically, this "old-guard" style propagandistic argument soon became the new target of *e gao* practitioners online.[50]

In fact, there exists a cyclical relationship between official discourse and *e gao* texts. While the former feeds to the latter as source materials and the official condemnation adds to the canivalesque pleasure of creating and distributing *e gao*, the proliferation of *e gao* also prompts stronger reaction from the establishment, which, as suggested in the previous discussion, includes political and cultural elitists, administrative bodies and legal entities.

Conclusion

The empowerment potential of the Internet use has been the central theme for discussions on communication in the digital environment. For optimists like Negroponte, the digital age will achieve ultimate triumph due to its "decentralizing, globalizing, harmonizing, and empowering" qualities.[51] In his famous *Declaration of Cyberspace Independence*, John Barlow also proclaimed with great pride that "We will create a civilization of the Mind in Cyberspace. May it be more humane and fair than the world your governments have made before."[52] For media scholars, the excitement of the Internet mostly comes from its interactive nature, which allows people to "talk back" in a much easier and effective fashion than in the non-digital environment. Lance Bennett identified four aspects of new media empowerment:[53]

> (1) the production of high-quality content by ordinary people, (2) the creation of large-scale interactive networks engaged by that content, (3) the transmission of that content across borders and continents, and (4) the convergence of media systems so that personal (micro media) content has more pathways through which to enter mass media channels.

The key issue, however, is how these potentials can be realized and how the dialectic of control vs. change will play out on the digital frontier. Many scholars have criticized the technological deterministic tendency in discussions about the Internet as a great democratizing force[54]. They point out that such expectations could be completely misguided, if the dynamics of power does not become a focal point of the analysis. A concentrated media ownership structure, which could be either controlled by the government or by a few private media conglomerates, is another antithetical force against the decentralizing potential of new media. From this perspective, *e gao* and the regulatory attempts associated with it are yet another example of struggles between the establishment and the rebels.

When addressing the theme of control vs. change in the Chinese context, some scholars pay more attention to the ongoing censorship and the power of the so-called "Great Firewall,"[55] while others emphasize how the Internet offers an alternative space for political discussion[56] or interacts with civil society in promoting civic engagement and political mobilization.[57] The *e gao* phenomenon suggests that on one hand we need to be aware of the multiple dimensions of the control mechanisms, which do not always come in the form of censorship. In this case copyright law could just be as effective in curbing the availability of certain content. On the other hand, political communication could also take place in non-conventional formats with non-conventional styles. From a Bakhtinian perspective, carnival is not simply an invitation to individual freedom. Rather, it is an invitation to become a part of a complex unity, a bodily collectivity.[58]

Obviously *e gao* practices are rather dispersed and those who engage in this activity do not have a common agenda or coherent strategy, let alone any explicit political goals. This is an important distinction between *e gao* and culture jamming in the West that specifically targets corporate domination and commercialism. Nonetheless, not having a political agenda does not mean *e gao* is void of political significance. After all, Marx and his contemporaries in the 1830 and 1840s also used the "underground languages" of parody and irony to evade censorship. For them parody is the stylistic means of "smuggling ideas past a censor."[59] A closer examination of the relationship between media and power structure reveals that online spoofs did at least magnify some major tensions with regard to the digital communication environment in China. Regulatory attempts boil down to three fundamental questions. First, who can be recognized as author and enjoys corresponding legal protection. Second, how media content should be produced and distributed. Third, what kind of content is allowed and in which style they shall be presented. It is still too early to draw any conclusions on the effect of tightened copyright enforcement and the new regulation on online audio-video service. We may not want to be too hasty in celebrating the political function of *e gao* either. The negotiation between decentralized form of communication and the state's constant effort of recentralizing will certainly go on in the digital environment and the openness of the network is always contingent upon social, political and legal conditions.

Notes

1 Tencent is a leading operator of the Internet community in China. Its instant messaging service platform, "QQ," is the most popular online chatting software in China.

2 For critical view on copyright, see R. Bettig, *Copyrighting Culture: The Political Economy of Intellectual Property* (Boulder: Westview, 1996); J. Boyle, "The Second Enclosure Movement and the Construction of the Public Domain," *Law and Contemporary Problems*, Vol. 66, No. 1–2 (2003), pp. 33–74; N. Dyer-Witheford, "E-Capital and the Many-Headed Hydra," in G. Elmer (ed.), *Critical Perspectives of the Internet* (Lanham: Rowman & Littlefield, 2002); L. Lessig, *Free Culture: The Nature and Future of Creativity* (New York: Penguin, 2004); J. Litman, "Sharing and Stealing," *Hastings Communication & Entertainment Law Journal*, Vol. 27 (2004), pp. 1–50; C. May, *Global Political Economy of Intellectual Property Rights: The New Enclosures?* (London and New York: Routledge, 2003).

3 N. Couldry and J. Curran, "The Paradox of Media Power," in N. Couldry and J. Curran (eds.), *Contesting Media Power: Alternative Media in a Networked World* (Lanham: Rowman & Littlefield, 2003), p. 7.

4 See Wikipedia entry at http://zh.wikipedia.org/wiki/恶搞 (accessed February 10, 2008).

5 S. Dentith, *Parody* (London: Routledge, 2000), p. 10.

6 L. Hutcheon, *A Theory of Parody: The Teachings of Twentieth-Century Art Forms* (New York: Methuen, 1985).

7 M. Bakhtin, *Problems of Dostoevsky's Poetics* (Minnieapolis: University of Minnesota Press, 1984), p. 193.

8 G. Debord, "A User's Guide to Détournement," in K. Knabb (ed.), *Guy Debord Completed Cinematic Works* (Oakland: AK Press, 2003), p. 208.

9 Quoted in B. Cammaerts, "Jamming the Political: Beyond Counter-hegemonic Practices," *Continuum*, Vol. 21, No. 1 (2007), pp. 71–90.

10 B. Cammaerts, "Jamming the Political: Beyond Counter-hegemonic Practices," *Continuum*, Vol. 21, No. 1 (2007), pp. 71–90; C. Harold, "Pranking Rhetoric: 'Culture Jamming' as Media Activism," *Critical Studies in Media Communication*, Vol. 21, No. 3 (2004), pp. 189–211; W. Pickerel, H. Jorgensen and L. Bennett, "Culture Jams and Meme Warfare: Kalle Lasn, Adbusters, and Media Activism" (Seattle: University of Washington, 2002), online, available at: http://dept.washington.edu/gcp/pdf/culturejamsandmemewarfare.pdf (accessed January 10, 2008).

11 T. Jordan and P.A. Taylor, *Hacktivism and Cyberwars: Rebels with a Cause?* (New York: Routledge, 2004).

12 For more discussion on the agenda of culture jamming, see the website of Center for Communication and Civic Engagement at the University of Washington:

http://depts.washington.edu/ccce/polcommcampaigns/CultureJamming.htm (accessed February 10, 2008).

13 J. MaCartney, "Director all Steamed up over Web Parody of his Film," *The Times* (February 22, 2006), online, available at: www.timesonline.co.uk/tol/news/world/asia/article733376.ece (accessed February 10, 2008).

14 Ibid.

15 Y. Qiao, "HuGe niruo pochan women weini juankuan" (Hu Ge if you go Bankrupt, we will Donate Money), *Nanfang Dushibao* (Southern Metropolis Daily), online, available at: http://news.xinhuanet.com/comments/2006–02/15/content_4181491.htm (accessed February 10, 2008).

16 See the online forum dedicated to this topic, "*The Promise, The Steamed Bun* and Intellectual Property," online, available at: http://it.people.com.cn/GB/8219/58496/index.html (accessed February 10, 2008).

17 *Zhonghua renmin gongheguo zhuzuoquan fa* (Copyright Law of People's Republic of China), promulgated on September 7, 1990, revised version adopted on October 27, 2001, English translation available at www.chinaiprlaw.com/english/laws/laws10.htm (accessed February 10, 2008).

18 Ibid.

19 This idea is believed to emerge during the Romanticism movement in the eighteenth century, when authors like William Wordsworth and Samuel Coleridge began to emphasize the connection between individual talents and their creative works. See M. Woodmansee, "The Genius and the Copyright: Economic and Legal Conditions of the Emergence of the 'Author'," *Eighteenth-Century Studies*, Vol. 17, No. 4 (1984), pp. 425–48; T. Pfau, "The Pragmatics of Genre: Moral Theory and Lyric Authorship in Hegel and Wordsworth," in M. Woodmansee and P. Jaszi (eds.), *The Construction of Authorship: Textual Appropriation in Law and Literature* (Durham: Duke University Press, 1994), pp. 133–58; M. Ross, "Genius of Print in Eighteenth Century England," in M. Woodmansee and P. Jaszi (eds.), *The Construction of Authorship: Textual Appropriation in Law and Literature* (Durham: Duke University Press, 1994), pp. 231–58.

20 R. Barthes, "The Death of the Author," in R. Barthes (ed.), *Image-Music-Text* (New York: Hill and Wang, 1978), p. 146.

21 M. Foucault, "What is an Author?" in J. Harari (ed.), *Textual Strategies: Perspectives in Post-Structuralist Criticism* (Ithaca: Cornell University Press, 1979), pp. 141–60.

22 N. Frye, *Anatomy of Criticism* (Princeton: Princeton University Press, 1957), p. 96.

23 Ibid., p. 97.

24 M. Woodmansee, "The Genius and the Copyright: Economic and Legal Conditions of the Emergence of the 'Author'," *Eighteenth-Century Studies*, Vol. 17, No. 4 (1984), pp. 425–48.

25 *Copyright Law of the United States of America*, § 101.

26 L. Lessig, *Free Culture: The Nature and Future of Creativity* (New York: Penguin, 2004).

27 Y. Zhu, "Wangluo e gao yu caogen wenhua" (Online e gao and Grassroot Culture), online, available at: http://culture.people.com.cn/GB/22219/4971934.html (accessed Feburary 10, 2008).

28 W. Jiao, "*E gao*: Art Criticism or Evil?" *China Daily* (January 22, 2007), online, available at http://english.cri.cn/3100/2007/01/22/63@187447.htm (accessed February 10, 2008).

29 Y.Y. Dou, "Wangshang *e gao* aoyun biaozhi jiangbei qiangxing guanbi" (Online Spoofs of Olympic Symbols will be Stopped), *Xin Jingbao* (Beijing Evening News) (January 17, 2008), online, available at: http://it.sohu.com/20080117/n254723903.shtml (accessed February 10, 2008).

30 Y. Zhao, "From Commercialization to Conglomeration: The Transformation of the Chinese Press within the Orbit of the Party State," *Journal of Communication*, Vol. 50, No. 2 (2000), pp. 3–26; Y. Zhao, "Transnational Capital, the Chinese State,

and China's Communication Industries in a Fractured Society," *Javnost: The Public*, Vol. 10, No. 4 (2003), pp. 53–74; Y. Zhao, "The State, the Market, and Media Control in China," in P. Thomas and Z. Nain (eds.), *Who Owns the Media: Global Trends and Local Resistance* (Penang, Malaysia: Southbound Press, 2004).

31 A. Ong, *Neoliberalism as Exception: Mutations in Citizenship and Sovereignty* (Durham: Duke University Press, 2006); Y. Zhou, "Privatizing Control: Internet Cafes in China," in A. Ong and L. Zhang (eds.), *Privatizing China, Socialism from Afar* (Ithaca: Cornell University Press, 2007), pp. 214–29; L. Tsui, "The Panopticon as the Antithesis of a Space of Freedom: Control and Regulation of the Internet in China," *China Information: A Journal on Contemporary China Studies*, Vol. 17, No. 2 (2003), pp. 65–82.

32 For analysis on the inherent bias of commercial media system, see for example, B. Bagdikian, *Media Monopoly* (Boston: Beacon Press, 2004); R. McChesney, "The Communication Revolution: the Market and the Prospect for Democracy," in M. Andersen and P.H. Collins (eds.), *Race, Class, and Gender: An Anthology* (Belmont: Wardsworth, 1997), pp. 57–78; E. Herman and R. McChesney, *The Global Media: The New Missionaries of Corporate Capitalism* (London: Cassell, 1997); R. Hackett and Z. Yuezhi, *Sustaining Democracy? Journalism and the Politics of Objectivity* (Toronto: Broadview Press, 1998); J. Curran and J. Seaton, *Power without Responsibility: The Press and Broadcasting in Britain* (London: Routledge, 1997).

33 Z. Hu, "The Post-WTO Restructuring of the Chinese Media Industries and the Consequences of Capitalisation," *Javnost*, Vol. 10, No. 4 (2003), pp. 19–36; Y. Zhu, *Chinese Cinema during the Era of Reform: The Ingenuity of the System* (Westport: Praeger, 2003); Y. Zhao, "From Commercialization to Conglomeration: The Transformation of the Chinese Press within the Orbit of the Party State," *Journal of Communication*, Vol. 50, No. 2 (2000), pp. 3–26.

34 Y. Wang, "Difang guangdian, 'zhuhou' buzai? – guanzhu zhongguo dishi, xianshi dianshitai biange" (Local Broadcast "Lords" are Doomed? Focusing on Metropolitan and County Television Reforms in China), *Meijie* (Media), No. 4 (2002), pp. 12–26.

35 G. Gerbner, *The Electronic Storyteller: TV and the Cultivation of Values* (Northampton: Media Education Foundation, 1997).

36 Online, available at: http://blog.sina.com.cn/huge (accessed February 10, 2008).

37 N. Couldry, "Beyond the Hall of Mirrors? Some Theoretical Reflections on the Global Contestation of Media Power," in N. Couldry and J. Curran (eds.), *Contesting Media Power: Alternative Media in a Networked World* (Lanham: Rowman & Littlefield, 2003), p. 42.

38 S. Li and J. Huang, "zhongguo zheng zhiding dui egao wangzhan zhuize tiegui" (China is Making New Iron Laws to Regulate Online Video), *Fazhi ribao* (Legal Daily) (November 13, 2006).

39 G. Li, "guangdian zongju zaichushou weijiao wangshang weigui shipin" (SARFT Once Again Striking Down Heavily on Illegal Internet Videos), *Diyi caijing* (Financial News) (August 12, 2006).

40 G. Wang, "wangshang egao youbei hexie linian" (*E gao* on the Web is Against the Idea of Harmonious Society), *Guangming ribao* (Guangming Daily) (November 17, 2006), online, available at: www.gmw.cn/content/2006–11/27/content_513840.htm (accessed February 4, 2008).

41 J. Zhang, "Network Convergence and Bureaucratic Turf Wars," in C. Hughes and G. Wacker (eds.), *China and the Internet: Politics of the Digital Leap Forward* (London: Routledge, 2003), pp. 83–101.

42 Beijing-based telecoms consulting firm Marbridge published a translation of the new regulation on their website: www.marbridgeconsulting.com/marbridgedaily/2007–12–29/article/7063/sarft_mii_co_issue_online_video_regulation (accessed February 10, 2008).

43 J. Goldkorn, "Updated China Video Website List" (2006), online, available at: www.danwei.org/business_and_finance (accessed February 10, 2008).

44 M. Bakhtin, *Rabelais and His World* (Bloomington: Indiana University Press, 1984).
45 Ibid., p. 10.
46 Ibid., p. 11.
47 Ibid., p. 7.
48 Quoted in M.B. Hull, "Postmodern Philosophy Meets Pop Cartoon: Michel Foucault and Matt Groening," *Journal of Popular Culture*, Vol. 34, No. 2 (2000), p. 64.
49 A complete report is available at: www.gmw.cn/CONTENT/wseg.htm (accessed January 10, 2008).
50 See, for example: http://hi.baidu.com/lewenge/blog/category/%D7%A8%BC%D2%B9%DB%B5%E3/index/3 (accessed October 10, 2007).
51 N. Negroponte, *Being Digital* (New York: Vintage, 1995), p. 229.
52 J.P. Barlow, "A Declaration of the Independence of Cyberspace" (1996), online, available at: http://homes.eff.org/~barlow/Declaration-Final.html (accessed February 10, 2008).
53 W.L. Bennett, "New Media Power: The Internet and Global Activism," in N. Couldry and J. Curran (eds.), *Contesting Media Power: Alternative Media in a Networked World* (Lanham: Rowman & Littlefield, 2003), p. 25.
54 R. Mansell, "Political Economy, Power and New Media," *New Media and Society*, Vol. 6, No. 1 (2004), pp. 96–105; V. Mosco, *The Digital Sublime: Myth, Power and Cyberspace* (Cambridge: MIT Press, 2004). R. McChesney, "The Communication Revolution: the Market and the Prospect for Democracy," in M. Andersen and P.H. Collins (eds.), *Race, Class, and Gender: An Anthology* (Belmont: Wardsworth, 1997), pp. 57–78.
55 J. Goldsmith and T. Wu, *Who Controls the Internet? Illusions of a Borderless World* (Oxford: Oxford University Press, 2006); J. Zittrain and B. Edelman, "Empirical Analysis of Internet Filtering in China" (Berkman Center for Internet and Society, 2003), online, available at http://cyber.law.harvard.edu/publications/2003/Empirical_Analysis_of_Internet_Filtering_in_China (accessed October 16, 2007); G. Wacker, "The Internet and Censorship in China," in C. Hughes and G. Wacker (eds.), *China and the Internet: Politics of the Digital Leap Forward* (London: Routledge, 2003), pp. 58–82.
56 Y. Zhou, *Historicizing Online Politics: Telegraphy, the Internet and Political Participation in China* (Stanford: Stanford University Press, 2006).
57 G. Yang, "The Internet and Civil Society in China: A Preliminary Assessment," *Journal of Contemporary China*, Vol. 12, No. 36 (2003), pp. 453–75; G. Yang, "The Co-evolution of the Internet and Civil Society in China," *Asian Survey*, Vol. 43, No. 3 (2003), pp. 405–22; Z. Tai, *The Internet in China: Cyberspace and Civil Society* (London: Routledge, 2006).
58 K. Clark and M. Holquist, *Mikhail Bakhtin* (Cambridge: Harvard University Press, 1984).
59 M. Rose, *Reading the Young Marx and Engels: Poetry, Parody and the Censor* (London: Croom Helm, 1978), p. 81.

4 In the name of good governance

E-government, Internet pornography and political censorship in China

Guoguang Wu

The emergence of digital communication, while providing enormous opportunities and potentialities for human development, presents immense challenges to the governing of human society at the same time. Authoritarian governments face particular challenges, because the nature of the Internet and the way it spreads information are in principle at odds with monopoly of public power and state control of mass communication which feature political authoritarianism. Special skills and sophistication are required of the Chinese authoritarian regime to be able to manage the nation's involvement in the worldwide revolution of information and communication technologies as it struggles to maintain the difficult balancing act between global economic and technology participation and resistance against the political values this participation may bring to China.[1]

To take advantage of information technologies to serve the political purpose of single-party monopoly of public power has motivated the Chinese regime to develop a series of sophisticated responses to the Internet. The bottom line of these responses is still media censorship, as this chapter shall demonstrate, and the emergence of the Internet in China does not change this. However, this chapter argues that the involvement of the Chinese Party-state in advanced communication technologies has widened and sophisticated the state's effort to control information flows, and that this sophistication of governmental control of the Internet has complicated the political ramifications in the context of globalization for both Chinese domestic politics and foreign relations.

One trait that reflects such sophistication lies in the Chinese government's intentional mix-up of Internet governance and political censorship. As in many other fields and activities of human society, the Internet and the communications via it need state regulations; in the context of the so-called late development such as in China, the prosperity of the Internet as a new industry also requires an active role of government to invest and promote. The authoritarian regime of the Chinese Communist Party (CCP) is obviously enthusiastic to develop and utilize the digital resources for economic purposes, and there are, doubtlessly, efforts for good governance of China in general and of the Internet in particular. At the same time, however, the regime always keeps high vigilance about any possible way which may help stimulate free expression and exchange of ideas among citizens, because such freedom would inevitably lead to the questioning of monopoly of public power by the CCP, and perhaps to the actions to change such monopoly. The Internet is, of course, a powerful invention for convenient communications; in many cases it has well demonstrated its power for fostering liberal and democratic political changes.[2] To contain and even to control such a political threat presented by the Internet thus becomes a challenge to the Chinese Party-state. Moreover, in this post-communist world where globalization and democracy claim their victories, the communist Party-state needs to legitimize such containment and control, and to utilize the same tool, i.e. the Internet, for its own benefits. The trinity of Internet management, as this chapter shall illustrate, has been invented for dealing with this multifaceted challenge, a trinity that combines together the Internet industrial development, legitimate regulations of digital communications, and political censorship.

Further, this chapter argues that, despite such an artificial Chinese trinity of Internet management, the authoritarian regime does much better in political censorship than in other functions a government should perform for the healthy development of high technology communications. In other words, the Chinese Party-state, which is often powerful, capable, efficient and effective in political control, performs relatively poorly in providing citizens with e-government services, a major function for public goods in Internet industrial development, and in the crackdown over Internet pornography, which legitimizes government filtering and censorship of the Internet. Chinese political institutions have often constrained the efforts in providing services while well accomplished in political control; furthermore, the regime turns those efforts to the direction of tightening political control over the Internet rather than providing public services through digital facilities. As the Chinese Party-state legitimizes its censorship with the claim to good governance through the Internet and legitimate administration of the digital world, it actually victimizes good governance for benefiting the single party's monopoly of political power.

The chapter therefore first of all investigates the systematic political skills (as well as technical, which is not a focus of this chapter) and discourses the Chinese Party-state has developed to legitimize its control, monitoring and censorship of the Internet, which undermines the freedom of expression the Internet might otherwise bring to Chinese users. It shows that promoting good governance in general and regulating the Internet to avoid its negative impacts, such as pornography in particular, are often used as excuses by the Chinese authoritarian regime to legitimize political censorship. The next inquiry of the chapter turns to how the doctrine of good governance in terms of Internet development is implemented in China. The chapter develops two sets of parameters to measure the successes or failures of good governance of the Internet. One parameter is positive, by which we look at, through the effort of promoting e-government, how the Internet provides services to citizens and stimulates political transparency and even citizen participation. Another is negative, by which we examine how the governmental regulations of the Internet help reduce pornography, which powerfully legitimizes the state's control and censorship of the websites. It is against these two parameters that the chapter examines the

Chinese government's effort at and impact on the online political discussions. Finally, based on the three-dimensional investigation of how the Chinese state works to govern the Internet, the discussions are then unfolded around the connections between those skills and discourses on the one hand, and the attempt of the regime to gain domestic and international legitimacy for political authoritarianism on the other. The chapter concludes that the authoritarian state of China is incapable of providing online public services, and often likely to tolerate and even tacitly promote pornography for its political purposes, while its control of the Internet essentially focuses on political censorship to undermine the digital potential for shaping public space in the country.

Web governance in China: institutions and discourses

To manage and regulate the Internet, the vast and complicated governmental machine has been invented and set into operation in China. Basically, website governance in China serves three major functions:

1 fostering the industrial development of the Internet for various purposes, including for benefiting economic development, strengthening China's national defense power in the information age, and providing online public services through e-government;
2 regulating Internet activities, particularly containing and reducing the unhealthy and criminal activities that take place via the Internet, such as pornography and terrorism;
3 preventing the Internet from acting as a channel of criticism of the Party-state, as a resource for political dissident activities, and as whatever kind of help to whatever the regime discretionally sees as a threat to its monopoly of public power.

Corresponding to these triple functions of development or service, administrative regulation and political control, the machine involves many governmental organizations and their departments, ranging widely from the Ministry of Electronic Industry, General Bureau of Postal and Telecommunications and the Central Military Commission, to Ministries of Public Security and State Security, the CCP's Propaganda Department and the State Council Information Office, while some new decision-making bodies and administrative offices have been created, together with new branches within the existing Party and state organizations.

Among the newly established the most prominent, and interesting to our purpose of study, is the National Leadership Group on Informatization (*Quanguo xinxihua lingdao xiaozu*, the Leadership Group hereafter) and its office, and the Web Propaganda Bureau of the Central Propaganda Department (*Zhongxuan bu wangluo xuanchuan ju*, the Web Bureau hereafter). The Leadership Group was set up in 2001 as a high-ranking decision-making body in charge of the development of the information industry, with Zhu Rongji, the then Premier, as the head. The extraordinary importance of this Group was also reflected in the fact that it included three of the seven members of the Standing Committee of the CCP Politburo, the top body which rules China, while some other Politburo members also joined in. First of the four deputies to Zhu was Hu Jintao, who was then PRC state vice-president and ranked number five among the CCP leadership.[3] After the leadership transition during 2002–2003 from the so-called "third generation" to the "fourth generation," the new Premier Wen Jiabao took over Zhu's job in the Group, with the other three of his Politburo colleagues joining him as deputies.[4] The significance was obvious, just as the then Party chief and state president Jiang Zemin emphasized: "None of the four modernizations can be accomplished without informatization." In both tenures of Zhu and Wen, the Leadership Group paid much attention to the establishing of e-government. While Zhu's term emphasized the significance of the information industry, the Wen administration added state security and national defense to the continuous efforts in e-commerce and e-governance.

With this strategic emphasis on informatization, numerous offices and branches have been set up in various Party and government organizations for multiple functions in e-governance. An office with Chinese characteristics of Web governance is the Web Bureau of the CCP's Central Propaganda Department, set up in recent years for the purpose of political censorship. It also has an equal in the government, i.e. the Web Bureau of the State Council Information Office. As some young blood has been recruited to the Bureau for a better grasping of high technologies, a group consisting of mainly retired Party managers of mass media and veteran journalists whose loyalty has repeatedly passed tests since the Tiananmen massacre in 1989 was organized as an ad hoc task force to monitor, filter, check and even distort the contents of the Internet from the political point of view according to the Party's guidelines. This Web examination group (*Zhongxuanbu wangluo shendu xiaozu*) is powerful, as in collaborations with other Party-governmental offices such as the Public Security Ministry and the State Security Ministry, it has the power to decide which websites must be closed down due to their political views, and to make a list of web users who are regarded as "threats" to state security – in the Chinese context it primarily means the "security" of the regime.[5]

The management structure clearly indicates the extraordinary attention the Chinese Party-state pays to the Internet. The leadership often, in many ways with the Chinese style of politics and governance, pours further energies to run the huge machine for the effective governing of the digital world. On January 23 and April 23, 2007, for example, Party chief and state president Hu Jintao twice chaired a collective study of the Politburo and a Politburo meeting respectively, on information industrial development. Hu gave speeches on the occasions, in which he urged that "the state bans the spreading of any news with content that is against national security and public interest," according to a statement from Xinhua, the official news agency. This kind of statement is of course rightful everywhere, even under a democracy, but it is necessary to point out that such concepts like "national security" and "public interest" in the Chinese context have their specific meanings, highly political or even partisan, largely referring to security and interest of the regime itself. Keeping this discourse in mind, one may better comprehend what Hu meant when he called on all Communist Party members to take action to "purify" the Internet, and understand why Hu linked the "purification" of the Internet with his urging of the Party's endeavor to ensure its control over Chinese Internet users, which reached 137 million at the end of 2006, with a growth of 23.4 percent from the previous year.[6]

This is not the first time Hu organized a national campaign to crackdown on free discussions on the Internet. In May 2005, he called for a "smokeless war" against "liberal elements" during a secret leadership meeting, and in the fall of the same year he continued to call for blogs and personal web pages "to be directed towards serving the people and socialism and to insist on correct guidance of public opinion for maintaining national and public interests."[7] Xinhua has collected Hu's major speeches about the Internet since 2000, from which one can find that Hu constantly emphasizes "taking the initiative in guiding online opinions" and "building up the powerful positive opinions online," while "fending off the negative influences brought by the Internet."[8]

Hu and other Chinese leaders' speeches are a major source for shaping the official Chinese discourse of legitimizing governmental control and censorship of the Internet. In essence, this discourse emphasizes the negative social, cultural and political impacts of the Internet, while fully acknowledging the significance of the Internet for economic development and for the loosely defined "national interest" which includes, for example, international competitiveness and national defense. It extends further to focus on the regime's maintaining of its monopoly of political power, and enthusiastically harnesses the Internet to serve all of those interests. To manage this double-edged communication technology, the Chinese regime has developed, as is indicated in Hu's speeches, a statist authoritarian doctrine of Internet regulations, which consorts with the authoritarian developmentalism that China has practiced during the reform era. First of all, this authoritarian state with such a doctrine plays a leading role in promoting economic development in general and that of the Internet in particular, and the state pours numerous resources to build up the Internet industry in this context. Meanwhile, the state takes every possible measure to contain the non-economic dimensions of the Internet, attempting to channel, circumscribe and even control spontaneous digital communications among citizens, including both the positive and negative sides of such communications. Both dimensions, however, are not constrained within the general conception of ordinary authoritarian developmentalism, as, through reading Hu's statements, two points become clear for understanding the Chinese doctrine of Internet governance:

1 the role of the state in promoting digital development of China has something more than the so-called "strong state" in the Asian developmental state model of economic development, and the extra functions are ideological and political;
2 while generally rather than specifically talking about the "negative influence brought by the Internet," the Chinese regime intentionally mixes up the real

negative stuff, which are those harmful to universal human values, with the politically negative that are at odds with the regime's ideological and political standards of correctness.

Further, it is not difficult to sense that, as a principle, the regime pays much more attention to crackdowns over the political negative rather than to contain other harmful contents.

Economic development and political authoritarianism here are institutionally combined to serve the double purpose of promoting prosperity under the monopoly of public power. However, this doctrine, or "the Beijing consensus," does not work as well in governing the Internet as it has been in promoting economic prosperity of China. Before we go into details of how this strategy fails in terms of governance, it is worthwhile to point out that this failure results from the incompatible nature of the Internet as a way of free mass communication with the authoritarian political institutions that govern its actualization in China. While the Chinese model is successful in stimulating economic growth through the freer exchange of goods and capital,[9] its management of the non-material world has been greatly and fundamentally handicapped by the regime's insistence on the tight control of free exchange of non-economic information.

Big-government online with little service

E-government has developed fast in China during the last decade. After the Government Online Project was formally launched in 1999, now about 80 percent of all government agencies, local and national, have websites.[10] Usually the application of the Internet in governance in general and e-government in particular is regarded as a powerful help for increasing democratic participation everywhere, including developing countries, as it provides citizens more public space, convenient civic networking, interactive communications with government, and the like.[11] One has no reason to expect that China's e-government does nothing for this, even though it runs within the non-democratic political framework. At least, as the Chinese Party-state is making efforts to promote "good governance," e-government can help to increase governmental information transparency and to provide more public services to the citizens, especially if we take the geographic and populace sizes in China. According to recent assessments made by government-affiliated Chinese scholars, however, China's e-government services are still "extremely backward," particularly in two fundamental functions, namely, interactive communications between Internet users and government, and online services provided by the e-government websites.[12] Although most governmental websites provide users with interactive communication (*hudong jiaoliu*) and transaction or online services (*wangshang bangong*, or *zaixian banli*), those listed choices are usually functionless when a user tries to activate the link, as a research group based at Peking University has found out during their study on Chinese e-government.[13] In addition, led by a vice-president of the leading university in China who obtained a doctoral degree of economics from Oxford, this group compares

Table 4.1 Comparison of government online services in China and EU, 2006

	Highest score	*Lowest score*	*Average*
China	59.85	0	15.15
EU	83	10	49.86

Source: Zhang, *Zhongguo dianzi zhengwu yanjiu baogao*, p. 5.

China's online services with those of EU, and their assessment result is summarized in Table 4.1.

The gap of about 35 points is remarkable, but it is even much greater in practice, because, according to the statement about how the scores are assessed in the research project, the EU's government online services cover much more items than those in China, and the comparison is actually not conducted based on the same criteria, which greatly favors China. For example, the scores of EU e-government assessments cited in the table are based on 20 categories of public service a governmental website may provide to its citizens, including income tax, enterprise tax, job seeking, personal files, business registration, automobile registration, construction project permission, environmental permission, custom service, public library service, public health service, marriage and birth, public security case reporting, statistics information, education, social welfare and benefits, social donation, and more. At the same time, the Chinese scores are based on only five categories, which are governmental guidelines, business consultation, application, online payment and inter-governmental departmental coordination. As the last category is not really about anything between citizens and government, but just an intra-bureaucratic activity, there are only four vague and general categories concerning governmental services that citizens may seek through websites, against 20 concrete items which residents may need to turn to for daily life and they are able to do so in Europe through e-government. Since the criteria are widely different from the Chinese ones which are apparently and greatly less demanding, a Chinese website, as the Chinese scholars admit, may obtain a score much higher than an EU website provided all conditions are equal.[14] In other words, the same score in the table indicates much less quantity and much poorer quality of governmental services provided by Chinese e-government.

As investment in e-government keeps growing in China, there have been no signs, however, that in the foreseeable future this problem will be remedied. Peking University researchers conclude that government–user interaction and online public services have already become the bottleneck for the development of e-government in China.[15] One may ask why the government has invested in establishing e-government as a digital extension of the government and yet provides very little function of the government? A possible answer lies in China's pre-digital resources performance. In totalitarian China, governmental services were also of low quality even though the communist regime had a government of a vast size that extended its reach to society in a degree that any other government is not able to. State control, rather than governmental services, was a major function of the state machine in that historical circumstance.[16] This logic has seemingly not been altered with the economic marketization under political authoritarianism, nor by the flourishing of advanced information technologies. The expansion of the government in digital space thus means more for the presence of the state than for the service delivery by the state, and more for the bureaucratic purposes than for the administrative functions, as will be further illustrated below with the performance of Chinese e-government in other dimensions.

One of the significant functions of e-government is to facilitate citizens' greater and more convenient access to government information. China is not an exception, but basically in the sense that e-government serves as the convenient outlet to publicize government information which is not so relevant to ordinary citizens, let alone citizens' in-depth knowledge about governmental operation. Similar to the Party organ newspapers, Chinese government websites are, first of all, full of news about leaders' activities. They are, nevertheless, more similar to the pre-modern chronological records of an emperor's daily business (*qi ju zhu*) than to the essential information for a modern citizen to become knowledgeable about public affairs. Space with fewer limits in the digital world than in the printed media also provides facilities for government to post various documents online, which are somehow helpful for Chinese citizens to know more about governmental attitudes and policies on various matters. Further information is not available, however, if one likes to know why the government has such a policy and how the government reaches the policy decision. In Chinese scholars' vague phrase, the "key information" (*guanjian xinxi*) of governance is often unavailable on government websites,[17] and it is still a big question in China whether, through e-government, "the information that the population really needs can be effectively conveyed in time."[18]

The Chinese assessment report admits that China's e-government is more propaganda-and management-oriented rather than service-oriented,[19] and more with "self-service" rather than public service.[20] So, why does the Chinese Party-state invest so much to build up e-government? There is a GDP drive, according to the research.[21] But it is also revealed that e-government can "greatly perfect and lift our international attraction and image."[22] The formalistic trend is reported as strong, which is reflected in the more and more beautiful technologic designs and faces of governmental web pages without improvement of functions and services. Some government websites even made fake statistics to boast their service functions.[23]

An independent researcher out of China has also found that, through the websites, Chinese governments of various levels try to report favorably on government activities.[24] Meanwhile, according to the Peking University report, they try to avoid reporting those negative events such as coal mine accidents.[25] For example, as non-government websites reported 19 mine disasters during the period from October 5 to November 5, 2006,[26] only five of them were reported by all municipal-level government websites, three by national government websites, and five by government-sponsored media's Internet outlets. Moreover, when government websites are forced by various elements to cover such disasters, they often highlight how the governmental officials did well to rescue the victims rather than focusing on the events and the victims.[27] If one simply trusts the positive functions of e-government in promoting public transparency, one must be easily fooled by such a highly selected and incomplete coverage of what is going on in China. In this regard, the digital expansion of the Chinese government increases both the possibilities of more public access into government information than otherwise and of more sophisticated and efficient propaganda of authoritarian messages. In practice, as has been discovered by various research, the latter potentiality, namely, the empowering of the authoritarian regime for public relation games and for sophisticated political propaganda, has so far overwhelmed the former with the emergence of e-government in China.

E-inclusion is also a problem to China's e-government, as the Chinese assessment report points out. In particular, farmers and the so-called "weak groups" including laid-off workers, female residents and the disabled often have tremendous difficulties gaining access to e-government services, if such services are provided. It rarely mentions the factors such as education level, urban–rural divide and age which also significantly hinder many poorly-educated, rural and aged Chinese residents to utilize the Internet in general and e-government in particular. According to the report, nationwide in China less than 9 percent of the government websites are aware of this function of e-inclusion.[28] What is ironic, and perhaps more important, to this issue is the fact that even those active Chinese users of the Internet are not attracted to e-government. In a 2004 national survey, the China Internet Network Information Centre (CNNIC) asked respondents how much they knew about e-government websites. Fifteen percent of the users said they never heard of e-government and 35 percent had heard about it but never used it. There were 36 percent who admitted to having some knowledge about e-government but only 14 percent of respondents claimed to know it well.[29] While indicating that the technologic expansion of the Chinese government has not achieved its expected social reach and political purposes, this further enforces our observation that the huge investment in e-government matters little for improving Chinese citizens' information acquisition.

How and why web pornography prevails

Traditionally, the Chinese communist regime is strong in banning something it does not like, either for the regime's selfish benefit or for the society's public interest, although it may not be capable of accomplishing the beautiful promises it makes, such as equality or communism. For governing the Internet, this could mean that for the positive purpose the Chinese e-government cannot provide substantive services to citizens. The Party-state is still powerful and effective enough to eliminate those negative digital phenomena which are harmful to social interests. As we have seen, the Chinese Party-state does repeatedly emphasize the negative influence of the "unhealthy" information, and much attention, at least rhetorically, has been paid to circumscribe the flow of such information. The Chinese accomplishment in this regard, however, is highly problematic, as many negative or harmful digital content and behaviors are prominent in China and have become prevalent in China's cyberspace along with the flourishing of websites, which include copyright infringement, security problems such as virus and hacker attacks, privacy invasion and Internet pornography.

The issue of pornography is of special interest for the examination of governance in the contemporary Chinese context, because one of the social accomplishments that the communist regime likes to boast has been its cleaning up of prostitution and the like after it took power of China from the old, backward, corrupt and impotent KMT regime. The post-Mao reform, nevertheless, has essentially ruined this proud record, but the impulse to make Chinese people live "clean" still drove the regime to launch a series of powerful campaigns to crack-down on the social activities and information related to pornography both before the Tiananmen massacre and after. The accomplishment in this regard apparently helps to legitimize the regime's concentration of public power; it also assists the regime to gain the upper hand over free society in ideology as in the latter there seems to exist an inseparability between market activities and civic rights on one hand, and sales of sex and pornography on the other. The Chinese regime always intentionally mixes the two together, giving both pornographic information and political dissent messages the same label as "unhealthy." As we will discuss later, this is a political strategy that is unhelpful to the "healthy" governance of society in general and of the Internet in particular.

One may easily spot many pornographic photos when visiting the official websites of various Chinese governmental branches and of the government-sponsored media, including *Renmin Ribao* (People's Daily), the mouthpiece of the Central Committee of the Chinese Communist Party. Some may take a relaxed definition of pornography and regard such stuff as not really pornographic. But I argue that first, to various degrees, pornography and quasi-pornography is almost everywhere in China's cyberspace, which indicates a failure of the Chinese Party-state's effort for "good governance" of the Internet in particular and Chinese society in general; second, it may appear to be unreasonable to blame the Chinese government for such a failure because there are also such phenomena outside China. However in China those governmental websites are also promoting themselves through their posting of or links to those items with sexual elements. The second point is more important to our discussion, as it involves politics rather than administration of the Chinese regulations of the Internet.

A political trick of the Chinese campaign against pornography, as indicated previously, is the Party-state's purposeful mixture of pornography and other negative things, such as crime, with political dissents, grouping them in the same category of "unhealthy" information. This is not a strategy newly invented to deal with bottom-up activities of criticizing the government which have become much more convenient for citizens while more difficult for the regime to contain in cyberspace, but it has been well developed and refined by the regime since it is engaged with the Internet use and regulations. In the early reform years, there was an "anti-spiritual pollution" campaign in 1983 and an "anti-bourgeois liberalization" campaign in 1987, both targeting political dissents which also included both the lifestyle of the West and those truly unhealthy "spirits" such as pornography into the "bourgeois pollution" or "liberalization."[30] The regime started to adopt a strategy after Li Ruihuan was appointed the ideological tsar in 1989, to "clean out pornography and crack down over illegality" (*saohuang dafei*) in order to implement the social stabilizing measures targeted at both political dissents and non-political "dissents." As Li was a well-known protégé of Deng Xiaoping, this strategy in the early 1990s partially served as a political leeway for economic reformers like Deng and Li to promote economic liberalization while avoiding ideological debates with their conservative colleagues.[31] But the continuous battles in this regard soon became meaningless in intra-Party politics for the post-economic reform China, where the division between reformers and conservatives became blurred during the overwhelming embracing of marketization by the whole Communist Party for making profits for both the regime and for the Party members themselves.

It therefore turned out to be an intentional muddling up of the government's legitimate regulation to crackdown over unhealthy publications and the regime's political censorship, using the former as a camouflage for legalizing and legitimizing the latter.

The Chinese regime applies this strategy to the Internet with even more sophistication, including taking advantage of the high technology that allows interactive communication and participatory discussion to "guide" public opinions. The single dimensional crackdown on sensational, sexual and pornographic contents of mass communication is now replaced by a double-edged handling of them. While the containment, control and crackdown are still constantly exercised by the Party-state to manage political dissent activities on the Internet and the critical voices online, the government and its sponsored media now also employ the attraction of those negative elements to entice Internet users. Though there is no evidence showing that this helps increase the visits to those official websites, it is obvious that it more or less works to divert some of the attention of Internet users, particularly those who are at an age with growing gender curiosity, away from political dissent information.

The advantage of this distorted mix-up is apparent. For example, in the 12 days of the "Civilized Web" campaign in April 2006, "almost 2 million unhealthy postings and photos" were deleted and "600 forums" closed from 14 Chinese web portals. Seven major Chinese web portals are openly criticized for their "bad information postings," whose "billions" of web pages are to be further "cleaned."[32] The voice of political dissents has thus been successfully contained and controlled within the scope that does not threaten the authoritarian regime, though the consciousness of civic rights and the mass actions to defend the rights have been growing in recent years. While both pornography and political dissents struggle for their influence in the digital world vis-à-vis governmental regulations, if one assesses the effectiveness of the Chinese government to deal with both pornography and political dissents, it becomes easy to tell that the regime has done more successfully to crackdown on political dissents than to contain pornography. To assess the regime's intention is relatively difficult, but a recent comment by a governmental official in charge of publications is revealing: "it is much more important for the government to fight against the politically harmful information than against pornography."[33] He is honest, though shamelessly.

Political censorship, political reform and Internet hypocrisy

In this section, we move our focus to the interplays of those three dimensions of governance of and through the Internet, namely, the digital expansion of Chinese government as venues of public services for citizens, the legitimate control of the webs by the government for reducing unhealthy information such as pornography, and the partisan crackdowns of public opinions that criticize government. The niche is to look at how the Chinese citizens' web criticism of government that apparently aims at promoting the nation's good governance through political reform is cracked down by the regime, while the regime, ironically, camouflages such actions with rhetoric of good governance.

Political reform has since the late 1970s been a major topic of Chinese debates among Party officials, intellectuals and ordinary citizens.[34] The Chinese leaderships from Deng Xiaoping to Hu Jintao never openly deny the necessity of reforming the existing political institutions, including, prominently, the necessity of expanding the civic rights of Chinese citizens and increasing the democratic participation of citizens in governmental decisions. Democracy and rule of law are repeatedly claimed to be the goals of China's political transition toward modernizations.[35] The Seventeenth Party Congress in October 2007 continued this claim, giving rise to a new round of debate about political reform in today's China.[36] It seems political reform is no longer a taboo if we believe in the statements by the Chinese regime and its leaders.

The reality is tricky, however. Common sense tells that citizens' discussions of political reform are not harmful to either governmental policy-making or the implementation of political reform, but it is also a common sense in China that this is a highly dangerous topic because the Party-state often bans such discussions. The emergence of the Internet may provide more convenient channels for more people to join the discussion, but it does not change or redefine the political fine line the participants have to carefully follow when expressing their opinions. Further, the regime discretionally intervenes in the discussions with its arbitrary decisions as to what opinions benefit the nation and what are "subversive" and the holder of the opinion deserves imprisonment. The regime always keeps high vigilance on the online discussion of political reform, and at times takes action to "clean" the discussion from the Internet and close down those websites devoted to such discussions, even though occasionally the regime officially announces that it welcomes suggestions on political reform. For example, as the Chinese official media thought the new opportunity of discussing political reform and even democratization had arrived, following Premier Wen Jiabao's press conference of March 2007 at which he mentioned "democracy" several times,[37] a new wave of Web crackdowns targeting online discussions of political reform began. Also in March 2007, Zhang Jianhong, a 48-year-old Internet blogger, known to readers as Li Hong, was sentenced to six years in prison for posting more than 60 essays and articles on Chinese and overseas Internet sites, which the court in Ningbo, Zhejiang Province saw as "slanders" of the government and China's political system.[38] He is of course not the single victim of the latest web crackdown, nor the only one who got punished. The PRC constitution that guarantees citizens the right to express their ideas is obviously violated by the government.

On the other hand, numerous essays and reports are published in government-affiliated media and posted on their digital extensions to praise both "democracy" and the achievements of China to advance it.[39] Constitutionally and legally equal, why are some Chinese citizens allowed to talk about their favorable assessments of "democracy," while others are punished due to their advocating of the same concept? Similarly, why are some articles talking about political reform encouraged and assisted by the government, with their printing and digital mouthpieces circulating them, while others cost their authors their civil freedom? Though the Chinese government or courts have never been troubled to explain this discrimination, this indeed reveals China's hypocrisy and the regime's playing with rhetoric about political reform. In particular, the Internet and its Chinese governance have significant functions to construct this hypocrisy, as imbedded in at least three aspects that the following paragraphs will demonstrate.

First of all, the Chinese regime pays special attention to the development of the so-called "informatization," as evidenced in our previous discussion of Chinese institutions and leaderships of the program. This special attention not only implies that the regime is fully aware of the economic and technological benefits the Internet may bring to China, it is also a political speculation of the utilization of this huge market potential to allure international investors and entrepreneurs in the industry of high-tech information and communication for their cooperation with the otherwise-disadvantageous Chinese Party-state. In other words, this cooperation between the Chinese regime and international capital works powerfully to support the authoritarian regime's legitimacy, as it often forces multinational corporations of the information industry to exchange access into, and the opportunity to enhance the competitiveness of, the Chinese market, for the assistance that the Chinese regime needs in monitoring the Internet and muting dissenting voices online. The Yahoo Company's notorious provision of information about the Chinese journalist Shi Tao's online activities is the best example in this regard, in which Shi Tao was sentenced to serve nine yeas of imprisonment because, according to the record that Yahoo supplied to Chinese authorities, he sent his critical opinions about the Chinese regime to overseas news web pages via Yahoo's digital facilities.[40] The monopoly of political power which is used to distort the Chinese web market and, accordingly, the behaviors of Internet companies, therefore, lays down the institutional foundations on which the government's attention to informatization becomes the unchecked power to manipulate market resources for partisan political purposes.

The official rhetoric of democracy and political reform thus becomes significant in the fact that it offers international capital some moral excuses to cooperate with Chinese authoritarianism. At the same time, the banning of spontaneous discussions on democracy and political reform is necessary, as such discussions may help to lay bare the government's political bubbles based on the same wording. In the information age, with the invasion of government and its affiliated media to cyberspace, this kind of governmental rhetoric has two advantages: one is its communicational advantage, through which the governmental messages are expected to widely spread; another is the technological advantage, by which the government's imperatives for modernization is convincingly evidenced. Together, the digital extension of the Party-state fights back the attempts of the dissidents to employ new technologies like the Internet and the democratic concepts which the regime now tries to monopolize. That is why the Chinese leadership urges the whole Communist Party to get equipped with the knowledge, skills and technologies of electronic communications in order to "occupy the battlefield of informatization." As the printed media is almost monopolized by the Party-state or at least more easily controlled by the government,[41] political dissent voices often seek their outlets on the Internet. This makes the Internet the primary target for the government to crackdown on free expression, with more sophisticated and hypocritical political censorship.

In comparison with the political censorship practiced by the CCP in the pre-information age however, this political hypocrisy is more easily accepted than criticized, by international society. It is so mainly due to the emergence of cyberspace and, accordingly, the global consensus about the necessity of governmental regulations of the Internet and even of governmental control over unhealthy phenomena online. While the huge potential mass communication via the Internet offers to human life is unprecedented in history, the challenges to the balance between freedom of speech and the press, on one hand, and governmental regulations and good governance on the other, also become unparalleled. The Chinese Party-state quickly harnesses this international norm to smuggle its fierce attacks on Chinese citizens' constitutional right to political criticism, and a series of government campaigns to silence unofficial voices and re-assert control over the new media have been openly launched in the name of Internet governance.

Sophistications of censorship, failures of governance: conclusions

The above investigations have demonstrated that the Chinese Party-state has invested huge energies, attention and resources in the governance of the Internet for two self-claimed purposes: promoting the positive functions of the Internet, particularly informatization including building-up the capacity of e-government, and preventing the negative side of digital communications such as Internet pornography. These two goals certainly appear to be consistent with the global trends of governing the Internet and they are of course legitimate for the healthier development of online communications. The problem, however, is that both are utilized by the government as the legitimate camouflage of political censorship that contains Chinese citizens' constitutional rights of freedom of speech and the press and their participations in the discussions of public affairs. The trick lies in the institutional arrangement of developmental authoritarianism: it expands the Internet market but controls capital's access into it; it stimulates informatization of government while the informatization of public power means stronger capacities of the state to intervene in, if not to totally control, citizens' online activities at the ruling party's discretions. While the regime blends its political censorship into its programs of Internet development and web governance, both of the latter are also harmed.

The first conclusion, therefore, is about the imbalance of the huge size of Chinese e-government and the little services it provides to ordinary citizens, as well its very limited impact on promoting government transparency or enhancing popular participation in public decisions. Instead, China's e-government stays propaganda-oriented and, to a great degree, it is a digital extension of the old-fashioned authoritarian government. Further, the Chinese government's capacities for its governance and its political control of the Internet are not balanced as it mixes the two dimensions of governance for its political benefits at the cost of public interests. In other words, the performance of the Chinese Party-state is not as good on the negative front, as exemplified in its mute tolerance of, and even intended collaborations with, Internet pornography, despite its loud claim of having cracked down on it. By contrast, the Chinese state's capacity to clean websites politically has been powerful and often effective, as is demonstrated in its attempts to circumscribe online expressions of citizens' political ideas, including the censorship of web pages, e-discussions of sensitive political topics and, most recently, bloggers.

Chinese users have, of course, also found and often enjoyed the functions of the Internet for convenient discussions on public affairs, but, quite different from their counterparts using the Internet under democratic political institutions, there is a huge governmental machine supervising, monitoring and channeling their opinions and, when the government feels it is necessary, interrupting and banning their discussions. Although the difficulties of control are tremendous, one has to admit that this effort of controlling the uncontrollable has so far been successful in at least two senses: first, the websites run by the Party-state and their media or business affiliations are prevailing at least technologically, and are often making the "mainstream" of Chinese digital communications; second, supported by high technology and authoritarian institutions, the regime usually responds effectively to the online emergence of political dissent, having remarkably contained those opinions defined by the regime as "hostile." While economic development and other factors including the limited improvement of governance are certainly among the most significant that have contributed to the sustaining of Chinese authoritarianism, effective control of public opinions is doubtlessly a key, too, for the post-Tiananmen regime's accomplishments for survival and prosperity. The emergence of the Internet has so far not changed this, and seemingly will not do so in the foreseeable future. This, the chapter argues, should be attributed to the Chinese Party-state, which has, along with the Internet's emergence and spreading, developed strengths and sophistications in controlling online opinions.

This control is promoted in the name of good governance, and camouflaged with the fashionable vocabularies of development, regulation and globalization. The development of the Internet itself, as we have seen in the building-up of Chinese e-government, also serves as a way to occupy the digital "smokeless battlefield." Moreover, it shows the enthusiasm of the Chinese Party-state on the Internet, which often gains applause from abroad and at home, is helpful to weaken the negative image of the regime which exercises online political censorship. At the same time, the campaigns to crack down over pornography are always intentionally mixed with the political cleaning up of the Internet, enabling the regime to loudly announce that its repressive actions are finely legitimate even according to international norms. While the dark side of the Internet provides a desired excuse for Beijing to defend its smuggling of political censorship, the regime's endeavors to regulate online activities are clearly inclined to tolerate pornography while suppressing freedom of speech.

This deliberative connection between web governance and Internet regulation on one hand, and authoritarian surveillance of online communications on the other, is not only imbalanced, it is institutionally and strategically so constructed by the Chinese Party-state. It is institutional because the authoritarian capacity of management is traditionally rooted in omni-control of society by the state, and there is not a line which the Party-state is not allowed to cross at its own will between legal regulation and punishment on one hand and political surveillance and deprivation of civic rights on the other. The Internet does not change this. It is also strategic, because, as such institutional capacity of the regime has been eroded by market reform and globalization, the regime deliberately muddles the opportunity the Internet brings to Chinese citizens for expanding their rights of expression with the pitfalls there might be in the online magnification of the human weaknesses, and utilizes the latter against the former. I am not arguing that the Party-state of China totally ignores the harms of those negative things like pornography, but I do argue that the Chinese Party-state is doing poorly to provide service and fight against unhealthy stuff, while it deliberately utilizes the pursuit of good governance often as the rhetoric to legitimize political censorship.

Notes

1 For this strategy China takes in a comparative perspective with broader backgrounds of globalization of culture, see Peter L. Berger, "Introduction: The Cultural Dynamics of Globalization," in Peter L. Berger and Samuel P. Huntington (eds.), *Many Globalizations: Cultural Diversity in the Contemporary World* (New York: Oxford University Press, 2002), pp. 1–16.

2 See, for example, P. Ferdinand (ed.), *The Internet, Democracy, and Democratization* (London: Frank Cass, 2000).

3 "Zhu Rongji zhuchi Guojia xinxihua lingdao xiaozu diyici huiyi" (Zhu Rongji chaired the first meeting of the NLOGI), December 28, 2001, at www.e-gov.org.cn/Article/news001/2001–12–28/1131.html. Those followed Zhu and Hu among the deputy heads of the Group were: Li Lanqing, then first deputy Prime Minister; Ding Guan-gen, then head of the CCP Central Propaganda Department, and Wu Bangguo, another deputy Prime Minister.

4 See, for example, "Wen Jiabao zhuchi zhaokai Guojia xinxihua lingdao xiaozu diwuci huiyi" (Wen Jiabao chaired the fifth meeting of the NLOGI), November 3, 2005, at www.gov.cn/ldhd/2005–11/03/conten_90748.htm. The new deputies were (at the time they were appointed): Huang Ju, first deputy Prime Minister and a Politburo Standing Committee member; Zhou Yongkang, Minister of Public Security, and Guo Boxiong, Chief of the general staff of the PLA, both are members of the CCP Politburo. The new personnel seemingly also indicated a shift of the major task of Chinese informatization from industrial development to its military application and political/security control of it.

5 Interviews of Chinese journalists, April 10 and July 29, 2006, Hong Kong.

6 Xinhua, January 24, 2007.

7 Benjamin Joffe-Walt, "China's Leaders Launch Smokeless War Against Internet and Media Dissent," *Guardian*, September 26, 2005.

8 Xinhua, January 25, 2007.

9 Of course, these achievements under authoritarianism are obtained with the costs higher than that otherwise. For this, see, for example, Minxin Pei, *China's Trapped Transition: The Limits of Developmental Autocracy* (Cambridge: Harvard University Press, 2006).

10 Xia Li Lollar, "Assessing China's E-Government: Information, Service, Transparency and Citizen Outreach of Government Websites," *Journal of Contemporary China*, 15: 46 (February 2006), pp. 31–41.

11 See, for example, C.J. Alexander and L.A. Pal (eds.), *Digital Democracy: Policy and Politics in the Third World* (Toronto: Oxford University Press, 1998); R. Tsagarousianou, D. Tambini and C. Bryan (eds.), *Cyberdecmoarcy: Technology, Cities, and Civic Networks* (London: Routledge, 1998); B.N. Hague and B.D. Loader (eds.), *Digital Democracy: Discourse and Decision-Making in the Information Age* (London: Routledge, 1999); J. Hoff, I. Horrocks and P. Tops (eds.), *Democratic Governance and New Technology* (London: Routledge, 2000); P. Ferdinand (ed.), *The Internet, Democracy and Democratization* (London: Frank Cass, 2000); and Cass Sunstein, *Republic.com* (Princeton: Princeton University Press, 2001).

12 Zhang Weiying (ed.), *Zhongguo dianzi zhengwu yanjiu baogao, 2006 nian* (Report on China's E-Government, 2006) (Beijing: Beijing daxue chubanshe, 2007), p. 3.

13 Ibid., p. 12.

14 Ibid., p. 5.

15 Ibid., p. 12.

16 For totalitarian political institutions, see Carl J. Friedrich and Zbigniew K. Brzezinski, *Totalitarian Dictatorship and Autocracy* (Cambridge: Harvard University Press, 1956); and Juan J. Linz, *Totalitarian and Authoritarian Regimes* (Boulder: Lynne Rienner, 2000).

17 Zhang, *Zhongguo dianzi zhengwu yanjiu baogao*, p. 3.

18 Ibid., p. 63.

19 Here 'management' is the conventional but inaccurate translation of the Chinese term '*guanli*,' as '*guanli*' first implies control, or *guan*.

20 Zhang, *Zhongguo dianzi zhengwu yanjiu baogao*, pp. 6, 63, 132.

21 Ibid., pp. 8, 63.

22 Ibid., p. 1.

23 Ibid., p. 37.

24 Lollar, "Assessing China's E-Government," p. 33.

25 Zhang, *Zhongguo dianzi zhengwu yanjiu baogao*, p. 16.
26 As the researchers correctly point out, this number is not the actual number of such disasters that took place during the period, as some are covered by no news reports.
27 Zhang, *Zhongguo dianzi zhengwu yanjiu baogao*, pp. 129–32.
28 Ibid., p. 15.
29 China Internet Information Centre, "Semiannual Survey Report on the Development of China's Internet (2004/8)," online, available at: www.cnnic.net.cn.
30 For the two campaigns and their implications to Chinese politics, see, for example, Merle Goldman, *Sowing the Seeds of Democracy in China: Political Reform in the Deng Xiaoping Era* (Cambridge: Harvard University Press, 1994).
31 Joseph Fewsmith, *China Since Tiananmen: The Politics of Transition* (New York: Cambridge University Press, 2001), p. 34.
32 *Renmin ribao*, April 23, 2006.
33 *Zhongguo chuban bao*, May 17, 2007.
34 Goldman, *Sowing the Seeds of Democracy*. Also, Wu Guoguang, *Zhao Ziyang yu zhengzhi gaige* (Zhao Ziyang and Political Reform) (Hong Kong: Pacific Century Institute, 1997).
35 For Deng's calling for political reform, see *Deng Xiaoping wenxuan* (Selected Works of Deng Xiaoping) (Beijing: Renmin chubanshe, 1993); for the official statements about the leadership's rhetoric commitment on political reform after Deng, see, Jiang Zemin's reports to the Fifteenth and Sixteenth Party Congresses and Hu Jintao's report to the Seventeenth Party Congress. Also, Goldman, *Sowing the Seeds of Democracy*; Fewsmith, *China Since Tiananmen*; and Merle Goldman and Roderick MacFarquhar (eds.), *The Paradox of China's Post-Mao Reforms* (Cambridge: Harvard University Press, 1999).
36 Hu's report to the Seventeenth Party Congress.
37 *Renmin ribao*, March 12, 2007.
38 Peter Goodspeed, "China Cracks Down on Dissident Bloggers," *National Post*, March 22, 2007, p.A11.
39 For example, Yu Keping, "Minzhu shi ge hao dongxi" (Democracy is a Good Thing), *Beijing ribao*, October 23, 2006.
40 This case was widely reported. See a report, for example, in BBC, "Yahoo Helped Jail China Writer," online, available at: http://news.bbc.co.uk/1/hi/world/asia-pacific/4221538.stm (accessed January 18, 2008).
41 Though semi-independent media has been struggling to emerge in reform China, the state–media relationship is still essentially dominated by the Party-state. See, for example, Chin-Chuan Lee (ed.), *Power, Money, and Media: Communication Patterns and Bureaucratic Control in Cultural China* (Evanston: Northwestern University Press, 2000), particularly Guoguang Wu, "One Head, Many Mouths: Diversifying Press Structures in Reform China," pp. 45–67.

5 Chinese intellectuals and the Internet in the formation of a new collective memory

Junhua Zhang

Introduction

The world is witnessing a tremendous change in global communication. Thanks to the emergence of telecommunication technology, people everywhere can, in theory, communicate with each other in real time regardless of distance. However, communication is not merely a matter of technology. It is embedded into much more profound political, cultural and psychological contexts. Memory, more exactly, collective memory, is one of these configurations.

The significance of collective memory can be easily felt if one follows the recent protest wave by (mostly) young Chinese people in the country and abroad against Western media since March 2008 before the Olympic Games. Regardless of what has caused the dispute, the collective memory both sides (Western societies and China) possess has strongly influenced the trajectory of the anti-Western attitude and vice versa. While Western societies have their positive memory of Dalai Lama, the Chinese young protestors have a completely different perception of this spiritual leader and his exile government.

In this chapter, I attempt to show how the Internet in China, primarily in a "bottom-up" form, helps enhance a collective memory which was first forged by official media in a "top-down" way. The chapter examines the impact of bloggers (both users and audience) on the process of constituting this kind of memory in a Chinese context. In order to explore the relations between intellectuals, the Internet and public audience, the following questions are conceptualized as guidance of the chapter:

1 What is collective memory? What are its functions?
2 Has China entered a cyber-society through which the civil journalism has become possible?
3 Can the Web 2.0 really help people in China create a sound collective memory?
4 Who is playing a decisive role in the formation of a new collective memory in the Chinese society?
5 What does the relationship between media-oriented intellectuals and official memory policies look like?

6 What impact does it have on the political behaviour of the young generations?

By answering the questions above, I intend to show that a new collective memory in China has already gained ground and a controlled Internet in terms of Chinese blogs as an important tool of mass journalism cannot achieve any breakthrough at least in the near future.

Collective memory and its functions

Human beings are characterized as holders of memory. Like individuals, each society has a dominant collective memory or historical consciousness. The more democratic and liberal a society, the more pluralistic and communicative the collective memory can be.

Generally, memory is regarded as a result of selection, exclusion and preservation of the past. That is to say, memory is closely connected with history. Yet memory is not fully identical with history. Maurice Halbwachs – the grand old theoretician of social memory, has established a clear distinction between memory and history. In his seminal study, *The Collective Memory*, he contrasted memory and history as two contradictory ways of dealing with the past. History aims to reconstruct the past in an impartial and objective account, whereas memory relates to the past as an emotional presence. Halbwachs holds that there is only one history, but there are as many collective memories as there are human communities.[1]

Like Halbwachs, many other social scientists assume a fundamental gulf between history and memory. For instance, Simnine[2] sees history as changes established by distance, as differences and discontinuities between present and past, while memory does not reflect the past but recognizes itself in the past. To him, memories are highly selective and are based on a reduction of complexity.

Starting from the 1980s, this split between history and memory has been challenged fundamentally by many academics, and a more fluid transition between memory and history was proposed instead. Among them, the German scholar Jörn Rüsen holds that memory and history are phenomena parallel to each other, each equally being an expression of history culture.[3] Patrick Geary takes the similar position by saying that all memory, whether collective or historical, is "memory for something": this political (in a broad sense) purpose cannot be ignored.[4]

In spite of the controversies around the link between history and memory, the functions of collective memory seem to be obvious. Following Maurice Halbwachs' view in his groundbreaking study *Les cadres sociaux de la mémoire*, all types of memory have a social dimension. Society strongly influences individual memories. In his work Halbwachs emphasizes that social groups, be they families, generations, institutions or nations, share narratives of the past and hand them down, re-tell and modify them. Collective memory is shared, passed on and also constructed by the group, or modern society.[5]

Before I discuss the dominance in constituting collective memory by answering the questions of who is dominant in a society and who plays a decisive role in forming social memory, the functions of collective memory need to be examined first.

A solid collective memory is the basis of a nation's identity, which can be used to stabilize certain ideologies and to enhance the legitimate basis of the ruling elites. A nation's as well as individual's identity depends upon an organic and conscious connection between the present and the past. In this sense, the history of civilization and political life is the history of remembrance.[6] Collective memory is important, because it is not just about the past. Collective memory brings the past into present consciousness and it can be mobilized for decisions about the future.

Given that human beings are capable of learning, a sound collective memory forges the learning process or the process of maturity of respective groups or nations, both in terms of political life and social-economic development. However, an artificially created, or a distorted memory can also lead to certain political behaviour, which might become a hindrance of democratization of respective countries.[7]

Having discussed the entity of collective memory, it is also important to demonstrate how it is shaped. Obviously, collective memory is a result of socialization process. In a Chinese context, it is important to tell the difference between dominant official efforts in socialization and the unofficial socialization process, which is not deliberately conceived. While the first one is realized through narratives with a "top-down" character, such as state-owned TV, press and school textbooks, the second one is embodied by bottom-up or horizontal communication via the Internet or among friends and family members. The official efforts in socialization are more target-oriented and visible. In contrast, the socialization process at the unofficial level is invisible and latent.

One important aspect of collective memory is its stark dependence on communication devises and technology. It is simply impossible for collective memory to be consolidated and spread without media. In this sense, any type of collective memory is mediated memory. Since the late 1990s the so-called digital revolution has strongly accelerated the pace and increased the dimensions of (re)constructing collective memory.

The emergence of the Internet especially the Web 2.0 in the last decade (such as weblogs, podcasts, YouTube) has changed greatly the way of diffusion of information. Many Western scholars hold that the Internet certainly enables the users to become a member of the civic or participatory journalism. Shayne Bowman and Chris Willis expressed their very optimistic view on the new generation of the Internet by saying that Web 2.0 creates grassroots journalism and it will become a big challenge to the existing conventional media.[8]

But the widely spread euphoria over the positive effect of the Internet in terms of mass journalism and democratization seems to be retrenched due to the "China fact", which will be explained in the following parts of the chapter.

The development of Chinese blogs

Similar to China's achievements in the economic sector, the increase of Internet users in China in the last ten years is astonishing. Today, more than 10 per cent of the population have become members of the digital world. In comparison to the developed industrial countries, China still lags behind in respect to the proportion of digitalized families even though the absolute number of Internet users is enormous. However, in comparison to India and many other developing countries, China takes a clear lead in Internet penetration (see Table 5.1).

In contrast to the developed countries, in which there is a parallel between conventional media and new media, TV and radio still maintains its monopoly on everyday life in terms of effective diffusion of information to the population in China. There are altogether 282 radio stations and 314 television stations as well as 60 education TV stations in the country. The radios in China have covered 94.5 per cent of population while TV stations have reached 95.8 per cent of the public.[9] Thanks to the newly built infrastructure, more than 30 cities in China are networked through digital TV, which is scheduled to be greatly extended in the coming years. It will be a reality in the near future that more than 400 million TV sets in Chinese households will be digitalized. As the next step, China's TV network will also be connected to mobile phone users. China has been promoting combined networks in terms of telephone, TV and the Internet in the last few years. At a conservative estimate, TV instead of the Internet will still prevail even in a digitalized China or thanks to the digitalization of the country.[10]

From this point of view, it is too early to say that China has entered a cybersociety in the sense that the Internet has become dominant in the everyday life of Chinese (including the rural population). Neither has it become a competitor of

Table 5.1 Top ten countries with highest number of Internet users

	Country or region	*Internet users, latest data*	*Population (2007 est.)*	*Internet penetration (%)*	*Source and date of latest data*	*Users of world (%)*
1	**United States**	**211,108,086**	301,967,681	69.9	Nielsen//NR Dec/06	18.9
2	**China**	**137,000,000**	1,317,431,495	10.4	CNNIC Dec/06	12.3
3	**Japan**	**86,300,000**	128,646,345	67.1	eTForecasts Dec/05	7.7
4	**Germany**	**50,471,212**	82,509,367	61.2	Nielsen//NR Dec/06	3.6
5	**India**	**40,000,000**	1,129,667,528	3.5	IWS Nov/06	3.6
6	**United Kingdom**	**37,600,000**	60,363,602	62.3	ITU Sept/06	3.4
7	**Korea (South)**	**34,120,000**	51,300,989	66.5	eTForecast Dec/05	3.1
8	**Brazil**	**32,130,000**	186,771,161	17.2	ITU Mar/07	2.9
9	**France**	**30,837,592**	61,350,009	50.3	Nielsen//NR Jan/07	2.8
10	**Italy**	**30,763,848**	59,546,696	51.7	Nielsen//NR Jan/07	2.8

Source: www.internetworldstats.com/top20.htm (updated on June 30, 2007).

conventional media in creating mediated memories, although the digitalizing TV will surely greatly promote the use of the Internet. TV in China will remain the dominant official medium in the future.

However, the Internet, particularly the Web 2.0, is gaining momentum among the young educated people. Weblog holders or bloggers have become an emerging community which attracts young audience increasingly in China (see Figures 5.1 and 5.2).

It is well known that the blog is one typical form of "bottom-up" journalism. In the Chinese society, it has already become part of socialization process in terms of informing the audience about the historical facts and events. Nevertheless, active bloggers still make a tiny part of the weblog community (see Figure 5.3) regardless of the rapid increase of the number of bloggers.

Bloggers are not simply Internet users. They are the people who have leisure time to tell stories and convey ideas on the one hand. On the other, they should also be greatly motivated to publish things continuously. In this sense, it is understandable that this group constitutes only 26.1 per cent, a small portion of all Internet users (see Figure 5.4).

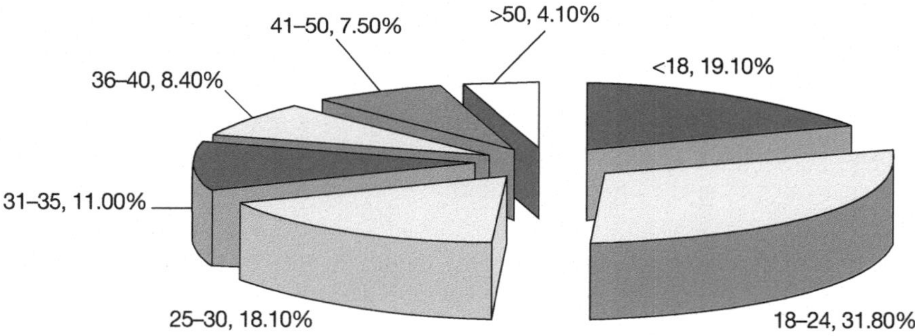

Figure 5.1 Age structure of Internet users in China (source: CNNIC Report, January 2008).

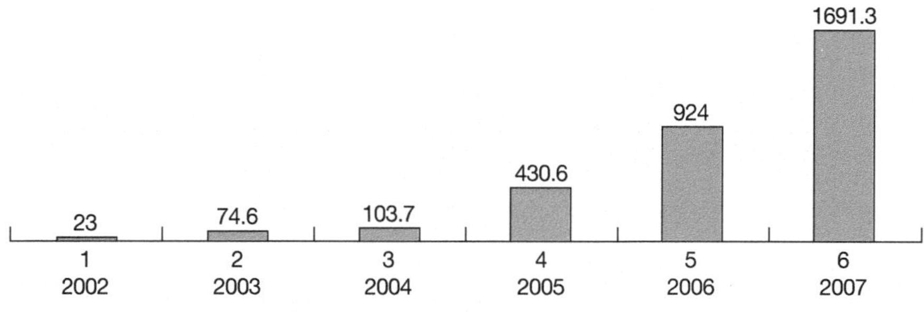

Figure 5.2 Increasing number of bloggers (10,000 persons) (source: CNNIC Report, January 2008).

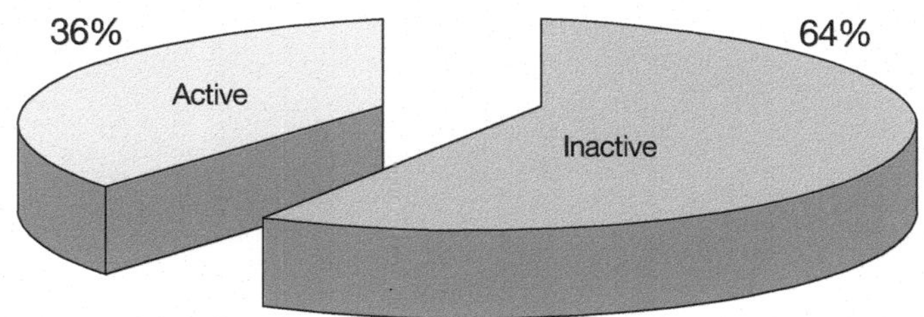

Figure 5.3 Active and inactive bloggers (source: CNNIC Report, January 2008).

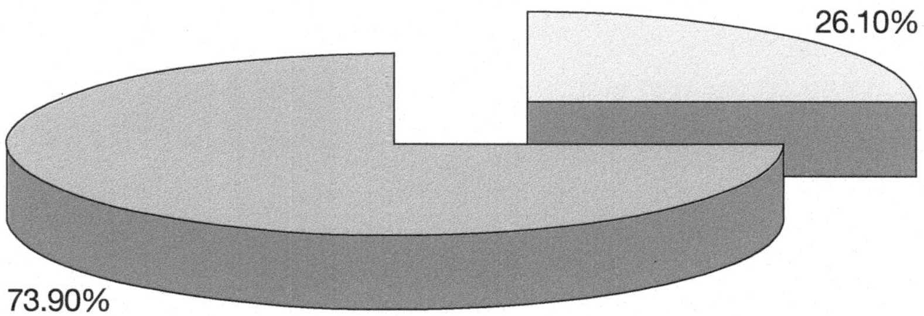

Figure 5.4 Share of bloggers among the Internet users (source: CNNIC Report, January 2008).

Judging from the professions of bloggers as Figure 5.5 shows, it is obvious that Chinese intellectuals are the main driver of this new trend. The notion "intellectual" refers in China to those who have obtained a higher education. In today's China 5 per cent of the population can be accounted as intellectuals.[11] Thanks to the reform of higher education, universities and colleges are "producing" more and more graduates (see Table 5.2), so that the real value and their status of intellectuals is declining. University students are usually viewed in China as "would-be intellectuals".

As to the age structure, it is notable that the majority of bloggers belong to the groups which are younger than 35 years old. It means that most of them have not experienced the "Cultural Revolution" (1966–1976). Also, the 4 June 1989 tragedy is part of their vague memory (see Figure 5.6).

Table 5.2 Number of graduates having obtained bachelor degrees in China (million)

Year	*2003*	*2004*	*2005*	*2006*	*2007*
Number	2.12	2.8	3.4	4.1	4.95

Source: http://job.liaon.com/datanews/200705/372.html (April 20, 2008).

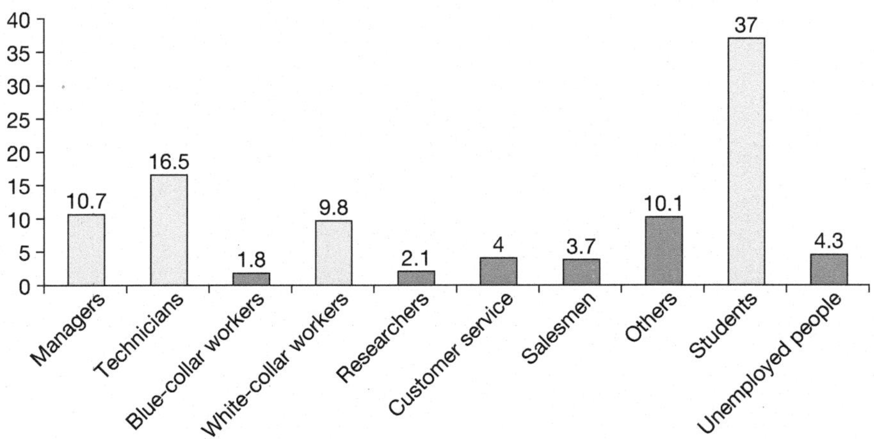

Figure 5.5 Composition of professions among the bloggers (source: CNNIC Report, 2007).

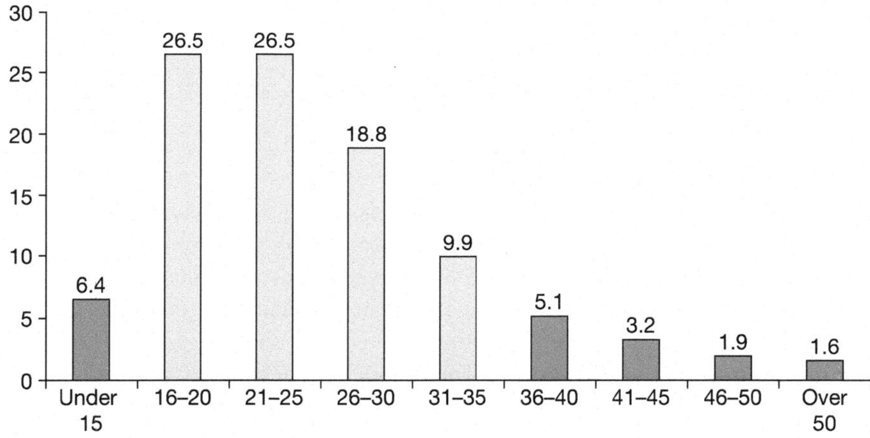

Figure 5.6 Age structure of China's bloggers (%) (source: CNNIC Report, 2007).

Asking about the motives of compiling weblogs, many bloggers show their great interest in expressing their feelings and views or sharing information with others. It indicates that weblogs provide Internet users with great space for outpouring of emotion, creating "public opinions", and there is a great need among the bloggers to present their views to the public (see Figure 5.7).

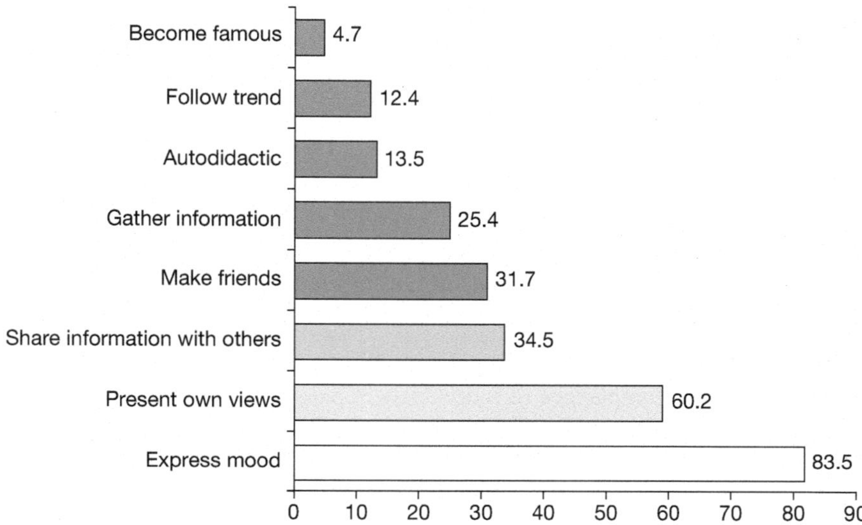

Figure 5.7 Motives of Chinese bloggers while compiling the weblog (%) (source: CNNIC Report, 2007).

China's memory policy

Before presenting my research findings on Chinese bloggers in connection with a new collective memory, it is necessary to get an overview of what the Chinese memory policy looks like.

The notion "information" in the Chinese context refers to not only facts and figures about the contemporary development of the world, it contains also knowledge about the past, especially the period starting from the foundation of the People's Republic of China (1949). In many countries, especially in non-democratic countries, the picture of the past is always a result of strongly controlled selection or even distortion made by the leading elites.

Obviously, China has been following a strict "memory policy" since opening up to the world. Although the citizens have gained more private sphere and individual freedom during the last three decades, the authorities have been keeping a tight rein on what should be memorized and what should be forgotten, especially when it concerns some "dark chapters" of modern history of the Chinese Communist Party (CCP). In other words, there is little space for the bloggers to gather information and dissimilate information related to these "dark chapters".

The memory policy in China is embodied by censorship of the press as well as the Internet. Journalists in China have been instructed what they are allowed to report and what they are not. In this respect there is an unwritten law which is in the journalist jargon called "the red line". Figure 5.8 shows which topics they are allowed to write about in local newspapers, or in officially controlled Internet news portals.

As Figure 5.8 tells us, the Taiwan issue and issues related to Tibet, Xinjiang are only ascribed to the Chinese Communist Party (CCP). The same is true of issues like foreign policy, territorial disputes, ethnic problems, social conflicts and democratization in China.

As to any criticism against the state or CCP, there is a differentiated censorship. For the last few years, China has welcomed public criticism (particularly criticism against corruption and fraud or pollution at the local level), only when the central government feels "safe", that is, the power monopoly of the CCP will not be challenged and the image of the state or the CCP will not be harmed. In this sense, criticism with a "happy end", from the point of view of the CCP, is the best form of reports for the public. The term "happy end" means that regardless of the problems caused by corruption and the like, the CCP is, in the end, capable of correcting the mistakes by itself and it is the single saviour of the country.

Looking at the competence of individuals imputed by the state in the sphere of disseminating information, there is little space left, especially regarding the information on one's own country. Journalists and Internet users have no problems when spreading soft information such as affairs of stars or things like the soap opera of everyday life. Also, commercial information is always allowed. Since almost 10 per cent of the population is engaged in the stock market, the country is experiencing a flood of this information.

As mentioned before, collective memory is mostly created by the ruling elites via selection. The main feature of the selection of historical facts is embodied by China's successful censorship of the Internet as well as conventional mass media. Both the English and Chinese versions of the "Wikipedia", for example, were not available for the users in mainland China for quite a long time, until very recently, when China lifted the blockage for the coming Olympic Games.

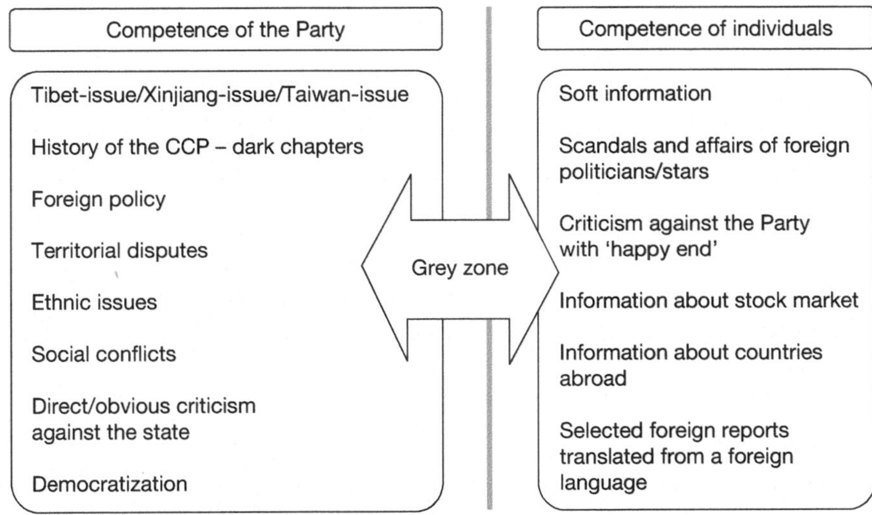

Figure 5.8 Dos and Don'ts – red line.

The second aspect of selection is to enhance the memories by presenting repeatedly certain "historical facts" and "events". In official CCTV news reports in the evening TV programme, for example, there was a series of documentary films called *Red Memory* which is integrated into the news report programme in the year 2007. By recalling events or personalities during the Civil War (1945–1949) or Anti-Japanese War (1938–1945) the glory of the CCP is purposely being propagated. This "strategic use" of memory has contributed greatly to the constitution of an artificial or a deficient memory in China.

As a result of an active selection process of historical facts on the one hand and deliberate evasion of reports of sensitive topics, there occurs a patched memory among the population, especially the young generations. As Zhang Yihe put it, people under 40 years old do not know what the "Anti-Rightist Campaign" (1958) is, in which a great number of Chinese intellectuals suffered due to the CCP's suspicion of educated people. Chinese under 30 are ignorant of the 4 June 1989 pro-democracy movement in Tiananmen Square, in which hundreds of young students and citizens lost their lives or got injured.[12]

The older generation of intellectuals and the official memory policy

Chinese authoritarianism has changed a lot since the last two decades. It has become more sophisticated and more flexible. One of the big changes of the regime is embodied in its differentiated intellectual policies.

Judging from the experiences gained by the intellectuals, there is a great gulf between the young and older generations of intellectuals in terms of their political attitude towards the political system and the CCP. Intellectuals, who have experienced the Cultural Revolution (1966–1976) and the Students Movement (1989), are mostly critical due to their own negative experiences with the regime before 1989. The CCP is quite aware of that. In order to stabilize the society, the older generation of intellectuals, especially those who are working at universities or research institutes, have become a notable "compensation" in terms of benefit in housing and chances of going abroad. By offering this group of intellectuals more material benefits and partly more privileges, the CCP imposed a kind of discretion on it. The so-called discretion refers to the obligation of not mentioning the "dark chapters" of the regime or at least not in an obvious way. This policy seems to work well in stabilizing the society, because the historical narratives are created either by the officially recognized ruling elites in terms of "establishment intellectuals"[13] or those who enjoy their academic reputation due to their professions (such as journalists, university teachers).

Apart from the official efforts in the formation of a collective memory which benefits the CCP, Chinese intellectuals also contribute a lot to this process, though in different ways and thus with different impacts on the political life of the population. Or, more exactly, the officially intended selected reconstruction of the collective memory is mostly realized by Chinese intellectuals. It is notable that more and more intellectuals have become increasingly interested in their publicity through media. The TV programme *Forum of 100 Schools* (*baijia jiangtan*),[14] in which university professors give TV transmitted public lectures on Chinese history of dynasties (not the modern history) and ancient Chinese philosophy, is one of these new developments in the efforts to "manufacture" a collective memory. Regardless of the very controversial views in their lectures, the narrative content of their lectures is overloaded with a surfeit of representations of Ancient China, partly because it is the single and secure way for them to reconstruct the collective memory.

In contrast to the relatively young bloggers, these intellectuals have the knowledge of the recent past, but they are not allowed to hand it down; they are quite afraid of annoying the authorities by telling the truth. Consequently, they deliberately keep silent when it concerns "sensitive" issues. This "cautious behaviour" has influenced the young generations on the one hand. On the other, it leads to a certain knowledge or information gap for the young generations including the majority of bloggers.

Findings from a content analysis of Chinese bloggers

In December 2007, the author undertook a content analysis of 600 blog texts compiled by 150 bloggers located in various Chinese providers. Only the bloggers with a narrative character (storytellers) were chosen as objects of analysis.

By analysing the authors' age structure, obvious differences are revealed between the age structure of Internet users provided by the CNNIC (see Figure 5.9) and the one discovered in the project. The reason for it is obvious: the bloggers who tend to tell stories are mostly those who have experienced quite a lot and they have mostly the need to express themselves via an official channel, such as a blog.

As to the professions the bloggers are in, four categories are found:

1 academics (working at universities or research institutes) and students;
2 media workers;
3 economists (in terms of managers and accountants) and technicians; and
4 others.

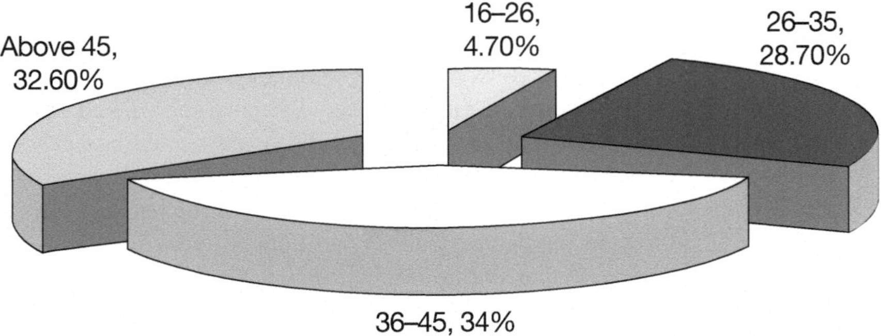

Figure 5.9 Age structure of the "storytellers".

Admittedly it is an enormous simplification. However, it made the statistics more understandable (see Figure 5.10). It is worth noticing that academics/students as well as media workers make up the biggest part of the storytellers. It is an assumption of the project that for the media workers, despite their work in a press or at a radio and TV station, there is still a great need to express themselves in an unofficial space.

The main purpose of the analysis is to examine what kind of historical events or facts were reiterated or narrated and which attitude the bloggers take while "telling stories". Three types of attitudes are defined according to the degree of either critical or uncritical stance taken by the bloggers:

1 "critical stance" indicates that authors purposely criticize the prevailing ideology or the authorities' memory policy while "telling stories";
2 "neutral stance" refers to that which does not fully conform with the official view, yet they do not intend to oppose the official memory policy;
3 an "uncritical stance" means that the bloggers are fully in conformity with the official version of historical facts and events in their narratives.

Based on the analysis of the bloggers' political attitudes found in their narratives or the way stories are told, the study comes to the conclusion that 12.16 per cent of bloggers took advantage of unofficial media to view the official version of historical facts critically. Most of the bloggers, however, do not care about the difference between the facts and fictions or distorted facts (see Figure 5.11).

Parallel to the three types of political stance, three categories of narratives are also found: stories with a pure cognitive and scientific character constitute obviously the biggest part (42.8 per cent of the 600 texts). These bloggers are also found to pour much emotion into their stories by conveying what they have experienced (37.3 per cent of the 600 texts). Only 19.8 per cent of the storytellers took a normative perspective in their narratives (see Figure 5.12).

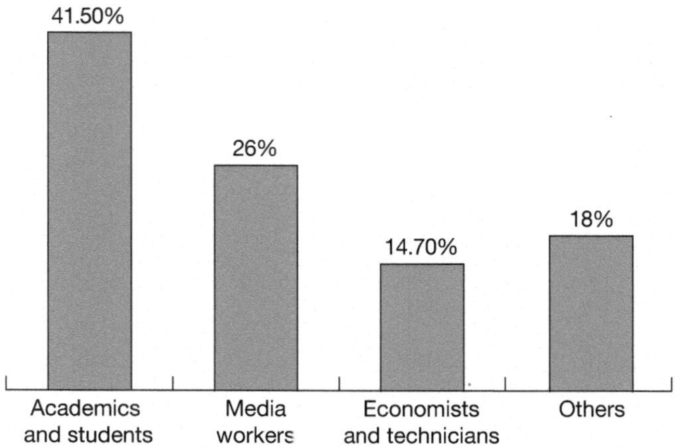

Figure 5.10 Professions of the "storytellers".

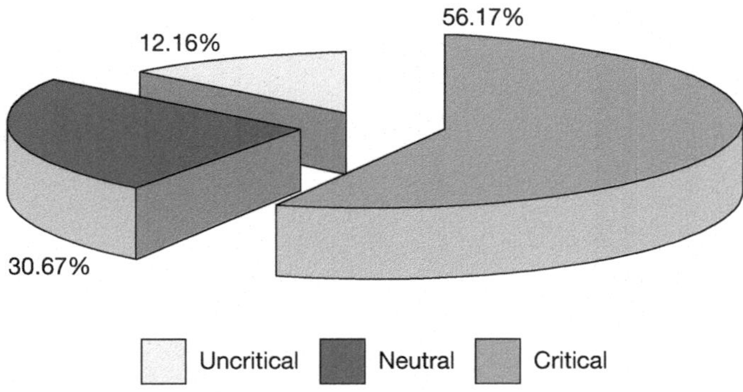

Figure 5.11 Stance taken by the bloggers.

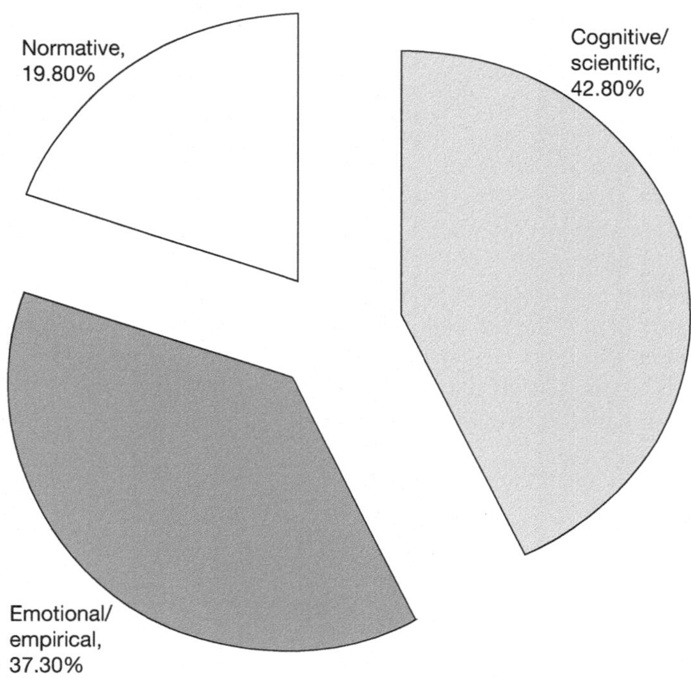

Figure 5.12 Scientific degree of the stories.

Regarding the time period the stories originated from all these 600 blogs, the project has artificially developed six periods. The first one begins with the pre-republic period, that is before the year of 1911. The second one refers to the period starting from the first republic in China (1912) until 1948 – the foundation of the PR of China. The third one is the so-called Mao Zedong's era (1949–1977); the

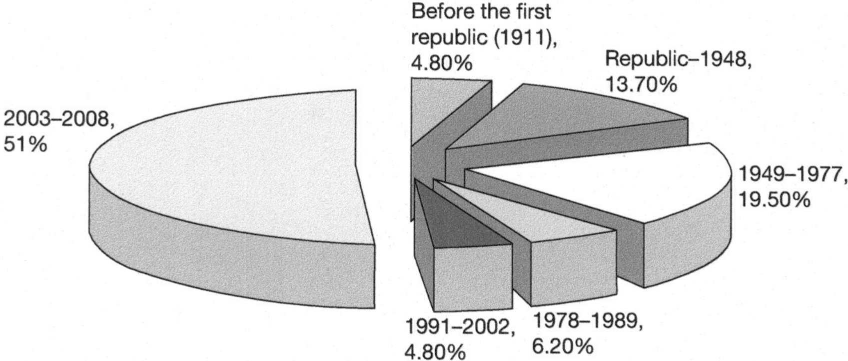

Figure 5.13 Time period of the stories.

fourth one Deng Xiaoping's era; the fifth Jiang Zemin's administration. The last one refers to Hu Jintao's administration (see Figure 5.13).

It is interesting to note that the events which took place during Hu Jintao's administration make up a big share of the whole timespan, followed by the time period of Mao Zedong's era. This indicates that bloggers are more concerned about the problems they are facing today than "yesterday", although Mao Zedong's era still remains a big issue among the storytellers.

As to the content itself, texts written by bloggers were divided into two parts – fully in accordance with Figure 5.11: one is called "blogs within the red line" and the other, "blogs outside the red line". As mentioned above, in the area of sensitive topics within the "red line", the policy of the Chinese authorities is either that you should follow the official version while talking about these issues or your publication will be banned within the territory of the PR of China. So far as the "blogs outside the red line" are concerned, they are mostly tolerated because they do no or little harm to the existing system.

During the research, it was noticed that those who attempted to exceed the red line or have already exceeded the red line via Internet publications are not necessarily taking an oppositional stance against the mainstream media. On the contrary, most of them keep strictly in line with the official version of the narratives, so that Figure 5.14 cannot fully reveal the real political stance of the authors having exceeded the red line.

According to the data collected in this project, the majority of bloggers are not interested in topics within the red line. Of 600 blogs, 184 contain issues listed within the red line. Among them, 44 texts imply narratives related to the Cultural Revolution (1966–1976), 29 texts show an interest in Mao Zedong's life. Only one text touched on the topic of the Falungong Sect. There is no mentioning of the Students' Movement in the year of 1989 or the Tibet issue. More importantly, only about 12 per cent of the bloggers take a critical stance while telling stories through sophisticated ways of expression. More than half of them,

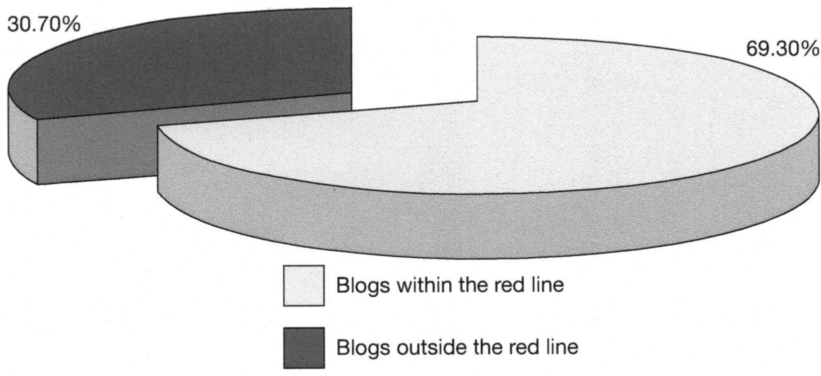

Figure 5.14 Blogs within or outside the "red line".

however, follow the official policy while about 30 per cent of them keep a distance from both sides. My findings from the above analysis can be summarized as follows:

1 In comparison to the academics/students and media workers, the so-called economists and technicians tend to conform easily with the mainstream narratives.
2 Authors with their narratives within the red line tend to identify themselves with the official version of the historical facts and events, while those who took a critical stance toward the authorities, conveyed their ideas mostly in the stories outside the red line.
3 The age group of 18–25 has seldom touched on issues within the red line, while the group of 36–45 was more keen on telling the stories within the red line.
4 Those who take a critical stance mostly have their narratives with great emotion while blogs with a more scientific character tend to be either uncritical or neutral.

Conclusion

The emergence of the Internet does not mean that it will lead an authoritarian country into speedy democratization. The optimistic view presented in Shayne Bowman and Chris Willis' study seems to have its limit. The Internet as informal media is surely providing people with a big variety of opportunities for participation in creating collective memories, be they public or private. However, the dominance of officially mediated collective memory is so strong in China that people are forgetting things exactly in a way that the authorities have wished. In addition, the unwritten regulations such as partly transparent, partly arbitrary restriction of narrative topics in terms of the red line effectively keep bloggers away from the critical issues. As a result, the Internet in China cannot be used, as many Western experts have expected, to create mediated social memories by the users. Rather, they are part of the victims of the prevailing memory policy while contributing to a certain extent to shaping a collective memory designed by the leading political elites. In China there occurs a de facto new collective memory which is politically harmless to the existing power. This task is being fulfilled firstly through conventional media, and TV in particular. Due to the effect of this kind of memory and rigorous implementation of CCP's memory policy, the space for the young bloggers remains very limited. Therefore they do not form a counterforce to the overwhelming power of conventional media. The memories produced by bloggers can only become at best a sub-collective memory or fragmented memory for a certain group, not the national collective memory at all.

The CCP is seemingly boosting the "achievement" of its memory policy by seeing that young generations do not know what they should remember regarding the contemporary history. Unlike the old generations who suffered a lot from the reprisals by the CCP, the young generations will take a more calm or indifferent stance towards the authorities because they know the related history either very little, or simply nothing of it. In this case, a new collective memory is de facto a patched memory, which is not compatible with an open society where people enjoy more autonomy in deciding what they like to know and how to judge the false and correct information by themselves.

The one-sided narratives of history could be the basis of legitimacy and they would lead young Chinese to radical views on the presumed enemies, be it Western societies or other ethnic groups. Nevertheless, the CCP is also reaping problems caused by the existing memory policy and its product. On 4 June 2007, a local newspaper in Chendu published an advertisement, more exactly, a commemoration of mothers who suffered the loss of their children during the 4 June massarcre in 1989. The young editors, all under 25 years old, lacked the background of this commemoration. They simply sent it to print without anticipating what would happen to them. As a result of their "negligence" they had to leave their workplace, because they had allegedly made a "serious political mistake".[15]

Regarding the development accompanied by the new telecommunication technology, it is too early to say that a global political communication has become possible at any time and anywhere. Since people from both worlds, that is, a democratic and "open society" (in terms of Karl Popper) on the one hand and a non-democratic society on the other, have created (sometimes totally) different collective memories, which have become, to a certain extent, hindrance to communication. The ongoing protest wave on the Chinese side against the Western societies triggered by the Tibet issue is a poster child for this phenomenon.

The process of creating a more or less fair mediated collective memory will take a long time, probably not thanks to, but also because of, the emergence of the Internet.

Notes

1 Maurice Halbwachs: *The Collective Memory*, New York and London: Harper and Row, 1980, Chapter 2.
2 Silde Arnold-de Simnine (ed.): *Memory Traces – 1989 and the Question of German Cultural Identity*, Frankfurt am Main/New York: Peter Lang, 2005, p. 9.
3 K.E. Müller and J. Rüsen (eds): *Historische Sinnbildung. Problemstellungen, Zeitkonzepte, Wahrnehmungshorizonte, Darstellungsstrategien*, Reinbek: Rowohlt, 1997, pp. 433–54.
4 Patrick Geary: *Phantoms of Remembrance. Memory and Oblivion at the End of the First Millennium*, Princeton: Princeton University Press, 1994, p. 12.
5 Maurice Halbwachs: *Das Gedächtnis und seine soziale Bedingungen*, Berlin: Neuwied, 1966, p. 20.
6 Stephen Bertman: *Cultural Amnesia – America's Future and The Crisis of Memory*, p. 31.
7 Ruth W. Sandwell (ed.): *To the Past – History Education, Public Memory and Citizenship in Canada*, Toronto: University of Toroto Press, 2006, pp. 11–12.
8 Shayne Bowman and Chris Willis (2003): *We Media – How Audiences are Shaping the Future of News and Information*, online, available at: www.hypergene.net/wemedia/weblog.php.
9 See: http://bk.51player.com/view/1123113.htm (accessed 20 April 2008).
10 See: www.dvbcn.com/news/cygc/2008418/1814241839.html (accessed 20 April 2008).
11 See: http://job.liaon.com/datanews/200705/372.html (accessed 20 April 2008).
12 See: www.dw-world.de/dw/article/0,2144,2426681,00.html (accessed 20 April 2008).
13 David S.G. Goodman: *Beijing Street Voices: The Poetry and Politics of China's Democracy Movement*, London/Boston: M. Boyars, 1981, pp. 29–31.
14 See: http://space.tv.cctv.com/podcast/bjjt.
15 See: www.rfa.org/mandarin/shenrubaodao/2007/06/08/chengdu (accessed 20 April 2008).

6 From "foreign propaganda" to "international communication"

China's promotion of soft power in the age of information and communication technologies

Xiaoling Zhang

Introduction

China's rise in economic power has been accompanied by a shift in its "foreign propaganda" from the defensive to the offensive. This shift is greatly facilitated by the technological conditions created by the rapid growth of information and communication technologies (ICTs) in China, both quantitatively and qualitatively. From the individualized computer to the more mass directed satellite television, ICTs have brought China a new form of publicizing itself to the world.

While much has been written on the effect of the rapid growth of ICTs in China, namely, whether the more liberal and open communication flows driven by the development of ICTs may lead to the development of a liberal public sphere, the rise of a civil society and, ultimately, democratization,[1] there have been few studies on how the growth of ICTs is empowering China to "have a bigger voice"[2] in the global competition for influencing, if not controlling, the political environment, or how China is trying to expand its soft power resources in the new world order. This chapter examines how China has shifted from defensive overseas publicity to the more offensive exertion of soft power, facilitated by the rise of ICTs. It looks at China's infrastructure, changing policies and strategies for overseas publicity on one hand, and the content on the key satellite TV channels and websites for foreign publics on the other. The chapter finishes with discussions on the possible impact China may have on the changing global information flow, the impact of China's unique pattern of "foreign propaganda" and its pursuit of soft power on users of Chinese TV satellite channels and websites, and the effect of the internationalization of Chinese media through ICTs for China itself.

From defensive to offensive – changing goals and strategies

China's shift from defensive to offensive for overseas publicity is well reflected in the themes of the annual national conferences on "foreign propaganda": for the first such conference in 1984, not long after China adopted the open-door policy, the theme was on how to publicize better the advantages of socialism in order to prevent illegal immigration to Hong Kong.[3] Conferences of this kind are presided by the head of the Propaganda Department (the English translation has been changed to "Publicity Department" but the Chinese term remains "Propaganda Department") and attended by heads of propaganda departments at the provincial level. They summarize China's "foreign propaganda" work for the past year and arrange concrete ideological and propaganda work details for the next to ensure that propaganda works of the year accurately reflect and support the achievements of the Party-state. With China's growing confidence that comes with its rapid economic development, the theme for 2005 became one on the building of an "all-dimensional, multi-channelled, wide-ranging and deep-levelled pattern" of "foreign propaganda" (*gou jian quan fangwei, duo cengci, kuan linyu de da waixuan geju*).[4]

The 1989 pro-democracy movement marked a turning point in both Chinese history and its "foreign propaganda" infrastructure in China. Leaders blamed the hostile international opinion environment after the 4 June crackdown for the slow response of the Foreign Propaganda Department and the backward technologies of information and communication. In the words of Zeng Jianhui, former deputy head of the Propaganda Department: while China sent out information via post only, Western countries sent out lies via satellite which could reach every corner of the world.[5] While positive reporting and the role of media in maintaining ideological control within China was re-emphasized, the Chinese government started to remould its overseas image by restructuring its overseas publicity system throughout the 1990s. The Central Foreign Propaganda Group, established in 1980 but dismissed in 1988, was re-established in March 1990 and, in 1993, it was upgraded to the Central Foreign Propaganda Office, directly under the Central Government, which was at the same time named the Information Office of the State Council. The same office at the provincial, municipal and city levels was also established. In addition, Chinese embassies also set up Foreign Propaganda Groups.[6] The Central Foreign Propaganda Office, more commonly known as Information Office of the State Council, thus becomes China's international public relations department,[7] to help the world see China in a positive light.

It was thus not until June 1989 that China discovered the importance of having the technological capacity to influence international attitudes. The technological conditions in China before 1989 did not include the most distinctive features of today: satellite channels and the Internet were either unheard of or had not yet been adapted for "foreign propaganda". Indeed in almost 60 years or so from 1949, the mix of resources that shapes "foreign propaganda" keeps changing. For a very long time, magazines and pictorials such as *Beijing Review*, *China Pictorial*, *China Today* and *People's China* were the main vehicles for publicizing China to the outside world. Newspapers such as *China Daily* and China's overseas radio broadcaster, China Radio International (CRI), were other important platforms for "foreign propaganda". Since 1989, however, China has been actively endorsing and improving information and communication technologies, and overseas publicity activities started to take advantage of the technological advancement for the reconstruction of its image abroad. In the early 1990s, satellite TV channels started to play an important role when Central China TV Station (CCTV) set up its first 24-hour satellite international channel in Mandarin Chinese. China Radio International (CRI) was also urged to develop new media forms to become a multimedia complex with radio and online broadcasting. Today, CRI broadcasts 1,100 hours of programmes a day in 38 foreign languages in addition to Mandarin Chinese and other four Chinese dialects. From 1995, all news media, publications, radio and TV stations started to run their own websites.[8]

In the past decade, China's growing significance in the world economy and its ambition for global political power have given rise to varying degrees of fear and scepticism in different parts of the world. The dominant media in the West has repeatedly used the term "China threat" since 1990s and "China Model of International Development" more recently, evincing China's rise as a destabilizing force ideologically, economically and militarily, a threat to the free world.[9]

Against this unfavourable backdrop, the capacity to influence international attitudes became paramount. The CCP launched another image-building campaign – nationally, to show that as a ruling party, it is open-minded, progressive, responsible, democratic and competent to lead the nation and to have its say in world affairs, and internationally, to show that China will emerge as a great power on the international scene in a non-threatening and non-confrontational manner. This seems to mark the beginning of China's pursuit for soft power, to "make its power seem legitimate in the eyes of others" so that "it will encounter less resistance to its wishes".[10] Since the Sixteenth National People's Congress of the Chinese Communist Party (CCP) in 2003 China has proposed the concept of "peaceful rise" (the leaders now use the less threatening term "peaceful development", and leave the nongovernmental experts to talk about "peaceful rise"[11]), an attempt at softening China's global image as an aggressive rising power. This involves shifting the focus from purely economic cooperation to other more subtle areas of cooperation such as culture. To that end, China has increased steadily its support for cultural exchanges, including staging heritage exhibitions and art performances overseas, welcoming students from other nations to study in China and paying for Chinese-language programmes abroad. In 2005, China's Education Ministry announced "Eight Measures to Boost Overseas Chinese Teachings" in universities and language institutes around the world, including the speeding up of the process of building the "Confucius Institute". By September 2007, over 170 Confucius Institutes have been set up around the world.[12] According to the plan of the State Leading Group for Teaching Chinese as a Foreign Language, 500 Confucius Institutes and Classrooms will be set up by 2010. Again, at the start of the year 2007, China announced a massive translation and publishing project "Greater China Library", the first attempt to translate thousands of years of documents into English and then into other languages. Through such endeavours, China is sending a double message to the international community: first, China is a peace-loving country, contributing to the building of a harmonious world[13] and will not interfere in other nations' internal affairs; second, other countries should not interfere with China's internal affairs.

China's overseas publicity activities have thus taken a step forward from the early 1990s, from being on the defensive to the offensive, with a more nuanced strategy but on a massive scale. In other words, they have taken on another objective – the pursuit for soft power for "publicizing China's assertions to the outside world, forming a desirable image of the state, issuing rebuttals to distorted overseas reports about China, to improve the international environment surrounding China, and exert influence on the policy decisions of foreign countries".[14] With the implementation of the policy of building an "all-dimensional, multi-channelled, wide-ranging and deep-levelled pattern" of "foreign propaganda", and the adoption of new media for the purpose of "foreign propaganda" as is shown in the following section, China is ready (technologically, socially and politically) for the exertion of soft power.

The expansion of ICT capacity

Joseph Nye aptly points out that "in a global information age, power is passing from the 'capital-rich' to the information rich".[15] As information becomes power, the ability to use information and communication technologies to pass information becomes an important source of attraction and power. In other words, communication instruments and effective communication become increasingly more important for a country to get its messages across and to affect the preferences of others.

"We should … establish a publicity capacity to exert an influence on world opinion that is as strong as China's international standing", announced Jiang Zemin.[16] Indeed, the economic success has given China the capacity to exploit the innovations in information and communication technologies which offer China unparalleled opportunities to reconsider conventional ways for influencing international attitudes and shaping the international symbolic environment.

Satellite TV channels

The mass media have been considered extremely powerful in political publicity in China. Television, which has been a national instrument for constructing the political and cultural discourse to create and reproduce national identity, loyalty and pride, is again taken up by the Party and state as the most effective way to improve China's image and for broadcasting China's voice to the world for its speed, clear image and popularity, and for enjoying unique privileges in overcoming the obstacles of languages and cultures. In 1998, a "go-out" or "go global" project was launched for the international expansion and multi-language coverage of China's satellite TV channels.

CCTV started its satellite broadcasting in 1984, which proved to be especially effective for transmitting its programming (and hence the Party's voice) throughout the country. Since 1999, all 31 provincial TV stations, driven by economic or political interests, have set up their own satellite channels and by the end of 2005 there are altogether 72 satellite channels.[17]

Working within the new framework of "foreign propaganda", TV stations at all levels are to work together for the expansion of activities abroad. As it has been for providing and shaping the political environment domestically, at the centre of this new pattern is CCTV as the station of the central government. TV stations at all other levels are requested to supply programmes to the CCTV international satellite channels.

CCTV-4, China's first international channel in Mandarin Chinese, started its operations in October 1992, targeted at overseas Chinese, especially those in Taiwan, Hong Kong and Macau. From the beginning it is clear that it is a not-for-profit channel despite the fact that CCTV spends about US$5,000,000 a year on running it.[18] With China's growing ambition CCTV's target audience shifted. In 2000 another 24-hour satellite English Channel, CCTV-9, was launched for the non-Chinese speaking international audience. In May 2003, CCTV-9 took on a whole new look, with many changes in its programming and even started to employ foreign anchorpersons to make the programme more palatable to Western viewers, a practice unprecedented in the recent history of Chinese media. The set up of the E&F channel (Spanish and French) in 2004 completes CCTV's major-language coverage. Although overseas Chinese remain the target audience, "they are minorities in Western societies and therefore the focus for 'foreign propaganda' should be the mainstream society in the U.S., Europe and our neighboring countries".[19] Therefore, "of all the TV channels for 'foreign propaganda' and for the exertion of soft power, the most important are the ones in English and other foreign languages".[20] Within a few years of its startup, CCTV-9 claims to be covering 98 per cent of the land in the world[21] via its six satellites, a great achievement for an English TV channel in a non-English environment. At the same time CCTV-4 has branched into CCTV-4 Asia, CCTV-4 Europe and CCTV-4 America, varying the programmes to suit the perceived tastes and needs of the audiences in different regions.

From coverage to landing

However, the capacity to send out signals does not guarantee the landing of the programmes. To move from coverage to landing thus became the priority for China and the government adopted many measures to achieve that goal.

As Chin observed,[22] China opened up some of the TV market in Guangdong to a number of foreign media on a "reciprocal and mutually beneficial exchange of knowledge and expertise". For instance, "in exchange for being allowed cable access, News Corp agreed that its United States network, Fox, would carry the English-language channel of Chinese state broadcaster, *CCTV-9*".[23] Similarly, AOL Time Warner "agreed to broadcast Chinese state-owned English-language channel, *CCTV-9*, in the US".[24] The remark of the spokeswoman for the State Administration of Radio, Television and Film (SARFT) pointed to the purpose of this kind of exchange, "Americans want to come in. We of course want to go there too. It should be mutually beneficial".[25]

Chin's interview with the Director of the Chief Editorial Office at the Guangdong Bureau also reveals[26] that the landing agreement was made according to the "three equal criteria". Among others, the TV households of CCTV-9 and Xing Kong of Rupert Murdoch's News Corporation must be equal. If Xing Kong has 600,000 TV households in the Pearl River Delta region, then CCTV-9 must be accessed by the same number of cable TV households on News Corporation's Fox cable network.[27]

In addition to CCTV at the national level, provincial and city level TV stations along the border such as Xinjiang and Inner Mongolia form another important part of the new pattern of "foreign propaganda", beaming their programmes to the neighbouring countries via satellites. The Great Wall TV Platform (GWTV), set up in 2004 with the latest advanced transmission technologies, including digital satellite and fibre optical transportation services, is China's latest endeavour "to enlarge and enhance its penetration into the world media market"[28] for "foreign propaganda" and for the expansion of soft power resources.

The GWTV is a TV package under CCTV for the intended overseas Chinese and mainstream audience worldwide, with government-approved satellite channels mostly from mainland China (CCTV and other provincial satellite channels). It provides Chinese movies, TV drama series, sports, news, infotainment, children's programmes, music videos, documentaries and travelogues. The GWTV has so far launched its satellite direct-to-home (DTH) service in the US, Europe, Canada, Asia, Africa and Latin America. The platform has tried to provide a combination of programmers with format changes according to the perceived needs of the audiences in different regions. For instance, for audiences in Europe the GWTV provides channels in English, Spanish and French as well as Mandarin Chinese, while for the Asian audience, it consists mainly of channels in Mandarin and Cantonese as well as English.

The Internet

The Internet brings a whole new dimension to "foreign propaganda", just as Klotz argues, "[T]he Internet is at once like no other communication device and like every communication device",[29] as "the Internet simultaneously shares all the traits of television, newspapers, radio, books, and a countless number of other media. It provides people with an encyclopaedic information source, which is available anywhere at any time".[30] The Internet, compared with TV programmes for the competition of "my information versus your information", is also considered by China to be more cost effective.

The Internet was inaugurated in China in late 1994. In 2001 the setting up and development of government-controlled news websites on a massive scale in China took place, with the aim of adding new channels to the Party's propaganda and ideological work on one hand and taking over the emerging new platform for public opinion supervision on the other.[31] In 2007, Hu Jintao, at a meeting of the Politburo, urged officials to continue to be proactive in running and managing the Internet.[32] This new platform for propaganda and ideological work is composed of both national and provincial key news websites, many of which are born of traditional media and business gateway sites. By the end of 2003, news websites approved by the Information Office of the State Council reached over 150.[33] Naturally, many of the key news websites are also key "foreign propaganda" websites. *Beijing Review*, one of the key national websites for "foreign propaganda", is a good example: in addition to the English print edition, it also publishes online editions in English, Chinese, French, German and Japanese. All editions claim to offer authoritative news coverage, policy information and analysis, and special reports and columns to satisfy specific needs of different readers.[34] The websites of the Xinhua News Agency, *People's Daily,* China Radio International and Central China TV Station and the website of the State Council Information Office are some of the leading ones among such sites.

An example at the municipal level is the *Shanghai Daily* founded by Wenhui-Xinmin United Press Group on 1 October 1999. *Shanghai Daily* is an English-language newspaper supervised by the Foreign Propaganda Office of the Shanghai CCP Committee and the Press Office of the Shanghai Municipal Government. "To serve as a better platform for Shanghai's foreign propaganda, *Shanghai Daily* unveiled a new format (first version in PDF) and launched its website on October 8, 2005."[35]

In addition to the websites run by the traditional media organizations, China has created other sites specifically for "foreign propaganda", with China National Network (china.com.cn) in 1997 as the key state "foreign propaganda" website. Typically, these websites are multi-lingual (e.g. China National Network uses ten languages and 11 versions of the sites), and provide specific topics and design different layouts for the target regions. Parallel to the practice of the platform made up of satellite channels led by CCTV, all local websites are required to support and provide information to China National Network. In December 2001 China National Network signed a cooperation agreement entitled "Building a Common Network Platform for Foreign Propaganda Agreement" with 28 local news websites including Beijing Qianlong Net, Shanghai Oriental Net, Guangdong Zaman and Tianjin Herald. Under the agreement, all the websites are to share information resources, which primarily serves to enrich the information content of China National Network for a "comprehensive, systemic and in-depth publicity about China and establish a good image of China".[36] The reward for the local sites is, it is argued, that as it is at the national level China National Network serves better for local economic development.

CCTV-9 and China National Network

CCTV-9 and China National Network have obviously been the new vehicles for China to realize the objectives of "foreign propaganda" and to pursue soft power. By content analysis of CCTV-9 and China National Network, we can infer, to some extent, how well China is achieving its goals for reshaping the international public opinion about China and its policies.

CCTV-9

Although CCTV-9 brands itself as "the only English 24-hour news channel in China", its airtime is divided into news and cultural programmes, including a language programme. The news programmes consist of the following: *CCTV News, Asia Today; Biz China; Culture Express; Dialogue; Sports Scene; World Insight; World Wide Watch; China Today* and *China This Week.*

An examination of the news programmes shows that CCTV-9, the first TV media organization in Asia that can beam its signals to every corner of the globe,[37] not only provides more extensive coverage on China, Asia, and other developing nations than is offered by other international channels, but is also set on presenting its own version of issues and events happening in China, Asia, the developing world and other world affairs as an insider and an alternative voice to the dominating Western voice, just as *Asia Today*'s mission statement goes: "We report on Asia from the perspective of Asians."[38] Similarly *World Insight*, a weekly programme, also promises to "provide a Chinese perspective on major global events and Chinese foreign affairs",[39] and *World Wide Watch* offers "daily round up of world news with a Chinese perspective" and "extensive coverage on what's happening in the developing world".[40]

The fact that *CCTV News* has replaced *News Hour*, and "*CCTV International*, your window on China" has changed to "*CCTV International*, your window on China and the world" in 2004 show that CCTV is pushing for brand recognition, and is expanding its viewpoints on not only China but on global affairs as well.

Second, it is also obvious that CCTV-9 aims to derive its importance in world affairs from its viewers, an importance that exceeds the sheer number of viewers. *Dialogue* claims to be "an authoritative talk-show designed to inform and educate viewers worldwide and influence decision makers in governments, businesses and academia",[41] and *World Insight* "is a must watch program for the intelligent viewer. It is aimed at policy makers, business people and academics inside and outside China".[42] To take part in shaping world politics is obviously one of the ambitions of CCTV-9.

Finally, a considerable amount of the news reports are on sports (*Sports Scene*), cultural activities (*Culture Express*) and business (*Biz China*), especially on China's achievements in the business and economic sections. This is not surprising as it is the economic success that has enabled China to open many doors in the world and given China the leverage and confidence to assert itself as a global player. It is also the economic development in China that is possibly becoming a model of development to other developing nations.

The feature programmes include the following:

AROUND CHINA: a television magazine programme about people, culture and economic development of various regions and ethnic minority groups of China.[43]

CENTRE STAGE: an entertainment programme composed of a wide range of performing arts, including Chinese folk songs, dance, opera, popular music, and the latest trends in the performing arts scene in China.

CHINESE CIVILIZATION: a vivid presentation of the highlights of Chinese culture throughout her 5,000-year history. We bring to life the historical celebrities, historical sites, folk arts, literature, education, science and technology of mankind's most enduring civilization.

LEARNING CHINESE: a language programme.

DOCUMENTARY: a faithful record of the extraordinary undertakings by the Chinese people, with an emphasis on the period of reform that began in the late 1970s.

REDISCOVERING CHINA: contemporary Chinese culture and social changes through foreigners' eyes.

NATURE & SCIENCE: a wide array of subjects from environmental protection, wild creatures, geology, biology, chemistry, medical science, and various modern technologies.

TRAVELOGUE: explore China from east to west, but catch a glimpse of other countries as well.

UP-CLOSE: a weekly entertaining look into the lives of extraordinary individuals.

NEW FRONTIERS: a programme investigating the enduring mysteries in our past and in nature.

TECH MAX: a television guide to the latest development of technologies in our daily life. It focuses on the most up-to-date ideas and gadgets in the market and keeps a close eye on the latest technological changes that affect our living.

Unlike the news programmes, the cultural programmes are largely on China itself. Thanks to its long history and diverse geographical landscape, China is blessed with a wide spectrum of cultural resources that help produce soft power: natural wonders, cuisines, traditional medicine, literature, arts, philosophies and folk religions. CCTV-9 taps into multiple cultural and ethnic symbolic resources, be they traditional or contemporary, and becomes a showcase to the Chinese landscape, local customs, historical legends or stories, cultural artefacts and an interpreter of their cultural meanings. For example, the regular magazine programme *Around China*, much of which comes from local TV stations across China, introduces the people, culture and economic development of various regions and ethnic minority groups of China. It also offers viewers glimpses of the beautiful scenery and rich cultural heritage of China.

CCTV-9's promotion of Chinese culture and language is part of a broader effort at "soft power rise", as it is believed that promoting the use of Chinese language and culture will contribute to spreading Chinese culture and increasing China's global influence.

Officials and professionals alike all clearly recognize these shows as important vehicles for boosting China's image and for the promotion of China's concept of peaceful development and advocacy of a harmonious world. The "National New Year's Gala", which has been institutionalized as part of the ritual of the New Year celebration since 1983, is such an example. It is a continuous variety show of four to five hours on New Year's Eve on CCTV. Each year, there is an official statement of the show's theme, with "unity" and "happiness" as the most favoured. From 2004, with building a "harmonious society" and "harmonious world" as the main official slogan of the country,[44] the theme for 2005, 2006, 2007 and 2008 has been harmony: "harmonious family, harmonious society and harmonious world". The performance is staged to thread the kinship families to the political and cultural community of national family. With more than one billion people tuned in to CCTV-1 to watch this Gala every year, a unique situation in which families are wired via television to the central state, the ancient Confucian ideal of the state governed like one huge family becomes more real than ever.[45] Over the years, this event has been broadcast on CCTV-4 for overseas Chinese, extending the notion of family to Chinese all over the world. From 2006, the event is also broadcast on the English and E&F channels, linking audiences of all ethnic backgrounds, at least in theory, "watching little green screens in London, New York and Tokyo ... via satellites and fibre-optic cables instantaneously and continuously".[46] The world has now become one family.

To sum up, CCTV-9, which "represents the images of the Party and government domestically and the images of the country and nation internationally", as defined by Ding Guangen in 1994, then Minister of the Ministry of Central Propaganda,[47] has become more proactive in supplying information and providing its views as an insider from Asia and China, an effort to become a trans-national media to break the Anglo-American monopoly. Second, the information supplied is not only limited to politics but also on culture and economic development, actively publicizing China's achievements in all areas. While eliminating negative images of China is still important, it has become more active in promoting China's concept of "peaceful development" and "harmonious society", using culture as the main source of attraction. With the shift of its objectives, China's targeted audiences have also shifted from the peripheral (overseas Chinese) to the mainstream, especially the elite. Finally, as a state-owned TV organization, it is increasing its international competitiveness by asserting its brand and increasing reports not only on China, Asia and the developing countries but also on all global affairs.

China National Network

The Internet is an increasingly significant presence in international politics. Investigations into the key national "foreign propaganda" website China National Network show China's expansion of its global influence in order to create a friendly international public opinion environment. The new design in ten different languages highlights its main role for overseas publicity. The main columns of the Chinese version include *China's Relations with the World*, *China's Foreign Policy*, *News Conferences of the State Information Office*, *Cultural Exchanges Activities*, *Business Activities*, *the Colourful and Diversified Chinese Culture*, *China in the Eyes of Foreigners* and *Chinese Abroad*, *Statistics and Facts about China*, *China News* and *World News*. Similarly, the English version has *News Reports on China and the International, Business, Government, Education, Environment, Culture, Women, Books and Magazines, Sports, Health, Entertainment, Learning Chinese*, and *Statistics and Facts about China*.

The substance of the website yet again proves that the objectives of China's "foreign propaganda" currently are to highlight the key jobs the Party and state are doing in order to manifest increasing transparency of the government, to promote cultural and business cooperation between China and other nations, and above all to build a desirable image of the state as dedicated to building a harmonious world with permanent peace and common prosperity. By publicizing the achievements China has made in economic and social development, and by using culture as the main source of attraction, it hopes to "help people in other nations to acquaint themselves with the Chinese culture, including its traditions, religions and particularly the Chinese way of thinking", as Du Ruiqing, former president of the Xi'an International Studies University, was quoted saying at the seventeenth annual international conference of the Sino-American Education Consortium.[48]

In addition to the articulation of China's views on global affairs, much prominence is given to China's environmental protection, political and social stability, national cohesion (especially on Taiwan and Tibet), anti-corruption, human rights and reduction of poverty, which shows China's active defence on sensitive issues it is often criticized for. China has become offensively defensive of its policies.

Discussions

The end of the twentieth century has witnessed unprecedented changes in world political and economic structures. In the re-ordering of the structures, three aspects contribute greatly to the basis for the global competition for attractiveness, legitimacy and credibility – technological capacity (e.g. the ability to launch, track, monitor and operate satellite-based broadcasting), the content of what is being advocated, and management. Countries with multiple channels of communication that help to frame issues in the information age are likely to be more attractive and gain soft power[49] for shaping international public opinion.

China has experienced nothing short of a telescoped ICTs revolution since just the mid-1980s, both in terms of quantity and quality. Central to the Party and state for hegemony in contemporary China, ICTs have also become essential vehicles and central stages for China to publicize itself and to pursue and act out what it perceives to be soft power. During just a matter of few years, CCTV-9 and China National Network have claimed their stake in the global communication landscape. Of course, the development of ICTs will not be the only factor determining whether China will be the next greatest power; nor will it necessarily be the most important factor. But it will be one very important facilitative factor for the rise of soft power for China.

Obviously the Chinese political system has helped its "foreign propaganda" and the pursuit for soft power to have come so far: wielding soft power resources in the information age is easier for China than in democracies where, as Nye points out,[50] public opinion and parliaments matter, and where politicians have less leeway to adopt tactics and strike deals than in autocracies. Furthermore, in a liberal society, many soft-power resources are separate from the government, such as firms, universities, foundations, churches and other nongovernmental groups that develop soft power of their own that may reinforce or be at odds with official foreign policy goals.[51] In other words, soft power does not belong to the government in the same degree that hard power does in a liberal society and government cannot control the culture, whereas successive Chinese state authorities have resorted to coercion and commands, while drawing symbolic resources from the cultural and ethnic nationalism to strengthen and legitimate their statist claim of representing the Chinese. The state orchestrated "all-dimensional, multi-channelled, wide-ranging and deep-levelled" pattern of "foreign propaganda" is possible only in an authoritarian country such as China.

However, what has helped in the expansion of soft power resources may also turn against it. ICTs are often a resource that helps produce soft power, but no mistake should be made in confusing soft power with resources. The expansion of soft power is not only about having the "hardware", the best facilities, but also about "software", i.e. cultural and political values, something that China is not unaware of, as is shown by the words of Zhao Qizheng, minister of the State Council Information Office: "For a nation with over 5,000 years of history, to export TV sets without exporting TV programs, or the Chinese values, is making China a production site."[52] What China has to offer to the world are not just quality manufacturing goods but also distinctive and attractive cultural values and products. In convincing the outside world of its peaceful intentions China faces the following challenges, apart from the obvious, which include the use of foreign languages and shortage of media professionals who can meet the educational and professional standards for the job in the short term.

First, the nature of media in China certainly goes against the nature of real-time global communication by satellite television and the Internet which requires accuracy, objectivity and above all timeliness. The nature of media in China decides that satellite TV channels and websites are vehicles of the Party-led state. As part of the China's state-run news media they are to "voluntarily keep conformity with the Party Central Committee with Hu Jintao as its General Secretary".[53] "Guidance of public opinion" remains a key term in China's press control regime. Although the Party has kept commercial-oriented entertainment programmes at an arm's length, the reporting of news remains subject to strict control. For instance, any reports on breaking events are organized and managed by the State Council Information Office, which drafts the reportage on the incident, and after approval from the Central Government and the State Council, it will organize to report it to the outside world.[54] It is difficult for the Chinese media, with its lack of competitiveness caused by strict government restrictions, to win large audiences abroad.

Second, unlike other regions where limitations, restrictions or quotas were set out of considerations more economic than political or ideological, China's international reach of media is primarily a government undertaking driven by the Party-state's political imperatives, rather than for the purpose of raising the economic benefit of cultural/media industry. Although the "all-dimensional, multi-channelled, wide-ranging and deep-levelled" "foreign propaganda" pattern requires all local TV stations and websites to provide programmes and information to CCTV and China National Network, local TV stations and websites have little commercial incentive to produce such programmes.[55] On the other hand, provincial satellite channels are keen to get outside China, but in 2004, a notice from the SARFT on "Further Strengthening the Radio, Film and Television 'Going-out Project' Management" stipulates that the "going-out" project should be planned and managed by the SARFT and that without its approval no radio or TV stations are allowed to rent or buy radio and television channels (frequency), time or to establish radio and television stations outside China.[56] This notice effectively stops any TV stations expanding outside China without approval from the SARFT.

Third, although China is using more nuanced strategies, the lines between domestic propaganda and international communication are not always sharply drawn. Contrary to democratic countries, where "many governments make the mistake of explaining domestic decisions only to their internal audiences and fail to realise the effect of their actions and the explanations of their actions on the international image of their country", the Chinese government makes a difference between Chinese domestic propaganda and international communication: more relaxed to outsiders and stricter with insiders for the sake of domestic political and social stability. It is believed that

> if propaganda for domestic purpose was simply carried over into international communication, many people would not like it. This includes some propaganda methods such as yelling slogans, which is proper for domestic propaganda, but international communication should focus on what the foreign audience needs.[57]

Nevertheless a quick look at the programmes on CCTV-9 shows that for the news programme, a paternalistic tone has been carried over to try to educate the international audience. For example, *Dialogue* claims to be "an authoritative talk show designed to inform and educate viewers worldwide and influence decision makers in governments, businesses and academia". *World Insight* also claims to be a "must-watch program for the intelligent viewer".

Fourth, Chinese culture has been projected on CCTV-9 and China National Network as a significant component of China's soft power (in fact, in official and academic discourse the "rise of cultural soft power" is more often found than the "rise of soft power"). However, China has been relying largely on its traditional culture as the main source of attraction. Probably China knows better than any other nations that the success of China's "peaceful development" relies on national revival that includes not only a return to economic superpower status, but also a revival of its own culture, a culture that is relevant to today's China and attractive to people of other cultures. At the People's National Conference 2006, Zhao Qizhen pointed out: "culture, unlike fossil which has lasting value because of its age, needs to develop to keep its vitality. It needs to be publicized to have influence and only when it has influence will it make a country powerful."[58] Jia Qinglin, chairman of the National Committee of the Chinese People's Political Consultative Conference, also cautioned in 2007 that "to enhance cultural 'soft power', China should maintain its cultural liveliness by promoting innovation, drawing useful foreign experience, while preserving traditional cultural heritage as well".

With increasing discussions within China on national revival and cultural soft power, the Confucian focus on self-cultivation towards humaneness, benevolence, righteousness, trustworthiness and filial piety has regained broad recognition, and has been argued by some proponents to be the core Chinese value system. Confucian values such as social harmony and respect for authority could prove very useful to Chinese leaders trying to manage the inequalities and injustices that have played an unfortunate part in China's economic rise. A revival of the ancient philosophical traditions of Confucianism and a return to ancient wisdom, leaders hope, will create a more moral society with a heightened sense of the importance of relationships – especially the hierarchical relationships of Confucianism that command obedience.

However, with nearly a century of rebellion against Confucianism it is more than a daunting task to rejuvenate the value of Chinese traditional culture, especially Confucianism, and to make it attractive to both the Chinese people and people of other cultures: the May Fourth Movement from 1917 to 1923 demanded for a total re-evaluation of Chinese culture and civilization, with its political positions in rejection of traditional Confucian morality and values. Lu Xun, still considered forefather of modern literature today, wrote about 30 short stories, most of which were thinly veiled attacks on various aspects of Chinese society such as the hypocrisy of Confucianism. In the 1960s and 1970s, China again repressed much of Confucian culture as part of its Cultural Revolution, burning temples and smashing artefacts in an attempt to purge the country of traditional influence. The June Fourth Movement in 1989 has been very often compared to the May Fourth Movement in the re-evaluation of Chinese traditional culture. Indeed, traditional culture was at the centre of blame for China's weak position in the world.

Furthermore, the effectiveness of any power resource depends on the context. Promoting positive images of one's country is not new, but the conditions for projecting soft power have been dramatically transformed. It is true that in recent years foreign interest in China and its culture has blossomed worldwide as a result of its growing weight in the world economy and China's continued efforts in promoting Chinese culture and language around the world. However, post-modern publics are generally sceptical of authority, and governments are often mistrusted. While many aspects of Chinese traditional culture are unique and attractive, China's advocacy of a harmonious world with its core value of respecting authority and order is hard to achieve in the absence of universally shared values, ideals and practices.

Finally, effective publicity is a two-way traffic that involves listening as well as talking. While the impact of China's communication strategy should be measured continually on a country-by-country basis in years to come, for one thing, television appeals to a more segmented market and local content has proved to be more important in reaching national audiences than the peek into Chinese culture on CCTV-9. China is not alone in this and the causes seem related more to market changes and economies of scale in satisfying local tastes than to political reactions. How much effect "foreign propaganda" websites will have in the global flow of information remains speculative, particularly because they are run and managed by the Party-led state. In the era of proliferation of satellite TV channels and websites, when "attention rather than information becomes scarce resources",[59] and when "information is demand-driven rather than supply driven",[60] China has to work hard in order to reach better to the international audience. At the same time, China should understand that growing access of peoples throughout the world to information via satellite-based radio and television and in particular the Internet is also creating a very different and in many ways less welcoming environment for any government broadcasting services abroad. They are both a conduit and a competitor for official government public diplomacy efforts. On a positive note, the Chinese government must take on the new task of formulating policies more promptly, flexibly and efficiently as it has to give due consideration to people both within and outside the country who are faced with the unlimited, multi-directional and instantaneous transmission of information that could be accessed from both outside and inside China.

To conclude, the development of ICTs presents China and indeed the whole world a tremendous opportunity for a new direction in the discourse of global cultural and information flows. China has been altering and will continue to alter its strategies for overseas publicity and the pursuit for soft power in adaptation to the development of ICTs. How much effect will the emergence of Chinese international media have on the changed and changing media environment in the world is still open to further analysis and investigation.

Notes

1 See, for example, Tai Zixue, *The Internet in China* (London: Routledge, 2006); Shanthi Kalathil, "China's New Media Sector: Keeping the State in", *The Pacific Review*, Vol. 16, No. 4, 2003, pp. 489–501; Tony Saich, "The External Challenge: the Information Revolution", in *Governance and Politics of China* (2nd edn) (New York: Palgrave Macmillan, 2004), pp. 337–42; Guobin Yang, "The Internet and Civil Society in China: a Preliminary Assessment", *Journal of Contemporary China*, Vol. 12, No. 36, August 2003, pp. 453–75; Yongnian Zheng and Guoguang Wu, "Information Technology, Public Space, and Collective Action in China", *Comparative Political Studies*, Vol. 38, No. 5, June 2005, pp. 507–36.

2 Tian Congming, president of the state-owned Xinhua News Agency, on a commemorative seminar in Beijing on the sixtieth anniversary of the English service provided by Xinhua News Agency, from the website of *People's Daily* at http://english.peopledaily.com.cn/200409/03/eng20040903_155773.html.

3 From China.com.cn, at www.china.com.cn/book/zhuanti/qkjc/txt/2005–09/23/content_5979478.htm (accessed 2 January 2008).

4 Ibid.

5 Zeng Jianhui, *Melting the Ice, Building a Bridge and Breaking Through* (*rongbing, jiaqiao, tuwei*) (Beijing: Wuzhou Publishing House, 2006), p. 10.

6 Ibid., p. 2.

7 Susan Shirk, *China, Fragile Superpower* (Oxford: Oxford University Press, 2007), p. 95.
8 Zeng Jianhui, p. 12.
9 Litao Zhao and Soon Heng Tan, "China's Cultural Rise: Visions and Challenges", *China: an International Journal*, Vol. 5, No. 1, 2007, pp. 97–108.
10 Joseph Nye, *Soft Power, The Means to Success in World Politics* (New York: PublicAffairs, 2004), p. 167.
11 Susan Shirk, *China, Fragile Superpower*, pp. 108–9.
12 From the website of the Office of Chinese Language Council International at www.hanban.org/cn_hanban/kzxy.php (accessed 31 January 2008).
13 The Chinese-style "harmonious society" as a concept was first put forward at the Fourth Plenary Session of the Sixteenth Central Committee of the CCP in September 2004. In his report to the National People's Congress in February 2005, Prime Minister Wen Jiabao explained that democracy, the rule of law, justice, sincerity and a solid social balance are features of a "harmonious society". In the same year, Chinese president Hu Jintao has extended the idea of building a "harmonious society" to the international community. At the 2005 Asian-African Summit, he proposed for the first time to build a "harmonious world".
14 Rumi Aoyama, "Chinese Public Diplomacy in the Multimedia Age: Public Diplomacy and Civil Diplomacy", *Waseda chapters*, December 2004.
15 Joseph Nye, *Soft Power, The Means to Success in World Politics*, p. 164.
16 Ibid., p. 39.
17 From the website of *Economics Daily* at www.bmedia.com.cn/newshtml/JPWZ/20060818085647.htm (accessed 4 January 2008).
18 Yik-chan Chin, *From the Local to the Global: Chinese Television from 1996 to 2003* (2005) unpublished dissertation, p. 125.
19 Zeng Jianhui, *Melting the Ice, Building a Bridge and Breaking Through*, p. 12.
20 Ibid., p. 130.
21 Guo Ke, Wang Wei and Sang Cuilin, "Globalizing the Local: How China's English TV Media Influence the World?", *Media Research*, 4, 2004, online, available at: http://rirt.cuc.edu.cn/html/meijieyanjiu/2007/0612/262.html (accessed 7 January 2008).
22 Yik-chan Chin, *From the Local to the Global: Chinese Television from 1996 to 2003*, p. 191.
23 *Murdoch Wins China Cable TV Deal*, BBC News, 23 October 2001, online, available at: http://news.bbc.co.uk/1/hi/entertainment/1721160.stm (accessed 7 January 2008).
24 *China Offers Murdoch TV Deal*, BBC News, 6 September 2001, online, available at: http://news.bbc.co.uk/1/hi/business/1528011.stm (accessed 7 January 2008).
25 Ibid.
26 Yik-chan Chin, *From the Local to the Global: Chinese Television from 1996 to 2003*, p. 191.
27 The other criteria, according to Chin (see note 17), include the following: in the first year of landing, foreign satellite channels were only allowed to enter the Guangdong Cable TV station's network which has about 600,000 households. In the second year and thereafter, depending on mutual agreement, the coverage area could be enlarged. Second, each party, i.e. the Guangdong bureau on behalf of the Chinese government or the corresponding authority in the US, has the equal right to blank or suspend the other's satellite channel and programmes if its content break the host country's laws, regulations and rules. Last, each party has the equal right to insert advertisements in the other's channel. During prime time, this is two minutes of advertisements per hour, otherwise, three minutes.
28 From the website of the Great Wall TV Platform at www.gw-tv.cn/aboutus/ (accessed 7 January 2008).
29 Robert J. Klotz, *The Politics of Internet Communication* (Oxford: Rowman & Littlefield, 2004), p. 1.

30 Nicholas W. Geidner, "Looking Toward 2008: The Effects of New Media on the Political Process", *The Review of Communication*, Vol. 6, Nos 1–2, January–April 2006, pp. 93–100.

31 Zhan Xinhui and Yang Chunlan, *News Websites between Traditional Functions and Changes*, at the website of the Xinhua News Agency on 10 October 2006, at http://news.xinhuanet.com/newmedia/2006–10/10/content_5184606.htm (accessed 8 January 2008).

32 From a speech of Cai Mingzhao, deputy director of the Information Office of the State Council, from the website of China's State Council Information Office, at www.scio.gov.cn/gzdt/ldhd/zyjhyls/200702/t108311.htm (accessed 8 January 2008).

33 Shu Bin, Wang Zhonglang, "National Key News Websites, a Growing Force in China", from the website of *People's Daily* on 7 April 2005, at http://media.people.com.cn/GB/22114/46419/46420/3302778.html (accessed 8 January 2008).

34 www.bjreview.com.cn/txt/2006–12/20/content_51383.htm, accessed on 31.01.2008.

35 From the website of *Shanghai Daily* at www.shanghaidaily.com/about.asp, accessed on 08.01.2008.

36 "China National Network Builds up a Foreign Publicity Platform together with Other Local Websites", from *People's Daily* on 28 February 2001 at www.people.com.cn/GB/chapter464/5074/538650.html (accessed 8 January 2008).

37 Guo Ke, Wang Wei and Sang Cuilin, "Globalizing the Local:How China's English TV Media Influence the World?".

38 From the website of CCTV at www.cctv.com/program/asiatoday/01/01/index.shtml (accessed 18 January 2008).

39 Ibid.

40 From the website of CCTV at www.cctv.com/program/worldwidewatch/01/01/index.shtml (accessed 18 January 2008).

41 www.cctv.com/program/e_dialogue/01/about/index.shtml (accessed 31 January 2008).

42 www.cctv.com/program/worldinsight/01/01/index.shtml (accessed 31 January 2008).

43 Most of the descriptions of the programmes are taken from CCTV's website at www.cctv.com/english/index.shtml (accessed 10 January 2008).

44 See note 13.

45 Bin Zhao, "Popular Family Television and Party Ideology: the Spring Festival Eve Happy Gathering", *Media, Culture & Society*, 1998, pp. 43–58.

46 Joseph Nye, *Soft Power, The Means to Success in World Politics*, p. 161.

47 Yik-chan Chin, *From the Local to the Global: Chinese Television from 1996 to 2003*, p. 124.

48 From *People's Daily online* (English), 26 May 2006, *China Promotes its Culture Overseas to Dissolve "China Threat"*, at http://english.peopledaily.com.cn/200605/28/eng20060528_269209.html (accessed 9 January 2008).

49 Joseph Nye, *Soft Power, The Means to Success in World Politics*, pp. 31–2.

50 Joseph Nye, *Soft Power, The Means to Success in World Politics*, p. 16.

51 Ibid., p. 17.

52 From the website of Xinhua News Agency, at http://news.xinhuanet.com/newmedia/2006–03/10/content_4283141.htm (accessed 16 January 2008).

53 Liu Yunshan, *Publicity Work Must Serve Reform, Stability*, opening speech at a national conference on publicity work in April 2005, from the website of *People's Daily* at http://english.people.com.cn/200504/26/eng20050426_182683.html (accessed 6 June 2007).

54 Zeng Jianhui, *Melting the Ice, Building a Bridge and Breaking Through*, p. 27.

55 See *National TV Foreign Propaganda Co-operation Conference 2006 in Yunan*, from the website of CCTV at www.cctv.com/tvguide/special/wyh/20050907/100973.shtml (accessed 16 January 2008).

56 From the website of the SARFT, at www.chinasarft.gov.cn/articles/2004/10/26/20070919141825580844.html (accessed 18 January 2008).

57 Wu Zheng, "Transforming the Concept of the International Communication: Communicating A True Image of China to the World", in *China's Need for a Strategy of International Communication* (Beijing: Changzheng Publishing House, 2001), pp. 39–46, from the website of the US Embassy in Beijing at www.usembassy-china.org.cn/sandt/chinamedia.html (accessed 16 January 2008).

58 From China National Network at www.china.org.cn/chinese/zhuanti/2006lh/1148770.htm (accessed 16 January 2008).

59 Joseph Nye, *Soft Power, The Means to Success in World Politics*, p. 106.

60 Philip Seib, "New Media and Prospects for Democratisation", in Philip Seib (ed.), *New Media and the New Middle East* (New York: Palgrave Macmillan, 2007), p. 10.

7 Web engineering in the Chinese context

"Let a hundred flowers bloom, a hundred schools of thought contend"

Kieron O'Hara

Introduction

There have been a number of highly illuminating studies of the effects of the Internet or the World Wide Web on Chinese society and politics – indeed there are many fascinating ones in this book. The clash between the cutting edge of technology and a relatively conservative society, or, seen from another angle, between an American, liberal and liberalising technology on a giant nation still trying to find its post-Marxian ideological bearings, is obviously interesting, not to say dramatic, and is one of the key arenas for ideological conflict in the twenty-first century.[1] But social science, like any intellectual endeavour, must make simplifying assumptions, and one that is usually, if not always, made in this field is that the technology is exogenous, imposed from without, a black box with inputs and outputs, but which is not fundamentally changed by the interaction. This is, however, an untrue assumption; the Internet and the Web are defined by complex and well-planned sets of engineering protocols – human creations – and they can be changed, or broken, by anyone coming into contact with them.

In this chapter, I attempt to look at the problem the other way around, and consider the potential effects of Chinese policy towards the World Wide Web. I want to think about the Web endogenously, as a piece of engineering, what assumptions underlie it, how it has developed and how it works (avoiding technicalities as far as possible), and then I will speculate about how Chinese interaction with it could create change in it. In the opening section, I will briefly describe how the Web, and the Internet on top of which it sits, developed, and what it is *for*. Then, I will consider the assumptions and principles on which the Web is founded. In that context, I will then move onto thinking about China's Web presence, and the effect that that could make, before concluding with the fundamental dilemma that faces not only the Chinese government as it considers how to interface with the Web, but also the standards bodies which administer the Web as they export their technologies to China and other illiberal polities.

The history and architecture of the Web

So completely has the Web entered the lives of people in Western democracies (particularly those on the right side of the various perceived digital divides) in the last few years that it is easy to forget how recent a development it is. The present author got his first glimpse of the Web – downloading a paper in the UK from a server in Stanford – in 1993. Ho hum, thought he. By 2000, the Web was an indispensable tool for scientific research. This section will rehearse some of the recent history of information technology, showing how the Web has built on the earlier development of the Internet.

The development of the Internet

The Internet is basically a network of computer networks. Small networks of computers, linked by telephone line or other communication routes to allow information to be passed between them, are themselves linked together, allowing information from any machine on any of the networks to be passed to any other. The key to the success of the Internet (as opposed to other methods of computer networking) is the general-purpose and universal nature of the links. Before the Internet, smaller computer networks could be and were supported by those with sufficient resources (often for military, academic, governmental or commercial applications), and those networks could be connected together. But the connections between networks tended to be special purpose, individually-tailored for the anticipated transfer of specific items of information in a specific form. The beauty of the Internet – often unappreciated – is that its protocols, which we shall describe briefly below, make few assumptions about the information that will be passed between networks, making it a uniquely general purpose tool. Information held in a wide variety of electronic representations, most unanticipated by the Internet's developers, can be passed around, pretty efficiently too, which is the root of its success. The key developments of the Internet happened during the 1960s.

Defence

The original Internet was largely driven by the needs of the US defence establishment, and its main precursor (ARPANET) was named after the US Dept. of Defence's Advanced Research Projects Agency (ARPA), and made its appearance on 21 November 1969. The aim was to provide large-scale communications that were efficient yet resistant to combat disruption. The system devised for routing information was a method called *packet switching*, in which a message was, in effect, chopped into little pieces (packets), which were then sent to the destination computer by separate routes. The destination computer assembled the packets into a complete message when it had received them all.[2]

The packets would be sent by a method called *dynamic routing*, in which the path by which they were sent would not be determined in advance, but worked out at the time. The pathway would be along the connections between individual computers in the network; a packet would be received by a computer, which would then try to send it to another computer which it reckoned would be closer to the ultimate destination if possible. So, for instance, in Figure 7.1, the aim is to get information from computer A to computer B. There is a direct route, but this can easily be knocked out. If it is the only route, then we have a bottleneck, and the connection between A and B is highly vulnerable. But if A and B are connected in a network, then there are several alternative routes. For instance, there is a route A–F–E–B. The network structure is much more robust; if this more complex route is compromised by another attack (say, the link from E to B is knocked out), then other routes, such as A–F–E–I–D–L–K–B (pictured) can be used. This is certainly not an exact science, but electronic transactions happened quickly enough that the information would eventually reach the destination in a reasonable time (in today's high-bandwidth world, downloads happen almost instantaneously, and a delay of even ten seconds is regarded as unacceptable). The dynamic routing algorithms would send each packet by a different route to the destination.

Dynamic routing met the criteria for a system of information passing with defensive capabilities. The network was robust against attack, largely because it avoided communications *hubs*. A hub is an area with many connections, often crucial for a network. If the hub is knocked out by attacks, then the connectivity of the network is reduced dramatically – indeed, it can fall into separate disjoint networks. Similarly, if two halves of the network were connected only by a small number of communications lines, then the network can be subverted and may be

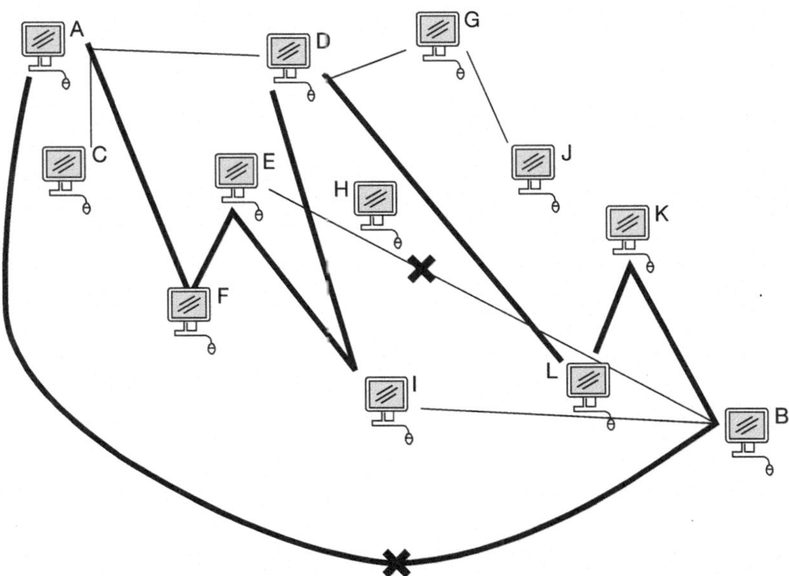

Figure 7.1 Getting information from A to B in a compromised network.

split by knocking out those lines. The packet switching system means that vulnerabilities stemming from hubs and/or crucial lines can be avoided by increasing connections between all parts of the network. Knocking out some telephone lines or computers will be damaging, inevitably, but not fatal to the network because there should always be alternative ways around. Even so, where there are bottlenecks there can still be problems. In February 2008, damage to the two undersea cables that carry 90 per cent of the data traffic through the Suez Canal caused severe disruption to connectivity in the Middle East.[3]

Packet switching is also efficient, as communications hubs can cause bottlenecks if information traffic grows too quickly for their infrastructure. If all messages have to pass through a central exchange, then every time an extra computer is added to the network, the number of potential sender–receiver pairs doubles. As the network grows arithmetically, the information traffic tends to grow geometrically, and if the traffic management system in the hub cannot scale, the growth of the system will be restricted by congestion. By allowing packets to be sent opportunistically from computer to computer along any line that is available and plausible, messages reach their destination more efficiently. If congestion starts to build up somewhere in the system, packets can be routed around it (and, with dynamic routing, these decisions can be taken instantly while the packet is en route).

Science and academe

But the ARPANET, and the Internet which followed (the term 'Internet' was first used in this context in 1974), obviously had advantages beyond defence – after all, their four desiderata: avoiding congestion; efficiency; allowing general purpose communications; and being scalable, are appealing to any organisation with large-scale information needs.[4] In particular, the scientific and academic communities, whose day-to-day activities concern the transfer of information to fellow researchers, students, the media and the general public, were obviously going to be interested. The Internet became, over the 1970s and 1980s, an important academic tool. When one was working on a computer connected to the Internet or its precursors, one suddenly had several informational and communicational options that were not available before. One could send messages (email) to people working on other computers using a system that imposed a low overhead for both sender and receiver (the sender did not need to leave his or her chair, while the receiver could access the message at a convenient time). One could get remote access to data or papers held on other computers. Files could be shared between communities. And two or more people, in remote locations, could collaborate in writing or editing files. Science and academic research became the driving ethos behind the Internet, and as a result Internet research tended to take the form of methods to *remove the friction* out of the journey of a piece of information, rather than methods to *restrict* the flow. One might wish to restrict the flow of information to promote security of intellectual property or state secrets, for instance, or the privacy of people referred to by that information. But since the user base of the Internet at this time was relatively small, and relatively well-behaved, these were not priorities.

Standardisation and protocols

For all its complexity, the Internet is basically a very simple device. It is made up of hardware and software; the hardware, computers, telephone lines etc., is not our concern. The software consists of a series of *protocols* that define how computers talk to each other. There are two levels of protocols.

The first level is the *Internet Protocol* (IP) itself. This is the heart of the Internet – a better definition of the Internet than the one given above is a network of computer networks linked using IP. This defines the packets that are routed about the system. Above that sits the *Transmission Control Protocol* (TCP), which defines the routing system for the information packets. In effect, TCP makes a virtual connection between the sender and the receiver, even if they are not directly connected. It also treats each packet equally – although each packet needs to indicate its relationship to the rest of the message and its destination, the content of the packet need not be read en route, and so the whole system treats the greatest works of philosophy and the least significant pieces of tittle-tattle with equal reverence and respect. This is a good thing from the network point of view, because any method of information transfer which involved reading the content of information packets would slow the system down and create bottlenecks.

There are alternatives to TCP and IP, but these have been easily the most successful. The two protocols are often referred to together, as the TCP/IP suite.[5] The TCP/IP suite provides a basic platform upon which further applications can be defined to use the Internet, exploiting the very clean method of transferring information across a network. The freedom of movement of information whatever form it takes means that TCP/IP is an extremely versatile platform which can be used by a wide variety of applications. One such application, sitting atop the Internet, has been very successful indeed – the *World Wide Web*.[6]

The development of the World Wide Web

It is fair to say that the World Wide Web (WWW, or Web – I will use these terms interchangeably) is the main application that nowadays brings people to the Internet, so that recent users come to other applications (such as email) afterwards. The essence of the WWW is to link hypertext documents using the Internet. A browser is used to access material that may be in any one of a number of media – text, pictures, video, sound – and then can follow hyperlinks from document to document. Key technologies include the Hypertext Transfer Protocol (http, and its secure variant https), which is a protocol telling computers how to access and retrieve hypertext pages, and the Hypertext Markup Language (HTML), which enables the description of the structure of a document to be seen online (e.g. in terms of *headings*, *lists* and so on), and its supplementation with other objects, such as embedded images, interactive forms, or links to other documents. There are other protocols, languages and technical requirements (in particular, more flexible markup languages, such as XML), but http and HTML are the basics. The China Policy Institute at Nottingham University has a homepage: www.nottingham.ac.uk/china-policy-institute/, which is written in HTML, and – as its address tells you – is transferred to your computer when you download it using http. This application – the WWW – sits neatly on top of the TCP/IP suite of protocols that defines the Internet. It is the neutrality and careful design of TCP/IP that has allowed the WWW to be created; if TCP/IP were designed less elegantly (if it made more assumptions about the information it was used to transfer), it would not be so straightforward to design something like the WWW that can sit on top of the platform. And, similarly, the WWW is designed to be as neutral as possible about applications that sit on top of it.

The end result is the huge hypermedia/multimedia space that is the WWW, which in effect allows you to treat every Web page as potentially sitting as a file on the user's computer. Markup languages such as HTML tell the individual machine how to display (or *render*, to use the technical term) the information. The way it is rendered will vary from computer to computer, and indeed window to window on a computer (open two windows with your Web browser, make them different dimensions, and then download the China Policy Institute's page onto each of them – it will appear differently, yet coherently, in both, thanks to HTML).

Navigating through the WWW is non-trivial, but made possible by various technologies. HTML allows links to be made democratically, from a page to any other you like; the reader, if she wishes, clicks on a link to go to the next page. http cleverly defines names of webpages in such a way that the computer can use the name to find the location of the resource that the name refers to. So, for instance, www.nottingham.ac.uk/china-policy-institute/ tells the computer to look for the contents of a directory called china-policy-institute on a computer server which is called www.nottingham.ac.uk. The name of the page is designed to be exactly the same as a conventional representation of its location (address). The simple idea of conflating names and addresses has proven to be very powerful.

A third method of navigation became required once the Web grew beyond a certain size, and people wanted access to Web pages with which they were not necessarily acquainted, and so the search engine was born (Google being the most successful at the time of writing). Search engines generally have three aspects: they must sample and store as much of the Web as they can (a huge engineering task), they must be able to search through their sample quickly and efficiently for a keyword or other method of identifying a potentially interesting page, and they must then present what may be a very large quantity of information to the user. This last is the most controversial; Google uses a variation of an algorithm called *PageRank* which orders the retrieved pages in order of presumed importance. The problem with search engines is to keep their performance acceptable as the size of the WWW increases – the search engines popular in the 1990s have not been able to cope, by and large, with the scale of the current WWW, and Google has claimed top spot.[7] To see how difficult a task that is, and what feats of engineering good search engines are, consider a Google search for the three keywords 'china' 'policy' and 'institute' performed on 4 January 2008. That search retrieved, from Google's stored model of the WWW, an astonishing 51,600,000 pages, all of which used the three keywords somewhere in their text. What is even more astonishing is that the retrieval took a mere 0.29 seconds. And the brilliance of PageRank is shown by the fact that, once it had ordered those 51.6 million pages on the basis of its assumptions about the searcher's requirements, the homepage of the China Policy Institute at Nottingham (for which I was indeed looking) was *first on the list*. Second on the list was the Wikipedia page describing the CPI (and including a picture of its lovely headquarters at China House). Any human attempt to perform this task on this scale would not only take weeks rather than fractions of a second, but would also be massively more error-prone.[8]

Properties of the WWW

This architecture means that the WWW has certain important properties, which are intended to be invariant aspects of the Web experience. In other words, if these properties were subverted, then the Web experience would be lessened, and the WWW would be reduced to something closer to the average information dispersal technology.

Such desirable properties include:

- **Decentralisation**. As a webpage author, you can link to any other page, resource or repository of data that has been published online, and indeed the creator of any other Web resource can link to you. There is no central hub to monitor linking – which helps efficiency of course, but also promotes the freedom to cite or reproduce the content of whomsoever one feels significant. Similarly, there is no hierarchical information structure, but rather a decentralised network, so information can be gathered direct from the appropriate source. The lack of a hierarchy rules out direct and pervasive censorship.
- **Open standards**. The growth of the WWW is down to the fact that several heterogeneous representation formats, languages and file types can peacefully coexist on it. This is because the WWW, which is defined by standards for the formalisms that make it up, uses open standards that can be accessed, for free, by anyone. The WWW is not a restricted piece of intellectual property. Someone writing an application for the Web can write their application, and connect it to the Web using these openly available standards. No one has to write in a particular computer language, or to pay a licence fee, in order to build an application on the WWW, which dramatically reduces the barriers to entry.
- **Living texts**. HTML is designed to allow texts to be commented on, added to, included in other texts, referred to and linked to. Digital technology keeps texts alive and open in a way that paper does not. Think, for instance, of the comments that follow an article in an online newspaper, compared to the closure that the paper version of the newspaper can rely on; any commenting would have to be done in subsequent editions of the paper, perhaps

on the letters page, and so the newspaper retains editorial control. In an online paper, the original article is often a seed for a long debate (which is admittedly often garbage!), and so the boundary between writer and reader is blurred. The author tends to lose control of his or her creation – ironically an effect that Plato, through the mouth of Socrates, predicted would happen (in the *Phaedrus*) with the invention of writing!

- **Non-linearity**. WWW texts can of course be linear, but equally they can exploit the hypertextual aspects of the WWW and adopt a non-linear structure, allowing the reader to follow links through a site as they interest him or her. So, for instance, a highly allusive text such as Eliot's *The Waste Land* can be rendered in such a way that one can follow the allusions around the WWW, or through the poem.[9]
- **Serendipitous reuse**. Because linking is so democratic, material can end up being reused serendipitously in contexts undreamt of by the author. In the paper era, the value of knowledge was created by *scarcity* – methods for allowing the collection of rents on intellectual property, such as copyright or patents, meant that knowledge was valuable by virtue of the restrictions placed on it. A user would have to pay (buy a book, or pay royalties or licence fees) to get hold of it. In the digital age, knowledge adds value through abundance – knowledge of little intrinsic value in an isolated context can have value added to it because it can easily be placed in a new context. So, for example, the diary of an ordinary person of the eighteenth century might be, in isolation, of interest mainly to the specialist historian. But in the context of a large number of such documents, it could be a great value for a range of social historians, philosophers and scientists – for instance, meteorologists could gain a lot of useful confirmatory evidence about weather patterns.

Use of the WWW

The WWW, then, is a decentralised information technology designed to have the properties outlined above. It has always, as we have seen, been defined by rules, and the rules that have determined its features have always depended on it context, and the perceived threats to it. How, then, has the WWW generally been used?

Science and the WWW

Perhaps the most important early adopters of the WWW were scientists. The performance of science, which not by coincidence has become much more data-heavy over the last few years, is now highly dependent on the Web and the Internet, serious disruption to which would produce something of a crisis. For the scientist, the WWW provides speedy access to documents, and data (and to the computing power to process those data). Various bottlenecks that typically slow down the dissemination of scientific research, such as the long period of time which publication of a book or journal article, and the limited amount of space and purchasing power available to university libraries, can be side-stepped by simply putting one's papers on the Web. This time factor is very important, as in many disciplines knowledge is advancing faster than it can be written about. The WWW also facilitates collaborative work – virtually all empirical work in the sciences and social sciences is now performed jointly by a number of researchers who are very often at different institutions.

Commerce and the WWW

During the mid-1990s, the use of the WWW moved from the universities to the private sector, with companies latching onto the commercial possibilities, and consumers relishing the opportunities to shop and bank online. These developments did require a change of culture of the WWW.[10] Conceived as a knowledge-sharing technology for the use of scientists and researchers, most WWW applications assumed a benign user base acting in good faith with the good of a community in mind as well as self-interest, and there was a clear instrumental value in the freedom to use knowledge created by others. These assumptions obviously do not hold in the commercial world.

In the first place, when money is being passed around during a commercial transaction, identity becomes important. It was famously pointed out in a *New Yorker* cartoon that "on the Internet no-one knows you're a dog", and this fluidity of identity was found attractive by many of its early adopters. In the world of science, hoaxes and forgeries are rare, so if a scientific paper appeared apparently written by, say, Kieron O'Hara, one could assume with some certainty that Kieron O'Hara was the author. However, the same is not true when presented with credit card details. The flip side of the *New Yorker* joke became apparent – sometimes it's useful to be able to prove that you are *not* a dog. Hence authentication procedures needed to be developed for online use. This, notoriously, created the concomitant problem that once an online identity was established, that in itself became a commodity of value, and the hitherto undeveloped crime of identity theft became the bane of many people's lives.

Similarly, other security measures were needed. Attempts to develop a purely online currency never really took off, but protocols allowing credit cards to be used online without giving away too much personal information were obviously required. One did not want fraudulent transactions performed using one's card, but equally one did want authorised transactions to go through relatively smoothly and easily. As with all aspects of commerce, complex security mechanisms (passwords, security codes) put off casual users and prevent sectoral growth.

Third, as users were putting information online, privacy protection was also needed. Avoiding identity theft is an aspect of this, but all online activity leaves some kind of trace, and those traces can be embarrassing. This is obviously true in industries such as pornography, but is also a factor in people seeking particular types of healthcare, buying subversive books or trading in shares, for example. It may be that people acting perfectly properly still do not want their details shared with others, perhaps because they do not want to be bombarded with marketing material.[11]

Fourth, there is also the important issue of intellectual property. Sharing data is of basic importance in science, but in popular music or literature, the artists' incomes are affected by royalties paid as a result of measurable purchases of their material. There are certainly good arguments that this sort of restriction of intellectual property is not the best thing for the arts, or even for the artists, but it remains the case that someone downloading a piece of music from a peer-to-peer file-sharing site is not contributing to the artist's income in the same way that a purchaser of a CD will be. Similar arguments surrounded the early recording industry (it was thought that records would destroy the sheet music industry, which they did, but of course no one minds that now), and the business model of the large record companies will change, but that innovating work still needs to be done.[12]

Finally, methods of communication that assume good faith can easily be undermined by those of bad faith. Several methods of swindling or pestering have been developed by people exploiting straightforward methods of transferring information, perhaps most notably spam and phishing, each of which is a serious problem in the online world which developed only as the WWW moved away from its academic roots.

The imperatives of the 1990s

The result of these developments in the WWW was that in the 1990s, the main imperative was to ensure that regulation was light, and governments were kept away from the Web as far as possible. It was felt that governments would interfere with the free flow of information, and free markets, and instead would try to impose restrictive security cordons on the WWW that would impede information flow, and the WWW's growth.

For example, Ira Magaziner, Bill Clinton's chief Internet policy advisor, argued that:

> Commerce on the Internet could total tens of billions of dollars by the turn of the century. For this potential to be realized fully, governments must adopt a non-regulatory, market-oriented approach to electronic commerce, one that facilitates the emergence of a transparent and predictable legal environment to support global business and commerce.
>
> Official decision makers must respect the unique nature of the medium and recognize that widespread competition and increased consumer choice should be the defining features of the new digital marketplace.[13]

Principles underlying the WWW

The result of this line of development of the WWW, and indeed the Internet, was a decentralised system designed to promote the free flow of information. In particular, the WWW became a system governed, explicitly or implicitly, on a series of principles or norms.

- **Liberalism**. The WWW is a space engineered on liberal principles, where freedom of speech is a privileged value. This is a particularly interesting point, as it has dual aspects. The WWW is a liberal space, where interactions are conceived of in a liberal manner. But also the success of the WWW, in terms of its growth (both of users, and of information held on it) depends on a liberal attitude to all the information packets moving around it.
- **Conversation and dialogue**. The WWW is intended to promote free, uninhibited self-expression, dialogue and compromise where possible.
- **The free flow of information**. Issues such as intellectual property and copyright intrude, but basically the more information flowing around the WWW, the better.
- **Adding value through abundance and reuse**. If the WWW had a single purpose, it would be to add value to information through its serendipitous reuse in novel situations, as noted above.
- **Promotion of science and human progress**. In all this, the WWW embodies a whiggish point of view that society can progress, and does so through the development of intellectual capacities, among other things. A WWW which promoted pseudo-science, conspiracy theories and pornography while failing to serve science would be seen as something of a failure.
- **A platform upon which undreamt of applications can be built**. As with TCP/IP, the WWW is intended to be a clean technological platform, making as few assumptions as possible about how it will be developed, upon which new applications can be built even though they are as yet unplanned. In this way, new technologies can appear almost overnight on the WWW, because once they are developed and made available, there is nothing impeding the rapid development of a user base. Examples of some of the technologies which have grown up on top of the WWW and the Internet include: the Semantic Web; Web services; Web 2.0 and social software; peer-to-peer systems; software agents; pervasive or ubiquitous computing; the mobile Web; grid computing; personalised computing services; e-commerce systems; revolutionary media such as Google; and massive multiplayer online role-playing games. All of these have high numbers of users, and none of them could work if it were not for the clean infrastructure below them.

It can be seen that many of these principles, though commonly accepted in the Western and Western-style democracies, are not universally accepted across the globe. There are many states of varying levels of illiberalism which would wish to oppose some or all of these principles, and it is to one of these, China, to which I will now turn.

China and the WWW

Chinese public policy in the twenty-first century can be characterised as continuing economic reform in advance of, or instead of, political reform. The government wishes to ensure the welfare and prosperity of its people, without accepting strong threats to its own position, or to a loosely-defined "social harmony". There are a number of potential threats to that harmony of course, including increasing inequalities of wealth, clear divides between urban and rural interests, major migrations both internally and externally, serious environmental issues looming and restive ethnic minorities in the West and South. But one major factor, as perceived (probably correctly) by the Chinese authorities is the WWW, which favours various social groups on the right side of the digital divide, and has also been used by subversive organisations. Indeed, the Internet and the Web have actually improved Chinese governance in some respects, as their provision of timely information undermined the attempts of regional and party officials to suppress bad news (perhaps most notably about the SARS outbreak and the rising number of riots across China).

However, as has also been pointed out, the WWW is an important part of economic reform, helping free up information in markets, and putting consumers and small businesses in touch with other businesses. The Chinese e-commerce site alibaba.com, and the associated auction site taobao.com, both founded and at the time of writing run by Jack Ma (Ma Yun), are among the most successful, and most heavily used, Internet sites in the world, for example. Furthermore, given that China has a number of ambitions in science and technology, the role of the Web in scientific research is, as has been noted, vital. The Chinese government, therefore, has in general tried to pursue a strategy of exploiting the WWW for commercial and scientific purposes, while trying to prevent it undermining social harmony.

The principle of abundance of information is replaced by restriction, notably on political commentary and political speech, as well as on "inappropriate" material such as pornography, and on technical information about how to get around security and censorship systems.[14] Control of the Web is shifted as far as possible from users to the government, and carriers of information, whose liability is in most polities limited, are turned into agents of the state.[15] And in part the hands-off strategy developed during the 1990s, to support the use of the WWW in science, research and commerce, which restricted the regulation of the Web, has allowed China (and other illiberal regimes) to flout liberal principles in this way. China now regularly uses Internet filtering technologies, looking for specific keywords or IP addresses, while regulating bloggers and Internet cafés, suborning big Western Internet firms such as Yahoo! and Google, all the while employing 30,000 secret policemen to trawl the Web for content of which it disapproves.[16]

There are arguments for censorship of course, and in many Eastern nations and cultures, social harmony is valued above individual freedom to some extent at least. But what is particularly worrying about the Chinese model in the context of the WWW is that it is particularly pernicious. For instance, in Saudi Arabia, censorship is transparent, and documented by the Internet Services Unit. The filtering is supported by a highly conservative society, to the extent that many Saudis report sites that should be made unavailable within Saudi Arabia to the authorities. There is a notification given when access is denied to a sensitive website, and there is a possibility of appeal; one can apply to the authorities that access be restored. In Singapore, there is relatively little direct filtering of the WWW by the Media Development Authority, and instead the authorities rely on muscular use of defamation laws and existing legal formulae, which are already used to suppress political comment in print and TV media. In North Korea, the entire country is pretty well cut off from the WWW, and a small number of individuals are licensed to trawl for content that can be made available to users of that nation's Intranet.[17]

In contrast, the Chinese approach is centralised, and more importantly, opaque. When, in China, one tries to download www.bbc.co.uk, the Web browser hangs. As a user, one is unaware whether there is a problem with the site, or whether it has been blocked (it will have been blocked). If one does a Web search in China, then pages are fairly likely to be blocked from one's search; even if one has used an unobjectionable keyword, sites which contain banned keywords (such as 'Falun Gong') will not appear. But again one is not notified that that has happened. As we have seen, the notions of transparency and equality of information are essential for the WWW to work on a number of levels, whether information is conceived in engineering terms as a packet of meaningful data encoded digitally, or in social terms as a series of informative propositions. The Chinese attitude is to replace transparency with opacity, making the operation of the Web unclear. Censorship is one thing – indeed, many users' computers censor content using spam filters or filters such as Net Nanny or CYBERsitter – but it is possible to censor transparently, making it clear what has been removed.

Conclusion: a dilemma

Does this matter? The short answer is 'yes' – perhaps most obviously in terms of sheer numbers. China's Internet usage is large and increasing. According to both the China Internet Network Information Centre[18] and Internet World Stats,[19] the Chinese online presence at the time of writing is second only to the USA, more than their next two rivals put together; it is widely expected that (particularly after the spectacular rates of growth recorded in 2007), China will overtake the USA in 2008. More to the point, Internet penetration (the number of people in the population using the Internet) is a very low 12.3 per cent, compared to relatively mature markets such as the United States (penetration 69.7 per cent), the United Kingdom (62.3 per cent), South Korea (66.5 per cent) and Japan (67.1 per cent). Only India and Indonesia, of the major Internet-using nations, have comparable "room to grow".[20]

The WWW has grown because of its support of the free and democratic flow of information; indeed, it is the free flow where value is added to information. The Chinese government, as part and parcel of its phased reform strategy, is much more interested in the value than the freedom – while for their part, those developing the WWW tend to work within a liberal paradigm, and are keener on the freedom than the regulation that must follow. This is a serious issue for those steering the development of the WWW.

Daniel J. Weitzner, at the time of writing Director of the World Wide Web Consortium's technology and society activities, has made the following suggestions for a way forward:[21]

- National sovereignty: accept the inevitable. China will clearly remain in charge of its own laws, and is entitled as a sovereign nation to regulate behaviour within its borders. This cannot be wished away. It may be that a "principled" approach to China could result in a vast reduction of digital contact, as urged by a number of NGOs including, for instance, Reporters Without Borders.[22] But this does ignore the possibility of using the WWW to ease China into a more liberal stance, as well as – given the size of the Chinese online presence – risking the integrity and connectivity of the WWW itself. A hardline approach to China could split the WWW into two more or less separate networks; currently it is not clear how damaging this might be.
- Support free expression. Having said that, it is clear that free expression is generally taken to be a human right by most international organisations, and that support – and criticism of countries that do not respect it – should be forthcoming in the context of the WWW.
- Global transparency. National laws and government actions should be transparent – if there is censorship of the WWW, then the extent of that censorship, and the principles underlying it should be made clear. Neither of these is true in the Chinese case; indeed, the uncertainty in the Chinese system leads, and is no doubt intended to lead, to self-censorship, as commentators are literally unaware of how much what they say will be tolerated.[23]

The very name "World Wide Web" is a statement of ambition. The WWW itself was founded by liberals, and has advanced on impeccably liberal principles.[24] It has become a space in which politics can take place,[25] and a key tool to support development, democracy and transparent governance.[26] As long as most users of the WWW were based in Western-style democracies, this was not a problem, but now that these markets are maturing, the Web's expansion in the next few years will inevitably be in illiberal communities. This is a problem for illiberal countries such as China, as has often been pointed out, but actually it is a problem for the Web too. The WWW is the most complex piece of technology ever built, yet also based on simple principles, and the idea of a democratic, decentralised space of linked information has proved to be incredibly powerful. There are serious issues about how to export that vision into illiberal polities, while preserving the essential invariants of the Web experience, to which can be traced its power.

Notes

1 Cf. e.g. Christopher R. Hughes and Gudrun Wacker (eds), *China and the Internet: Politics of the Digital Leap Forward* (London: RoutledgeCurzon, 2003); Françoise Mengin (ed.), *Cyber China: Reshaping National Identities in the Age of Information*

(Basingstoke: Palgrave Macmillan, 2004); Jens Damm and Simona Thomas (eds), *Chinese Cyberspaces: Technological Changes and Political Effects* (London: RoutledgeCurzon, 2005); Zixue Tai, *The Internet in China: Cyberspace and Civil Society* (New York: Routledge, 2006).

2 Janet Abbate, *Inventing the Internet*, (Cambridge: MIT Press, 1999), pp. 7–42.

3 "Of Cables and Conspiracies", *The Economist*, 9 February 2008.

4 Abbate, *Inventing the Internet*.

5 W. Richard Stevens, *TCP/IP Illustrated Volume 1: The Protocols* (New York: Addison-Wesley, 1994).

6 Tim Berners-Lee, *Weaving the Web: The Past, Present and Future of the World Wide Web by its Inventor* (London: Texere Publishing, 1999).

7 John Battelle, *The Search: How Google and its Rivals Rewrote the Rules of Business and Transformed Our Culture* (Boston: Nicholas Brearley Publishing, 2005).

8 For more on the architecture of the Web, the technologies it supports and its likely development over the near future, see Kieron O'Hara and David Stevens, *inequality.com: Power, Poverty and the Digital Divide* (Oxford: Oneworld, 2006), pp. 33–67.

9 Cf. e.g. http://eliotswasteland.tripod.com/.

10 Cf. Laurence Lessig, *Code and Other Laws of Cyberspace* (New York: Basic Books, 1999).

11 Kieron O'Hara and Nigel Shadbolt, *The Spy in the Coffee Machine: The End of Privacy As We Know It* (Oxford: Oneworld, 2008), O'Hara and Stevens, *inequality.com*, pp. 243–71.

12 Cf. Laurence Lessig. *The Future of Ideas: The Fate of the Commons in a Connected World* (New York: Random House, 2001).

13 Ira C. Magaziner, "The Framework for Global Economic Commerce: a Policy Perspective", *Journal of International Affairs*, 51 (1997).

14 Jonathan L. Zittrain and John G. Palfrey Jr, *Internet Filtering in China in 2004–2005: A Country Study*, Open Net Initiative, April 2005, online, available at: www.opennetinitiative.net/studies/china/ONI_China_Country_Study.pdf.

15 Daniel J. Weitzner, *China: A Broken Link on the Web?* Keynote speech, 2006 World Wide Web Conference, Edinburgh, 2006, online, available at: www.w3.org/2006/Talks/0424-chinabrokelink/#(1).

16 Zittrain and Palfrey, *Internet Filtering in China in 2004–2005.*

17 O'Hara and Shadbolt, *The Spy in the Coffee Machine*, pp. 168–75.

18 China Internet Network Information Centre, *Statistical Survey Report on the Internet Development in China*, CNNIC, January 2008, online, available at: www.cnnic.net.cn/uploadfiles/pdf/2008/2/29/104126.pdf. The figures are from December 2007.

19 www.internetworldstats.com/index.html, figures from June 2007.

20 Ibid.

21 Weitzner, *China: A Broken Link on the Web?* The comments following each suggestion are my own.

22 Reporters Without Borders, *Do Internet Companies Need to be Regulated to Ensure They Respect Free Expression?* Press release, 6 January 2006, onlinem available at: www.rsf.org/article.php3?id_article=16110.

23 Zittrain and Palfrey, *Internet Filtering in China in 2004–2005.*

24 Tim Berners-Lee, Wendy Hall, James A. Hendler, Kieron O'Hara, Nigel Shadbolt and Daniel J. Weitzner, "A Framework for Web Science", *Foundations and Trends in Web Science*, 1(1) (2006), pp. 1–134, at pp. 107–9.

25 O'Hara and Stevens, *inequality.com*, pp. 1–31.

26 Ibid., pp. 119–242.

8 The political cost of information control in China

The nation-state and governance

Yongnian Zheng

This chapter attempts to explore the political cost of information control in China. Information control involves high political costs of different types. The Chinese government controls information flow in order to maintain its dominance over society, but information control in turn leads to poor performance in governance. It seems that the government is "rationally" maximizing the benefit derived from Internet development while minimizing its cost. Nevertheless, in reality, it is difficult to define what the benefits are and what the costs are. In many cases, the boundary between the two is more often than not blurred. To look at the political cost of information control will lead one to rethink the sustainability of information control. At a certain point, the cost of information control might become greater than the benefit. If this is the case, the government, as a rational actor, will have to allow freer flow of information, and liberalize information control.

Information control comes with different forms of cost. This chapter focuses on the political cost of information control from two perspectives. First, it will look at how information control prevents China from developing rational forms of nationalism and thus modernizing the nation-state. Second, it will examine how information control prevents China from developing good governance. Good governance here is defined in terms of effective interaction between the state and society and is understood as a set of characteristics such as participation, rule of law, transparency and accountability. While this chapter will discuss how information control has prevented China from developing these characteristics, it attempts to go one step further and look at how information control has slowed down the process of developing China into a modern nation-state, which is a precondition for good governance.

This chapter is divided into two main parts. In the first part, I shall look at how information control often distorts nationalism and thus prevents China from developing rational forms of nationalism as the basis of a modern nation-state. I will explore the issue in the context of communicative nationalism literature. In the second part, I discuss the impact of information control on different aspects of governance. In discussion, I refer to the SARS case, partly because the SARS event provides a good example of the cost information control can incur, and partly because the spread of SARS is the very result of the Chinese government's practice in information control. In conclusion, I will draw some implications for the liberalization of information control in China.

Information distribution and nation-state building

We are now in an age of information and know how important information is for our daily life. However, less known is the importance of information for nation-state building. While information is regarded as an integral part of nation-state building in the literature of political development, it is hardly discussed in the literature of information studies today. One main reason is probably that most scholars have focused on well-developed nation-states, and usually democratic states, when examining the role of information in modern societies. Therefore, information is often linked to civil society, non-governmental organizations (NGOs), democracy, governance and human rights, but not to nation-state building. This is also true when scholars look at the case of China. While the importance of information to these aspects of political development should be studied, we cannot afford to ignore information as the key to nation-state building given the fact that China is not yet a modern nation-state.

Information and federalists

The importance of information to the nation-state was realized long before the age of information. We can find some strong arguments from state-builders of the United States of America, namely, the federalists. The federalists are a good example not only because they knew how important information was to a new nation-state, but also because they built a new nation-state in which information was the key to the functioning of the system.[1]

In the view of federalists, the new government was to be the center of information for the new nation. According to Alexander Hamilton, the distribution of political information is important to the health of the political system, and one of the several advantages of a large, more centralized federal republic over a system of decentralized confederated states was its superior information properties. In building a new state, the mediation of political information is more than a technical necessity. It is politically desirable because it permits the filtering and aggregation of local communication, as well as the building of larger views and a synthetic body of national-scale political information. The information tasks of central government are to aggregate information in such a way that a useful synthesis results, in which the information whole is greater and wiser than the sum of the individual facts about local problems. In the construction of a national view of problems, it is useful that some local details recede into the background.

Furthermore, the state governments have an important role to play in the flow of information because they can serve as information aggregators, standing between local problems and the larger national view. In the proposed system of government, local information is to be assembled into state-level information in the state governments. The state governments would then bring to the federal government a body of information already aggregated at the first level. In the Capitol, a second level of aggregation would occur as legislators inform themselves about the problems and interests of other states, melding these into a national conception. The result is to a balance of local, state and federal perspectives and information, rather than a simplistic summation of all local political facts and knowledge. Hamilton particularly emphasized that the health of a state or society is a function of many properties beyond size, especially the state of economic commerce. Therefore, there are the virtues of division of labor, improvements in work skills and expertise, organizational specialization and diversification, and other features of industrialization. However, more striking additional properties are the genius of its citizens and the degree of information they process. In this sense, possession of information can be regarded as a measure of a society's development.

In the same vein, James Madison provided a philosophical justification of the importance of information for the government. According to him, humans possess simultaneously the capacity for both good and bad actions, and the design of governments should serve to facilitate the good. The passions, that are a great threat to justice, thrive in information-poor environments. They are more likely to be subdued by reason and better judgment where information is rich. There are connections between information and deliberation. The entire problem of the passions is one of incomplete information. To achieve justice, the government should facilitate the inflow of information which would enable citizens to reach rational judgments.

Information and nationalism

In the contemporary era, we can find discussions of the importance of information to nation-state building in the literature of the communicative theories of nationalism, including the works of Karl Deutsch, Ernest Gellner, Benedict Anderson and Jurgen Habermas. In their works, there is a discernible line of argument that takes communication to be of central importance to nationalism, and thus nation-state building.

In many of his books,[2] Deutsch developed a powerful argument on the role of information in organizing nationality: "The essential aspect of the unity of a people ... is the complementarity or relative efficiency of communication among individuals – sometimes that is in some ways similar to mutual rapport, but on a larger scale."[3] Deutsch sees a "people" as providing the basis for the forging of a nationality. That in turn is distinct from nation-statehood, in which political sovereignty is harnessed to the pursuit of a group's cohesion and the continuity of its identity. Hence the exercise of national power relies on a relatively coherent and stable structure of memories, habits and values which in turn depends on existing facilities for social communication, both from the past to the present and among contemporaries.[4]

For Deutsch, nations and nation-states are strongly bound by their socially communicative structures of interaction: "People are held together 'from within' by this communicative efficiency, the complementarity of the communicative facilities acquired by their members."[5] Nationality is therefore an objective function of communicative competence and belonging. In other words, "national consciousness" and national self-awareness – or what today would be termed "national identity" – can be seen as an outcome of the structural cohesion that comes about through social communication.

While Gellner stressed the role of industrialization in creating nations, he also highlighted the social role of culture and communication in the same process.[6] Gellner argues that the formation of nation-states is the inevitable outcome of industrialization, with its concomitant complex division of labor. The new social relations of industrial society necessitate a universal, standardized system of education, using a standardized linguistic medium. Nationalism is to organize "human groups into large, centrally educated, culturally homogenous groups."[7] Culture thus refers to a distinctive style of conduct and communication of a given community, which in the modern world takes the modal form of a nation-state. For the members of such political formations "culture is now the necessary shared medium" and based in education and literacy.[8] He argues:

> The media themselves, the pervasiveness and importance of abstract, centralized, standardized, one to many communication, which itself automatically engendered the core idea of nationalism, quite irrespective of what in particular is being put into the specific messages transmitted.... The core message is that the language and style of the transmissions is important, that only he who can understand them, or can acquire such comprehension, is included in a moral and economic community, and that he who does not and cannot, is excluded.[9]

The media thus functions as a categorical system: widespread public identification with the national space is an effect of this form of cultural organization. Media are boundary markers, intimately related to the political roof that caps a culture and makes it into a nation-state. It is their function of sustaining a political community that is of prime interest.

In Benedict Anderson's work on nationalism, one can also find a similar line of argument on the central importance of information in the formation of a nationalist consciousness or national identity.[10] Anderson defines nationalism in the following way: "What, in a positive sense, made the new communities imaginable was a half-fortuitous, but explosive, interaction between a system of production and productive relations (capitalism), a technology of communications (print), and the fatality of human linguistic diversity."[11]

What Anderson tried to highlight was the importance of the media of communication in the construction of an "imagined community." The collective consumption of mediated communication serves to create a sense of national community. Anderson writes: "It is imagined as a community, because, regardless of the actual inequality and exploitation that may prevail in each, the nation is always conceived as a deep, horizontal comradeship."[12]

Social communication theories share a broad concern with how nations speak to themselves and mark themselves off as different from others. This is also a central theme of Habermas' works. His theory of communication and public space has exerted a profound influence in the recent debate about the role and quality of political communication.[13] The "public sphere" refers to the whole domain of debate in an institutional space that exists outside the state, but which engages all who are concerned with matters of public interest. The formation of the classic public sphere coincided with the growth of nationalism and nation-state formation. This theory stresses that public communication remains pre-eminently tied to the structure of meaning of nation-states. The boundaries of the public sphere therefore coincide with those of a political community conceived of as quintessentially national in scope. The nation-state, consequently, has provided the regaining Gellner-Anderson conception of social communication as national culture but also for the more narrowly conceived Habermasian domain of political communication.

Information and the Chinese communist state

As a state-builder, the CCP realized the importance of information. Put simply, the People's Republic was built through information control. It was a state imposed from above. In academic and policy circles, it was called a totalitarian state. According to Carl Friedrich, totalitarian regimes are characterized by a totalist ideology, a single party committed to this ideology, a fully developed secret police, and the monopoly of mass communications, operational weapons and all organizations.[14] The communist party defines "ideology" as what Karl Marx called the "second side" of the superstructure, namely, the ideas and convictions that support the existence of the system. This ideology broadly encompasses such elements as public opinion, morality, theoretical thought, political ideas, philosophy, religion, art and literature.[15] As Stuart Schram observed, "In China, as well as in the Soviet Union, ideology means the idea, theory or hypothesis recognized by the leaders."[16]

The communist state led the development of a mass communications system in order to mobilize mass support to the regime. According to Alan Liu, mass media was the communists' organizational approach to social mobilization. To make an organization effective, its members had to be dedicated to the goals of the organization and competent in their professional skills. The media had to disseminate ideology and educational matter in order to transform its population into efficient and dedicated members of the communist society.[17] The monopoly of information was also to cultivate a "new people" uniquely imbued with "socialist morality" who acted spontaneously and habitually in accordance with socialist values.[18]

In this sense, the monopoly of information ultimately empowered the state by enabling it to exercise both "formal" and "informal" control, to use Norbert Elias and Michel Foucault's terms. According to Elias and Foucault, the early modern state imposed control formally to encourage certain behaviors and threatened draconian punishments for their violation. In contrast, the modern state enlists its subjects as participants in their own governance. In the process, it shifts the locus of control internally.[19] It is hardly true that in China, citizens were allowed to take part in politics. As a matter of fact, the state instructs, commands and punishes on the one hand, and educates, informs, persuades and discourages on the other.

Information control and state–society relations

The monopoly of information flow has an important impact on relations between the state and society, as well as on individuals. There was little space for the existence of civil activities. After the CCP took power in 1949, the state adopted measures to reshape the sphere of intermediary organizations in the light of reordering class relations, restructuring the economy and legitimizing power. All organizations which were regarded or even suspected to be "counter-revolutionary" by the government were banned. On the other hand, in order to mobilize millions of people to implement public policies and to achieve the party's and even Mao Zedong's personal political purposes, enormous mass civilian bodies, or "administered mass organizations," were created by the party-state. Party cadres and governmental officials used such organizations to organize youths, workers, women and other social groups into bodies resembling a "conscription society."[20]

In terms of interpersonal relations, China in the pre-reform era was characterized by social atomization: the obliteration of social ties that are not directly harnessed to the party's aims. The state recognized no legitimate distinction between private and public spheres. Allegiances not subordinated to the party were regarded as subversive to its aims. Consequently, as William Kornhauser pointed out, an "atomized society" was formed, "a situation in which an aggregate of individuals are related to one another only by way of their relation to a common authority in a variety of independent groups."[21] The reason is simple. A totalitarian regime requires "atomized masses" not only to keep power, by preventing alternative loyalties independent of the regime, but also to ensure that there are no obstacles to inhibit the total mobilization of the population.[22] In such a situation, "alienation," "anomie" and "loneliness" are normal characteristics of the structure of social relations.[23]

Weak society and distorted nationalism

To build a nation-state from above is the only choice for many late-developing countries like China. A nation-state imposed from above means that it was created by an asymmetrical distribution of information between the state and social forces. While it is hard to achieve absolutely fair information distribution in any society, equilibrium must be achieved between the state and social forces in terms of information distribution if a state is to function and be maintained well. The scholarly community has debated on weak states versus strong societies. Many would agree that the interaction between the state and society is not a zero-sum game, and that state and society can be mutually empowering. The state is a part of society, and without a strong societal foundation, the state cannot be strong. In other words, without a strong society, a seemingly strong state could be very weak. Given the central role that information plays in nation-state building, the question of how information flows between the state and society becomes extremely important. If there is tight information control by the state, social forces will be in a weak position.

To empower social forces, political reform with the liberalization of information control among other goals is essential. Liberalization of information control was an important part of what Huntington called the "third wave of democratization."[24] Of course, information liberalization can take place in a radical way in some cases, and be incremental in others. Information must be liberalized for a nation-state to function in a normal way.

It is not difficult to see that despite all the reforms introduced since the late 1970s, information control remains in China. To promote the development of a market economy, the state has to liberalize its control of economic information. This is because without sufficient information, economic actors such as individuals, firms and local governments will not be able to make rational decisions. It is reasonably argued that (economic) information liberalization is an integral part of the market economy. Furthermore, economic transformation leads to a pluralistic, and indeed divided, society. Information on social matters has also been liberalized to meet the needs of different social forces.

However, information control in many key areas such as politics, religion and ethnicity remains tight. This means that genuine civil society does not exist in these areas. What the scholarly community calls "communicative community" is extremely weak in China. With society becoming pluralistic and divided, different social forces need to aggregate and articulate their interests before they can influence policy-makers. Without information liberalization, social forces can hardly achieve these goals. The government used to rule a very simple society, but now it is facing an increasingly complex one. To govern effectively, the government has to reach out to different social forces. Without information liberalization, the foundation of the Chinese state remains weak.

Moreover, without significant political reform, the government has to tighten information control in these areas in order to maintain socio-political order. Social pluralism resulting from economic growth is regarded as a serious political threat to the one-party rule. The government has introduced different methods to control the development of nationwide networks of information enterprises. While the government does not allow the establishment of nationwide civil society or non-government organizations, it also does not allow the formation of cross-regional media networks. For example, the Southern Newsgroup in Guangzhou is not allowed to set up a branch or to merge with a newspaper in Shanghai. Except for a few official media, the media industry is localized, and divided by administrative and political means.[25] Local residents now can learn local news, but not news in other regions unless the news becomes national. To a great degree, the regional limit of information circulation helps the strengthening of local identity and the weakening of national identity among local residents. As a matter of fact, local identity has been an important force behind growing localism since the reform and open-door policy.[26] The Internet has seriously challenged the efforts of the government to limit information circulation to a regional level. Again, the government has taken a measure of selective control over Internet information, meaning that sensitive information is not allowed to circulate over the Internet nationwide.[27]

Information control therefore leads to different forms of distorted nationalism in China. Indeed, to maintain the existing nation-state, nationalism has to be distorted. Information control is a serious constraint on ethnic nationalism among minorities. Minority groups are not allowed to develop their strong ethnic identity through the development of communicative communities among themselves. But information control also discourages national integration. When different ethnic groups are not allowed to communicate with one another freely, it is unlikely that they will understand one another, let alone develop shared values and a common national identity. Coercive information control plays an important role in preventing ethnic groups from separating from China on one hand, and serves as a barrier for further national integration on the other.

In terms of state–society relations, information control is in favor of state-oriented nationalism, but discourages liberal nationalism. Historically, the idea of nationalism is intimately connected with the idea of freedom. American political scientist Hans Morgenthau argued that:

> nationalism as a political phenomenon must be understood as the aspiration for two freedoms, one collective, the other individual: the freedom of a nation from domination by another and the freedom of the individual to join the nation of his choice.[28]

In China, while the Chinese communist movement brought about national freedom, liberal nationalism has been absent and replaced by state-centric nationalism. This situation has continued since the reform and open-door policy. The government allows more space and even encourages state-centric nationalism, but controls potential forces of liberal nationalism.[29] It is not difficult to find various "communicative communities" in favor of statism, but no liberal "communicative communities" are allowed to exist.

Information control has also distorted Chinese nationalism at the international level. In many scholarly works, nationalism is regarded as the mainstream of political ideology and China has been described as nationalistic in the post-Mao era.[30] While there is plenty of evidence to suggest the existence of increasingly strong nationalistic voices in China, it can hardly be argued that nationalism is the only voice in the country. There are different schools of thought among Chinese intellectuals and the general public such as conservatism, the new Left, and political liberalism. Nationalism is only one of these voices. Even within nationalism, there is no evidence to suggest there is only one voice. For example, nationalism can be divided into official nationalism and popular nationalism since the two forms of nationalism often contradict each other.[31] Nationalism can also be linked to democratization and liberalism.[32]

If there was no intervention from the state, especially from its propaganda department, the different voices of nationalism could contest one another and reach an equilibrium. Nationalism is not only about national identity and emotion, but also about different interests. With the presence of pluralistic interests, nationalistic voices present themselves in favor of the different interests which lay behind them. However, state intervention in the development of nationalistic voices has led to the distortion of nationalism. As a self-interested actor, the state understandably encourages nationalistic voices which are in favor of state power and discourages and even prohibits those which are against state power. Take Chinese nationalism versus Japan as an example. There were voices against the government's hard-line Japan policy, as represented in the school of "New Thinking."[33] However, the "New Thinking" school soon had to retreat from the public domain. It was not only under attack from hard-line nationalistic voices; more importantly, the government was in favor of the hard-line voice and did not allow rational debates between the "New Thinking" scholars and other nationalist scholars. Distorted nationalism against Japan was an important factor contributing to worsening China–Japan relations since the late 1990s. Recently the state intervened again to control hard-line nationalistic voices in order to stabilize China–Japan relations, and nationalism against Japan has died down.

There is a logic built into China's nation-state, which was built from above. In order to maintain this nation-state, the government has to intervene in the formation and development of nationalism which is increasingly becoming an important ideological base of the nation-state. In other words, it is rational for the state to distort nationalism. While nationalism could be distorted in many other places, not many states intervene in nationalism like the Chinese state does. Apparently, information control is an integral part of state intervention. While nationalism is distorted, it cannot be rational when dealing with other actors, be they internal social forces or foreign states. How to transform distorted forms of nationalism into rational ones is one major challenge facing China. Certainly, information liberalization must be a part of this transformation.

Information control and governance

I have so far discussed why without political reform, a nation-state built from above has to be maintained from above by distributing information asymmetrically. Information control and distortion is part of this maintenance. This leads to another type of significant political cost, namely bad governance. I believe that information control and distortion has a causal effect on governance.

Governance and information

The term "governance" is increasingly used in the development literature. Governance describes the process of decision-making and the process by which decisions are implemented. Hereby, public institutions conduct public affairs, manage public resources, and guarantee the realization of human rights. Good governance accomplishes this in a manner essentially free of abuse and corruption, and with due regard for the rule of law.

Good governance represents an ideal which is often difficult to achieve in its totality. However, measures must be taken to work toward this ideal to ensure sustainable human development. Many international organizations such as the World Bank view good governance as a set of eight major characteristics, including participation, rule of law, transparency, responsiveness, consensus orientation, equity and inclusiveness, effectiveness and efficiency, and accountability.[34]

Participation means that the views of minorities are taken into account, and that the voices of the most vulnerable in society are heard in decision-making. Participation also implies freedom of association and expression on the one hand and an organized civil society on the other. Rule of law requires fair legal frameworks that are enforced impartially, and full protection of human rights, particularly those of minorities. It also means independent judiciary and an impartial and incorruptible police force. Transparency means that decisions taken and their enforcement are done in a manner that follows rules and regulations.

Responsiveness means that institutions and processes try to serve all stakeholders within a reasonable timeframe. Consensus orientation means the need for mediation of the different interests in society to reach a broad consensus on what is in the best interest of the whole community and how this can be achieved. It also requires a long-term perspective for sustainable human development and how to achieve the goals of such development. Equity and inclusiveness ensures that all members of society feel that they have a stake in it and do not feel excluded from the mainstream. This requires all groups, and especially the most vulnerable, to have opportunities to maintain or improve their well-being. Effectiveness and efficiency means that processes and institutions produce results that meet the needs of society while making the best use of resources at their disposal. It also means sustainable use of natural resources and the protection of the environment. Accountability means that governmental institutions as well as the private sector and civil society organizations must be accountable to the public and to their institutional stakeholders. In general, organizations and institutions are accountable to those who will be affected by decisions or actions. Finally, a political system with the presence of these characteristics can assure that corruption is minimized.

There is little discussion in the governance literature on the role information can play in helping good governance. Given the fact that all these characteristics were drawn from political experiences in the West, it is understandable that information is not discussed in an explicit manner since in all democratic states, free flow of information has been a precondition for democracies to function. Apparently, to achieve good governance, information must be freely available and directly accessible to decision-makers and those who will be affected by decisions and their enforcement. Information must be distributed symmetrically between the state and social forces. In this section, I discuss how asymmetrical information distribution and measures for information control lead to bad governance in the case of the SARS crisis in 2003. The SARS crisis was high profile due to its scale and deep impact on the world. It has been regarded as a good example of China's bad governance. The case shows how institutions, which were built in China's political system, and how excessive measures for information control which were taken on the part of the government, led to the mismanagement of the SARS crisis. Also important is that these factors are consistent in affecting the Chinese government when it deals with crises and emergencies since the SARS crisis.

Chinese institutions and asymmetrical information distribution

As discussed in the last section, the Chinese nation-state was built through asymmetrical information distribution. Institutionally, information asymmetries are in favor of the lower-level bureaucrats and against higher-level leaders, and in favor of the state and against the public. Higher levels of the Party and government bureaucracy rely heavily on lower levels to report various types of information, including local disasters, diseases and other urgent problems. This gives local officials and lower-level bureaucrats an edge in information vis-à-vis their superiors. Furthermore, the Chinese state has been suppressing sensitive information. This gives the state, or officials, an edge in information concerning the political, economic and social state of the country and its external standings over the public.

Both asymmetries affect governance. Institutional authority of local governments and officials in handling information means that national leaders can be deprived of alternative sources of information. They have to rely on information transmitted from the lowest level inside the political system or bureaucracy. At each layer, bureaucrats who transmit the information have an incentive to distort it in order to protect their own careers. As self-interested actors, it is in the interest of local governments and local officials to report the good news and suppress the bad news.

Chinese officials are motivated to distort the information. Given the fact that the center is not able to gain sufficient information from the media, which is under tight control, it has to rely on government officials to report information. The center would have to commit a great deal of manpower and resources in order to produce an alternate source simply for any ad hoc case. This will be very costly and cannot be done for a large number of cases. The result is that the center falls back on localities for first-hand information and that the center has difficulties in finding out whether local officials distort the facts. Furthermore, even if the center knows local cadres lie, it still has to rely on them to implement its own orders. It will therefore be relatively lenient in penalizing them.[35]

Chinese officials, who are used to the autocratic information control, can be quite hostile to and ready to suppress any alternate source of information. Yasheng Huang observed that many Chinese officials feared negative media publicity more than administrative and political censure, because negative publicity could put an end to their careers once and for all.[36] Open media criticisms can inflict greater damage on an official's career than administrative censure. In this sense, administrative censure can be gentler and more humane. However, administrative censure can be effective only when reliable information is available for higher-level officials, and this is not easy in China. As a result, administrative censure is rarely used and is hardly effective in correcting mistakes in official conduct.[37] In this sense, Kenneth Lieberthal argued that the Chinese state is self-defeating. According to Lieberthal,

> Beijing's determination not to allow people to criticize the government has led to a policy of suppressing all independent sources of information gathering and transmittal, such as a free press. By thus denying themselves the one relatively systematic option for checking the accuracy of the information they receive, the top Chinese leaders have made themselves virtual captives of their own system and of the distortions it inevitably produces.[38]

The Chinese state monopolizes vital information regarding the regime and pending crises, information that can be highly useful for the state. It is expected that by suppressing all negative news about the government's performance, its external environment, and the scale of disasters in a given region and by feeding the population mainly good news, a high-level of confidence toward the government can be instilled in the populace.

However, as Hongyi Lai has observed, this practice more often than not leads to two main problems. First, in many cases the public can take necessary action to prevent the disaster only when it is informed. Suppressing negative information can only aggravate the disaster. Informing the public may lead to certain public panic in the short term, yet may induce it to behave in a rational fashion over a protracted period to avoid the disaster. Second, should the state suppress the information regarding a pending crisis and eventually fail to prevent it, the populace will be discontented over the state's performance. The state may lose credibility and even legitimacy.[39]

Information control and the SARS crisis

During the SARS outbreak, central leaders also relied heavily on local officials for information, especially regarding the nature and effects of the disease. However, many institutional barriers prevented the center from gaining vital information on SARS from different provinces. On March 12, 2003, the World Health Organization (WHO) issued a global alert on the outbreak of a new form of pneumonia-like disease with symptoms that are similar to those of a common flu. This illness, officially known as Severe Acute Respiratory Syndrome (SARS), was first found in the Guangdong province in China in November 2003 and then spread to many parts of the world in a matter of weeks. When it was found in China, the Chinese authorities lied to the whole world about the situation in the country. Consequently, when SARS spread to different parts of world, people, especially Asian people, were angry with China's initial lackluster reaction. The Chinese government faced the greatest international pressure since its crackdown on the pro-democracy movement in 1989.

How did the SARS crisis deepen? Information control played an essential role in the process. To examine this issue, it is important to note some important characteristics of China's political system, including political priority, political correctness, lack of transparency, and political fragmentation.[40] All these factors prevented the free flow of information and thus prevented China's political system from responding to SARS quickly and effectively.

Political and non-political information

In China, whether a matter including information is considered political or not is usually decided at the very top with almost no input from below. Not everything is regarded as political, and not every issue is resolved politically. In democratic countries, whether a given event is political or not is usually decided by a confluence of factors such as public opinion, public pressure and politicians' perceptions. This is because the public is an essential part of politics via political participation. When a given social event happens, the public can immediately contribute its part to politics. In China, the boundary of politics has to be perceived and defined by top leaders, collectively or individually. Of course, the public can express its voice by engaging in popular demonstrations or protests, but it is very risky to do so. Furthermore, only after a social event enters the boundary of politics and becomes political will top leaders begin to pay attention to it. A non-political issue, even if it is serious, could be dealt with by local governments or central bureaucracies, and top leaders are unlikely to be involved in the first place. In other words, only when information becomes politically significant will top leaders be informed.

The first two SARS cases were found in Guangdong in November 2002 and were defined as "unidentifiable" pneumonia. Although the early spread of SARS did cause local public panic, neither Guangdong nor Beijing perceived the matter as serious. In February and early March, when SARS spread to different parts of Guangdong and Hong Kong, it was still regarded as a medical issue, *not* a political one. Needless to say, a medical issue should be handled by local governments and at most by relevant central bureaucracies such as the Ministry of Health (MoH). At that time, those who were affected began to die, but SARS had not entered China's political domain. Only when SARS went beyond China's territorial boundary and reached Taiwan, Singapore, Canada and other parts of the world and generated mounting international pressure did the top leadership begin to regard SARS as a political issue and started to mobilize national resources to combat the disease.

Political correctness of information

Political correctness has been a common practice in China. Usual political practice is that good things can be exaggerated but bad things are not supposed to be publicized. SARS spread because it was not accorded sufficient attention in the first place. Several local newspapers in Guangdong did report SARS cases, including *Southern Weekend* (*Nanfang Zhoumuo*) with a circulation of over one million, *Southern Urban Post* (*Nanfang Dushi Bao*), and *Goat City Evening Posting* (*Yangcheng Wanbao*). However, all the reports were suppressed and journalists were criticized and even fired. Among many factors, the most important was that from October 2002 to March 2003 was the highest season of China's politics. In October 2002, the CCP held its Sixteenth National Congress, the most important event held every five years. The Sixteenth Party Congress handled the leadership succession from the third generation to the fourth generation. Then in March 2003, China held the Tenth NPC, during which a new government was formed.

Neither party leaders nor government officials are democratically elected. In order to justify the legitimacy of new leaders, a good "public opinion environment" has to be created. Prior to the party congress, the party propaganda machine drummed up political support to usher in a new set of leaders in a solemn environment. After the party congress, another campaign followed to promote the party's new policies. This was also true before and after the Tenth National People's Congress (NPC) in March 2003. All official newspapers devoted much attention to the new leaders and their policies. Indeed, during the Tenth NPC, one candidate from Guangdong formally raised the issue of SARS, but no top leader paid attention to it. Of course, no newspaper was allowed to report SARS during such a period of time. Actually, if SARS had been widely reported, popular awareness would have been created and preventive measures taken. It was unfortunate that SARS came to China during a season of high politics.

Information control and lack of transparency

China's political system also lacks transparency. China's system is not representative, and leaders are not chosen by the Chinese people. There are no effective mechanisms for people to take part in the political process. Because of the lack of mechanisms between the regime and the people, the process of decision-making and policy implementation occurs in a lockbox. It is difficult for those from the outside to find out what is happening inside the regime. In the case of SARS, when the regime was accused of withholding SARS information from the public and the international community, the world was told that the Chinese government had already begun to take measures against the spread of SARS. For the regime, news about the tenacious spread of SARS was detrimental to social stability. When SARS spread to different parts of Guangdong, there was some panic. The government seemed to believe that if SARS could be controlled silently, then social stability would not be disturbed. Furthermore, in order to ensure social stability, which is vital for economic development, releasing half-truths or withholding information from the public can also be justified. With non-transparency, the regime does not need to be sensitive to outside pressure (neither domestic nor international) unless the matter becomes a political issue.

Information control and political fragmentation

Political fragmentation often leads to poor policy coordination in China. There are tensions between the center and the provinces. In the case of SARS, there were conflicting interests between Guangdong provincial officials and top leaders, and between the Guangdong provincial government and the Ministry of Health in Beijing. Why did the Guangdong provincial government suppress reports on SARS? Guangdong did not have any incentive to publicize the SARS outbreak partly because of its economic rationale and partly because of its political rationale. As the largest trading province in China, Guangdong is highly dependent on foreign investments and tourism (from Hong Kong and Macao). Provincial officials were afraid that the publicity of SARS would cause chaos and social instability and thus affect foreign investments and local economic performances. Politically, from late 2002 to early 2003, Guangdong was also experiencing a local power succession. Guangdong party secretary Li Changchun was appointed member of the Standing Committee of the Political Bureau in Beijing. That meant that Li would leave Guangdong soon to take up this appointment. Within a month or so, Zhang Dejiang, who was previously party secretary of Zhejiang Province, was appointed to take over Li's position. When Zhang Dejiang came to Guangdong, SARS had already spread. Guangdong local officials did not want SARS to "welcome" the new party secretary. Needless to say, Zhang also did not want SARS to bring chaos to Guangdong, the new territory under his charge. Thus, local reports about SARS were suppressed. Neither the central government nor the public in Guangdong was able to get enough information on this new virus.

Tensions between the MoH and Guangdong were also obvious. The two units were of the same administrative rank, and there was a lack of coordination between them. While the Guangdong Bureau of Health was obliged to report to the MoH, no issue would be given priority as long as the MoH did not accord due attention to it. In the case of SARS, it was rational for the MoH to want to bring the issue under control. If an issue cannot be solved within the MoH, it can ask higher-level government units to intervene, meaning that the issue would go beyond the boundary of a medical problem and become political in nature. Nevertheless, the MoH from the very beginning regarded SARS as a medical issue. Even when the international community began to criticize China, the MoH viewed all kinds of critiques as politicizing a medical issue. No doubt, as long as SARS was regarded as a medical issue, top leaders were unlikely to get involved. Both the MoH and the Guangdong provincial government can report directly to the Political Bureau or the State Council, especially given the fact that Zhang Dejiang is a member of the Political Bureau. Information is not available as to whether the MoH and the Guangdong provincial government reported the SARS situation to the top leadership, but it can reasonably be assumed that even if they did, they did not provide enough information for the top leadership to realize the political significance of the SARS outbreak.

There was also bureaucratic fragmentation. Self-interested bureaucratic behavior played a role in China's delayed reaction to the spread of SARS. In this case, fragmentation happened between the party's Department of Propaganda (DoP) and the MoH not only because their interests conflicted with each other but also because they belonged to different lines of political authority, such as the CCP and the State Council, respectively. The DoP is the party's mouthpiece in charge of justifying the party's rule. Understandably, the interest of the DoP is not to report news that could have a negative impact on the party. In this regard, there is no difference between the Guangdong provincial DoP and the central DoP in Beijing. The DoP strictly constrained the flow of information and disabled both relevant government departments and the public from obtaining enough information on SARS. Apparently, like the MoH, the DoP should share the responsibility for the spread of SARS.

More seriously, there was a conflict between the civilian government and the military sector. This conflict is worse than the lack of coordination between the MoH and the DoP. The military is virtually an independent kingdom in Chinese politics, and the civilian government always has difficulty in bringing the military under its control. In Beijing, many SARS cases developed in military hospitals, and the Beijing government was actually not supposed to know what was going on within military hospitals. Of course, military hospitals did not have an obligation to inform the civilian government about SARS. So, when Beijing city officials claimed that the reported SARS cases included those in military hospitals, the world knew that this was not completely true.

All these factors led to the rapid spread of SARS from Guangdong to other Chinese provinces and to different parts of the world. What broke China's information control was information technologies. When all newspaper reports on SARS were suppressed in Guangdong, information on SARS did not stop circulating among people, regions and even countries via emails, short message service (SMS) transmissions, and other Internet-based communications. Despite tight information control by the regime, an essential portion of the population was aware of this deadly virus. Information technology played an important role in spreading the news about SARS. Take Guangdong as an example. There were 40 million SMS transmissions recorded on April 8, 2003, 41 million on April 9, and 45 million on April 10.[41] A few people who circulated such information were punished by Chinese authorities, but more people joined.

The unavailability or lack of information on SARS from official news media forced residents to turn to other sources such as the Internet, SMS and rumor. Needless to say, much of the news from such unofficial channels was frequently exaggerated. The widespread rumors actually led to several waves of panic among urban residents in cities like Guangzhou, Beijing and Nanjing. People rushed to stores to buy and stock up on daily necessities. Public panic generated enormous pressure on local government officials and pushed them to tighten information control in order to avoid further panic. Thus, a vicious circle developed in the interaction between the government and urban citizens. What broke this vicious circle was a brave act by Jiang Yanyong, a retired military doctor in Beijing. On April 4, after he saw on TV that China's Minister of Health had lied to the world one day ago, he wrote an open letter to the CCP leadership about the seriousness of the SARS situation. Jiang first emailed a TV station in China and a pro-China TV station in Hong Kong but got no reply from either station. Later, he mailed the letter to the *New York Times*, which published Jiang's letter immediately. Thus the whole world was informed of the actual situation of SARS in China, and what happened in military hospitals came to be known.[42]

Institutional roots of information control

Has the Chinese state learned a good lesson from the SARS crisis? There are signs to indicate that the government is becoming more transparent and accountable since this event. However, this change is more about leadership style than institutional. While the new leadership has tried to be more accountable to the people, it has hardly introduced meaningful changes into the existing political system. Indeed, information control tends to be tighter. The latest new Emergency Response Law (draft) would give local governments the right to "manage news media reports" about emergencies. Article 57 of the law would fine news outlets up to 100,000 yuan for reporting on those events without permission or in a way that "causes serious consequences."[43] The proposed media legislation does not define what constitutes "serious consequences." In the absence of further definition, officials could conceivably use the legislation to smother reporting on any events that might reflect badly on them, or on China in general. The central government continues to rely on its local units and officials for information. While the new law also emphasizes that the public has the right to access information, it is apparent that information must be censored by government at different levels. This situation was the main reason for the SARS crisis. As long as there are no institutional changes, asymmetrical information distribution will continue along with bad governance.

Conclusion

In this chapter, I have examined the political cost of information control from two perspectives, namely, nation-state building and governance. First of all, information control has led to a distorted nation-state. While it is a historical fact that the Chinese nation-state was built from above through asymmetrical distribution of information between the state and social forces, it is costly to maintain this nation-state by continuing information control. Information control has prevented national identity from forming among social groups, and local identity often prevails. In Anderson's words, information control has made it impossible for people to "imagine" their "community" across the whole country. In terms of national integration, coercive information control has perhaps prevented any independence movements among ethnic groups, but in the long run it can also prevent any shared values and thus state identity from developing between different ethnic groups. Needless to say, information control has become a barrier to the development of liberal nationalism, a force of China's democratization. At the international level, information control has distorted Chinese nationalism, and thus affects China's relations with other countries.

Second, information control has had a seriously negative impact on governance in China. When information is distributed asymmetrically between the state and social forces, good governance becomes an impossible enterprise. Information control seemingly enables the state to control society and leads to a situation of a "strong state and weak society." However, in reality, both the state and society can be weakened because of information control by the state. As discussed above, this is exemplified by the SARS event. Good governance results from the effective interaction between the state and society under a condition of free flow of information.

The distorted nation-state and bad governance imply that information control is not sustainable in the long run. It seems that many factors are facilitating a greater degree of information liberalization in China. It is doubtful whether information control is rational with the rise of information and communication technologies, especially the Internet. The Chinese state has attempted to tighten its control over the Internet, but apparently the cost is becoming increasingly high while effectiveness becomes increasingly low. Despite tight control, new technologies have facilitated waves of Internet-based social protests.

As mentioned at the beginning of this chapter, information is an integral part of state power. As shown by the SARS crisis, localization of information (in the hands of local governments and bureaucratic agencies) causes a weakening of central power. To manage a giant country like China, the national state has to centralize information in order to govern the country effectively. However, information centralization does not mean in any sense that information has to be monopolized by the national government. Information centralization means that information is available to the national government from different social channels. This can be achieved only through information liberalization. Information liberalization means that information is symmetrically distributed between the state and society and among social forces. Only by doing this will the central government be able to collect accurate information, and make the right decisions.

In a market economy, information access has become an integral part of human rights. The functioning of the market economy depends on the free flow of information. All individuals within this market make decisions according to the information they collect. With insufficient information, it is unlikely that they will make rational decisions. This is especially true for all investors, be they domestic or international. China has now been integrated into the world economy. Information control will not only affect the Chinese economy, but also the whole world economy. Furthermore, with its rapid economic transformation and globalization, Chinese society is becoming increasingly open, meaning that the functioning of society is also dependent on the free flow of information. This is also true in terms of political participation. China is not a democratic state yet, but different forms of political participation have taken place at different levels of government. Individuals participate in politics and express their voices according to available information. Without the free flow of information, there will be no meaningful political participation. All these developments require information liberalization. In other words, the cost of information control is becoming increasingly high. Whether the Chinese state is able to absorb these costs will decide whether information control is sustainable.

Notes

1 For a discussion, see, Bruce Bimber, *Information and American Democracy: Technology in the Evolution of Political Power* (New York: Cambridge University Press, 2003), Chapter 2.
2 Karl Deutsch, *Nationalism and Social Communication: An Inquiry of the Foundations of Nationality* (Cambridge: MIT Press, 1953); *The Nerves of Government* (New York: Basic Books, 1966); and *Politics and Government: How People Decide Their Fate* (Boston: Houghton Mifflin, 1970; 3rd edn, 1980).
3 Ibid., 1966, p. 188.
4 Ibid., p. 75.
5 Ibid., p. 98.
6 Ernest Gellner, *Nations and Nationalism* (Ithaca: Cornell University Press, 1983).
7 Ibid., p. 35.
8 Ibid., pp. 37–8.
9 Ibid., p. 127.
10 Benedict Anderson, *Imagined Communities: Reflections on the Origin and Spread of Nationalism* (New York: Verso, 1983).
11 Ibid., p. 46.
12 Ibid.
13 Jürgen Habermas, *The Structural Transformation of the Public Sphere: An Inquiry into a Category of Bourgois Society*, translated by Thomas Burger (Cambridge: MIT Press, 1991).
14 Carl J. Friedrich, "The Evolving Theory and Practice of Totalitarian Regimes," in Carl J. Friedrich, Michael Curtis and Benjamin R. Barber, *Totalitarianism in Perspective: Three Views* (New York: Praeger, 1969).
15 Su Shaozhi, "Chinese Communist Ideology and Media Control," in Chin-Chuan Lee, ed., *China's Media, Media's China* (Boulder: Westview Press, 1994), pp. 75–88.
16 Stuart R. Schram, *Ideology and Policy in China since the Third Plenum, 1978–84* (London: University of London, School of Oriental and African Studies, 1984), p. 112.
17 Alan P.L. Liu, *Communications and National Integration in Communist China* (Berkeley: University of California Press, 1971).
18 Su, "Chinese Communist Ideology and Medial Control."
19 Peter Baldwin, "The Return of the Coercive State: Behavioral Control in Multicultural Society," in T.V. Paul, G. John Ikenberry and John A. Hall, eds., *The Nation-State in Question* (Princeton: Princeton University Press, 2003), pp. 106–35.
20 Gregory J. Kasza, *The Conscription Society: Administered Mass Organizations* (New Haven: Yale University Press, 1995).
21 William Kornhauser, *The Politics of Mass Society* (Glencoe: The Free Press, 1959), p. 32.
22 Ibid., p. 62.
23 Andrew G. Walder, *Communist Neo-Traditionalism: Work and Authority in Chinese Industry* (Berkeley: University of California Press, 1986), pp. 2–3.
24 Samuel P. Huntington, *The Third Wave: Democratization in the Late Twentieth Century* (Norman and London: University of Oklahoma Press, 1991).

25 Personal interviews in Shanghai, May 2007.

26 Yongnian Zheng, *Discovering Chinese Nationalism in China: Modernization, Identity and International Relations* (Cambridge: Cambridge University Press, 1999), Chapter 2; Lynn White and Li Cheng, "China Coast Identities: Regional, National, and Global," in Lowell Dittmer and Samuel S. Kim, eds., *China's Quest for National Identity* (Ithaca and London: Cornell University Press, 1993), pp. 154–93.

27 Yongnian Zheng, *Technological Empowerment: The Internet, State and Society in China* (Stanford: Stanford University Press, 2007).

28 Hans Morgenthau, "The Paradoxes of Nationalism," *Yale Review*, xlvi (4) (June 1957), p. 481.

29 Zheng, *Discovering Chinese Nationalism in China*, Chapter 2.

30 The literature of Chinese nationalism is growing, some latest works include, Peter Hays Gries, China's *New Nationalism: Pride, Politics, and Diplomacy* (Berkeley: University of California Press, 2004); Suisheng Zhao, *A Nation-State by Construction: Dynamics of Modern Chinese Nationalism* (Stanford: Stanford University Press, 2004); Christopher R. Hughes, *Chinese Nationalism in the Global Era* (London: Routledge, 2006); and Xu Wu, *Chinese Cyber Nationalism: Evolution, Characteristics, and Implications* (Lanham, Boulder: Rowman & Littlefield, 2007).

31 Zheng, *Discovering Chinese Nationalism.*

32 For example, Baogang He and Yingjie Cuo, *Nationalism, National Identity and Democratization in China* (Aldershot: Ashgate, 2000), and Wu Guoguang, *Ziyou de minzu yu minzu de ziyou* (The Free Nation and National Freedom) (Taipei: Chinese Eurasian Foundation, 2002).

33 For a discussion of the "New Thinking," see Peter Hays Gries, "China's 'New Thinking' on Japan," *The China Quarterly*, 184 (2005), pp. 831–50.

34 See, www.worldbank.org/wbi/governance (accessed April 28, 2007).

35 Hongyi Lai, "Local Management of SARS in China: Guangdong and Beijing," in John Wong and Zheng Yongnian, eds., *The SARS Epidemic: Challenges to China's Crisis Management* (Singapore and London: World Scientific Publishing, 2004), pp. 77–98.

36 Yasheng Huang, *Inflation and Control in China: The Political Economy of Central-Local Relations during the Reform Era* (New York: Cambridge University Press, 1996), p. 228.

37 Lai, "Local Management of SARS in China."

38 Kenneth Lieberthal, *Governing China: From Revolution Through Reform* (New York: W.W. Norton, 1995), p. 175.

39 Lai, "Local Management of SARS in China."

40 This description is based on Zheng Yongnian and Lye Liang Fook, "SARS and China's Political System," in John Wong and Zheng Yongnian, eds., *The SARS Epidemic: Challenges to China's Crisis Management* (Singapore and London: World Scientific, 2004), pp. 45–75.

41 Zhou Xiaohong, "*SARS liuxing qijian de shehui chuanyan yu gongzhong yulun diaocha*" (An Investigation of Social Rumors and Public Opinions during SARS), in Ru Xing, Lu Xueyi and Li Peilin, eds., *Shehui lanpishu: Zhongguo shehui xingshi fenxi yu yuce, 2004* (Social Bluebook: An Analysis and Forecast of Social Situation in China, 2004) (Beijing: *Shehui kexue wenxian chubanshe*, 2004), p. 254.

42 Jiang Yanyong had first emailed his letter to CCTV and Phoenix TV (a pro-China TV station in Hong Kong) on April 4, 2003. After his email was ignored, Jiang was interviewed by Susan Jakes, a correspondent with *Time* Magazine, on April 8, 2003, and she published the interview the same day. See "Feature: A Chinese Doctor's Extraordinary April in 2003" at http://english.peopledaily.com.cn/200306/13/print20030613_118182.html.

43 For the text of the law, see, http://news.xinhuanet.com/ziliao/2006–01/17/content_4062615.htm (accessed April 31, 2007).

Index

1kg.org 24
4 June 1989 pro-democracy movement 95, 116

A World without Thieves 59
accountability 136, 145
Adbusters 54
alibaba.com 132
American Idol 42
Anderson, Benedict 138, 139, 152
"antibourgeois liberalization" campaign 78
Anti-Japanese War 95
"Anti-Rightist Campaign" 95
"anti-spiritual pollution" campaign 78
AOL Time Warner 107
Arnison, Matthew 59
ARPANET 122, 124
Article 10 56
Article 22 56
AOL Time Warner 107
Asian civil societies 20
atomized society 141

Bakhtin, Mikhail 60
Bakhtinian perspective 63
Bangladesh 37
Banquet 59
Barlow, John 62
Barrington Moore's theory 18
Barthes, Roland 56
BBS forums 20, 21, 22, 24, 26
BDA 1
Beck 35, 36
"Beijing consensus" 73
Beijing Municipal Copyright Administration 57
Beijing Qianlong Net 109
Beijing Review 104, 109
Beijing University 24; *see also* Peking University 73, 74, 75
Beijing Youth Daily 27
Bennett, Lance 63
"big, big brother" 39, 40; *see also Dageda* 39
Billboard Liberation Front 55
"black kiln" 27
biopower 30
Bloody Case that Started from a Steamed Bun, The 53–4, 55, 56, 59, 61
Blue Book of Civil Society Development in China 27
BMW 22
Bob Jessop 20
Bowman, Shayne 100
"Building a Common Network Platform for Foreign Propaganda Agreement" 109
biopower 30
"Bus Uncle" 7, 35, 38, 42, 43, 44, 47

Cannes Film Festival 55
carnival 60, 61, 63
CCTV-1 112
CCTV-4 107, 112
CCTV-9 107, 108, 109, 110, 111, 112, 113, 115, 117
Cell Phone 8, 35, 38, 42, 45, 46
Central China Television Station (CCTV) 55, 61, 62, 105, 106, 107, 108, 109, 111, 115
Central Foreign Propaganda Group 104
Central Committee of the Chinese Communist Party 77, 114
Central Military Commission 70
Chen, Kaige 55, 56, 57
china.com.cn 109
China's Copyright Law 56

China Daily 104
CCTV International 107, 110
China Internet Society 28
China Internet Network Information Centre 133
China Mobile 41
"China Model of International Development" 105
"China threat" 105
China Today 104
China Unicom 41
China Youth Daily 52
Chinese Communist Party (CCP) 2, 28, 68, 69, 70, 71, 81, 140, 141, 149, 152
Chinese Internet Network Information Center (CNNIC) 21, 26, 30, 76, 96
Chinese People's Political Consultative Conference 116
Cisco 2
Civil War 95
"The Civilized Web" campaign 79
Clinton, Bill 130
collective memory 11, 86, 87, 88, 93, 94, 95, 96, 100, 101
"combined modernization" 34, 35
"Computer Information Network and Internet Security, Protection and Management Regulations" 21
Confucius 24
Confucius Institutes and Classrooms 105
cultural jamming 54, 55, 63
Cultural Revolution 20, 95
Curse of Golden Flowers 59
cyber nationalism 22; *see also* Internet nationalism 3

Da Vinci 54
Dadaism 54
Dageda 39; *see also* "big, big brother" 39, 40
Dalai Lama 86
Debord, Guy 54
Declaration of Cyberspace Independence 62
Deng, Xiaoping 78, 99
Deng, Zhenglai 36
Department of Propaganda (DoP) 70, 104, 151
Deutsch, Karl 138
digital civil society 6, 17, 18, 19, 22, 24, 28, 29, 30; *see also* e-civil society 26
digital control 7, 14, 29
digital divide 7, 29, 30
digital formations 19
digital governance 6, 7
Ding, Guangen 112
disciplinary power 30
Du, Ruiqing 113
Duchamp, Marcel 54
dynamic routing 122

e-civil society 26; *see also* digital civil society 6, 17, 18, 19, 22, 24, 28, 29, 30
e-commerce 26, 71, 132
e gao 8, 9, 41, 52, 53, 54, 55, 56, 57, 58, 59, 60, 61, 62, 63, 64
e-government 10, 26, 68, 69, 71, 73, 74, 75, 76, 81, 82
e-inclusion 76
Education Ministry 105
Elias, Norbert 140
Eliot 128
Emergency Response Law 152
environmental NGOs (ENGOs) 22, 27
Esping-Anderson's theory 18
EU 74
Exxon Valdez disaster 55

Falun Gong 133
Fan, Yafeng 27
Farewell My Concubine 55
Feng, Xiaogang 42, 45
"Fifth Generation" 55
"first modernity" 6, 37, 47
Forum of 100 Schools (*baijia jiangtan*) 96
foreign policy 18
foreign propaganda 12, 103, 104, 106, 107, 108, 109, 112, 113, 114, 115, 117
Foreign Propaganda Office of the Shanghai CCP Committee 109
Foucault, Michel 56, 140
Foucaultian perspective 7, 30
Fox 107
fragmentation 148, 150, 151
France 38
"Freezing Point" 27
Friedrich, Carl 140
Frye, Northrop 57

Geary, Patrick 87
Gellner, Ernest 138, 139
Gellner-Anderson conception 140
General Bureau of Postal and Telecommunications 70
Gerbner, George 59
Germany 38
Goat City Evening Posting (*Yangcheng Wanbao*) 149

Golden Palm award 55
GONGO 28
Google 2, 13, 126, 132
governance 3, 14, 15, 19, 28, 68, 69, 70, 72, 73, 77, 79, 81, 83, 136, 137, 141, 144, 145, 146, 152, 153
governmentality 21
Government Online Project 73
governmentality 21
grassroots journalism 88
Great Northern Telegraph Co. 38
Great Wall TV Platform (GWTV) 108
"Greater China Library" 105
Gross Domestic Product (GDP) 35, 75
Guang Ming Daily 62
Guangdong Zaman 109
Guantanamo 62
Guo, Zhenzhi 7, 8

Habermas, Jurgen 138, 140
Halbwachs, Maurice 87
Hamilton, Alexander 137, 138
Helmut K. Anheier 18
historical imagination 17
historical sociology 17
Hong Kong 43, 103, 107, 148, 150, 152
Hu, Ge 55, 56, 59, 61, 62
Hu, Jintao 28, 71, 72, 99, 108, 114
Hu Jintao-Wen Jiabao leadership 3
Huang, Yasheng 146
Hunan Radio and Television Group 58
Hunan Satellite Television (HSTV) 42
Huntington 142
Hutcheon 54
Hypertext Markup Language (HTML) 125, 126, 127
Hypertext Transfer Protocol (http) 125

ICPs 21
ID cards 3
identity formation 7
India 37, 89, 133
Indonesia 133
Informatization 70, 71, 80, 81, 82
instant messaging 1, 2, 3
Internet cafés 1, 13
Internet Copyright Regulation 57
Internet filtering technologies 13
Internet nationalism 3; *see also* cyber nationalism 22
Internet Protocol (IP) 125, 126, 132
Internet World Stats 133
IP addresses 13
Iraq 54
ISPs 21

Jessop, Bob 20
Jia, Qinglin 116
Jiang, Yanyong 151, 152
Jiang, Zemin 28, 71, 99, 106
Jordan 54
Joyce, James 54

KMT regime 77
Kornhauser, William 141
"Kuso" 53

Lai, Hongyi 146
Latham, Robert 19
Lenin in 1918 54
Levinson, P. 46
LHOOQ 54
Li, Changchun 150
Li, Hong 80; *see also* Zhang, Jianhong 80
Li, Lianjiang 23
Li, Ruihuan 78
liberal principles 13
Lieberthal, Kenneth 146
Little Fatty (Xiao pang) 53
Liu, Alan 140
Liu, Yong 22
Lu, Xun 116

Ma, Jack (Ma, Yun) 132
Macau 107, 150
Madison, James 138
Magaziner, Ira 130
Mao Zedong 98, 99, 141
Marx, Karl 63, 140
Matrix 54
May Fourth Movement 116
media censorship 68, 69
media conglomerates 58
Media Development Authority 133
memory policy 11, 93, 95, 97, 101
Meng, Bingchun 9
Microsoft 2
Middle East 124
Ministries of Public Security and State Security 70, 71
Ministry of Central Propaganda 112
Ministry of Culture 52, 57
Ministry of Electronic Industry 70
Ministry of Health (MoH) 148, 150, 151
Ministry of Information Industry (MII) 39, 60
Ministry of Public Security 21
Mobile telephony 7, 34, 41

Mona Lisa 54
MSN Spaces 2
multidimension transition country 2
Murdoch, Rupert 108

nail household 23
nation-state 14, 136, 137, 138, 139, 140, 141, 142, 143, 144, 146, 152, 153
National Leadership Group on Informatization 70, 71
National People's Congress 4
"National New Year's Gala" 111
nationalism 14, 15, 136, 138, 139, 140, 141, 143, 144, 153
Negroponte 62
netease.com 54
Netease 56
New Left 143
New Media 28
New York Times 152
News Corp 58, 107, 108
NGOs 1, 12, 19, 28, 134, 137
Nigeria 37
Nike 54
North Korea 133
Nu River 27
Nye, Joseph 106, 113

O'Brien, Kevin 23
Odyssey 54
O'Hara, Kieron 13, 129
Olympic Games 86, 94
"Online Audio-visual Broadcasting License" 60
online campaign 3
online shopping 26
Oxford 73

P2P 57
packet switching 122, 124
PageRank 126
parody 53, 54, 55, 60, 63
Party-state 68, 69, 71, 75, 76, 77, 80, 81, 83
"peaceful development" 105, 111
"peaceful rise" 105
Peking University 73, 74, 75; *see also* Beijing University 24
"people-centred" approach 3
People's China 104
People's National Conference 2006 115
People's Republic (of China) 38, 93, 140
periodization 6, 17, 20, 21, 29
Philippines 37
political correctness 148
political cost 14, 136, 144, 152
populism 4
pornography 10, 68, 70, 76, 77, 79, 81, 83, 132
post-modern 34; *see also* "second modernity" 34, 34
Press Office of the Shanghai Municipal Government 109
Promise (*Wu Ji*) 55, 56
"public media event" 44
Publicity Department 104
punitive power 30

QQ 2

Rabelais and His World 60
reality shows 8, 42
"Realm of Ideas" 22
red line 93, 94, 99, 100, 101
Red Memory 95
Regulation for Online Audio and Video Services 60
Renmin Ribao (People's Daily) 77, 109
Reporters Without Borders 134
rule of law 136, 145
Rüsen, Jörn 87
Rwanda 37

"Safety and Protection Regulations for Computer Information Systems" 21
Salamon, Lester M. 18
Sassen, Saskia 19
Saudi Arabia 132
school of "New Thinking" 144
Schram, Stuart 140
"second modernity" 34, 35, 36, 37, 47
Seventeenth Annual International Conference of the Sino-American Education Consortium 113
Seventeenth Party Congress 79
Severe Acute Respiratory Syndrome (SARS) 28, 132, 136, 146, 147, 148, 149, 150
Shanghai Daily 109
Shanghai Media Group 58
Shanghai Oriental Net 109
Shi, Tao 80
Simnine 87
Sina 3
sina.com 54
Singapore 37, 133
Situationism 54
Sixteenth Party Congress 149

SMS 25, 34, 39, 40, 41, 42, 43, 46, 151
SMTH 24
soap opera 94
soft power 12, 103, 105, 106, 107, 108, 108, 111, 113, 114, 115, 116, 117
Sohu 3
Songhua River 28
Southern Metropolis Daily 60
Southern Newsgroup 142
Southern Urban Post (*Nanfang Dushi Bao*) 149
Southern Weekend (*Nanfang Zhoumuo*) 149
Soviet Union 140
Sparkling Red Star 61, 62
spoof 9, 52, 53, 54, 55, 56, 59, 61, 63
Standing Committee of the CCP Politburo 71, 150
State Administration of Radio, Film and Television (SARFT) 52, 60, 107, 115
state-centred theory 5
State Council 21
State Council Information Office 70, 104, 109, 114
State Leading Group for Teaching Chinese 4
Statism 5
stock market 94
Suez Canal 124
Sun, Zhigang 4, 22
Super Girls 7, 8, 34, 38, 42, 43, 46
Surrealism 54

technological determinism 19
Tencent 3
Tencent.com 52
Tenth National People's Congress (NPC) 149
Third China Internet Conference 21
Tiananmen massacre 71, 77
Tianjin Herald 109
Tianya.com 24
Transmission Control Protocol (TCP) 125, 126
transparency 136, 145, 148, 149
'trinity' 10, 69

Ulrich Beck 35
Ulysses 54
UN Security Council 3, 62
US Department of Defence's Advanced Research Projects Agency (ARPA) 122
user-generated content (UGC) 28

Viacom 58

Web 2.0 28, 86, 88, 90
Web Bureau of the State Council Information Office 71
Web engineering 13, 121
Web Propaganda Bureau of the Central Propaganda Department 70, 71
Weitzner, Daniel J. 133
Wellman, Barry 37
Wen, Jiabao 4, 71, 80
Wikipedia 94
Willis, Chris 100
Wilson, Ernest 21
Windows messenger (Microsoft's instant-messaging system) 2
Wolman, Gil 54
Woodmansee 57
World Bank 145
World Health Organization (WHO) 147
WTO 58
Wu, Guoguang 10, 11
Wu, Mei 7, 8
www.bbc.co.uk 133

Xi'an International Studies University 113
Xing Kong 108
Xinhua News Agency 71, 72, 109
XML 126

Yahoo 2, 13, 80, 132
Yan, Shouyi 45
Yang, Boxu 37
Yang, Guobin 6, 7, 9
Yitahutu (YTHT) 24
YouTube 43, 44

Zhang, Dejiang 150
Zhang, Jianhong 80; *see also* Li, Hong 80
Zhang, Junhua 11
Zhang, Xiaoling 12
Zheng, Yongnian 14, 15
Zhao, Qizheng 114, 115
Zhou, Yongming 22
Zhou, Zola 23
Zhu, Rongji 70, 71